IRELAND'S ROUND TOWERS

ORIGINS AND ARCHITECTURE EXPLORED

Round Towers are the only form of architecture unique to Ireland. The remains of over seventy survive, widely distributed throughout the island, from Cork to Antrim, in some of the most beautiful and historic areas of the country. They include the towers at Cashel in Co. Tipperary and Glendalough in Co. Wicklow, Ireland's most-visited monastic site.

In this fully illustrated guide, the Round Towers are listed county by county, allowing the reader to locate towers in their immediate area. The detailed study of each tower discusses the uniqueness of its site and examines its architectural design and construction, function and setting within the landscape.

Ireland's Round Towers is an informative guide to these intriguing products of the Celtic imagination.

'Be Thou my Soul's Shelter.
Be Thou my High Tower.'
Anon., *Be Thou my Vision*

IRELAND'S ROUND TOWERS

ORIGINS AND ARCHITECTURE EXPLORED

BRIAN LALOR

The Collins Press

Title spread: *Kilmacduagh, Co. Galway*

PUBLISHED IN THIS FORMAT IN 2016 BY
The Collins Press
West Link Park
Doughcloyne
Wilton
Cork

First published in hard cover 1999
Published in paperback 2005

A CIP record for this book is available from the British Library.

Paperback ISBN: 978-1-84889-264-4

Editor: Kate Duffy
Book design: Paradigm Publishing Services, Co. Cork

Printed in Poland by HussarBooks

Acknowledgments

I wish to thank all those who helped me in any way during my work on this book: the public bodies, custodians, landowners and clergy in whose care and on whose property individual Round Tower sites are located. No study of this topic should fail to acknowledge the invaluable work done by George Lennox Barrow in assembling a vast archive of reference material for Round Tower sites, and I am indebted to his pioneering publications. I am particularly grateful to Conleth Manning, Dúchas, The Heritage Service for his meticulous reading of the manuscript, and for his many valuable criticisms and observations. The Office of Public Works, Dublin; Department of the Environment, Northern Ireland; the librarians and staff of the Boole Library, University College Cork; Irish Architectural Archive; Cork City Library; National Library of Ireland; Royal Irish Academy; Royal Society of Antiquaries of Ireland; and branch librarians throughout the island who were invariably helpful and accommodating. I am also most grateful for the assistance from the boatmen and ferrymen who make access to the island sites possible.

Publishers and authors who have granted me permission to quote from copyright works are as follows: The Architectural Press for permission to quote from *Towards a New Architecture* by Le Corbusier; Dover Books for permission to quote from *Vitruvius, The Ten Books on Architecture* (trans M.H. Morgan); Dundalgan Press for permission to quote from *Irish Churches and Monastic Buildings* by Harold Leask; Penguin Books for permission to quote from *The History and Topography of Ireland* by Gerald of Wales (trans. John J. O'Meara); Minerva for permission to quote from *Irish Journal* by Heinrich Böll; Veritas for permission to quote from *Patrick in his own words* (trans. Joseph Duffy); Daphne D.C. Pochin Mould for permission to use her aerial photographs; Allegra Duvica Lalor for permission to use her photographs.

for Caoimhe and Eve

OTHER PUBLICATIONS BY BRIAN LALOR

The Jerusalem Guide 1973
Cork (with Eiléan Ní Chuilleanáin) 1979
Dublin 90 Drawings 1981
Voices from Stones (with Myrna Haugaard) 1983
Blue Guide Ireland 1988
Dublin Bay from Killiney to Howth 1989
West of West 1990
Ultimate Dublin Guide 1991
Archaeology and Biblical Interpretation (contributor) 1997
The Ballad of Reading Gaol, Oscar Wilde (woodcuts) 1997
The Laugh of Lost Men 1997
Dublin & Ireland 1997
Blue Guide Dublin 2001
The Irish Round Tower 1999
The Encyclopaedia of Ireland (general editor) 2003
I am of Ireland 2010
Ink-Stained Hands 2011
Rosenheim & Windermere 2011
Island of Shadow 2011
Forgotten Beauty 2015

Biographical Note

Brian Lalor, artist-printmaker and writer, has pursued a multidisciplinary career involving work in architecture, archaeology, fine art, and as editor and arts administrator.

He worked in architecture in the UK, Germany and Israel for a number of years and was prizewinner in the Max Reinhardt Theatre Competition, Tel Aviv. He subsequently directed the architectural department of the Hebrew University/Israel Exploration Society excavations at the Temple Mount, Jerusalem 1968–1973 where his proposal to solve the century-long debate concerning the monumental approach to the Basilica of Herod the Great received widespread critical acceptance. He also worked at the Neolithic city of Khirokitia in Cyprus with the Centre National de la Recherche Scientifique, Paris, and studied arch and vault construction during the Late Bronze Age at Tel Jemme with the Smithsonian Institution, Washington, D.C., where he identified hitherto unrecognised mud-brick vaulting systems. More recently he was a member of an international team excavating the classical hill town of Jotapata/Yodfat with Bar Ilan University/Israel Antiquities Authority/University of Rochester, NY.

As General Editor of *The Encyclopaedia of Ireland* (2003) he led a worldwide team of over 900 Irish-studies academics in the production of the largest single-volume publication produced by an Irish publishing house and was the recipient of many international awards, including the Association of American University Presses Award for a Work of Reference in the Humanities.

He lectured widely on the history of printmaking, was chairman successively of two fine-art print studios, Graphic Studio Dublin and Cork Printmakers, and has, in *Ink-Stained Hands* (2011), written the definitive history of Irish fine-art printmaking in the twentieth century. A thirty-year print retrospective exhibition, *Voussoir*, was held in 2010 and *Brian Lalor a Life in Books* was presented as part of the 2012 World Book Fest. In 2015 he donated to the National Gallery of Ireland an extensive collection of European sixteenth-to-twentieth-century historic master prints. Brian Lalor lives in West Cork and is joint curator of the Blue House Gallery, Schull.

MAPS AND ILLUSTRATIONS

CONTENTS

~

INVENTORY CONTENTS

★ Non-Tower Sites

Preface

Any comprehensive study of the Irish Round Tower, the only form of architecture which is unique to Ireland, must depend for its accuracy on the towers having been the subject of exacting archaeological investigation. In order to carry out such a study, all the towers would need to be studied at close quarters from scaffolding, both internally and externally, and their immediate environment excavated in order to establish their original ecclesiastical context. The fact that no such survey has ever taken place limits commentary to a more generalised overview. More surprisingly, the scarcity of recently published archaeological studies of individual Round Towers indicates the degree of invisibility into which these extraordinary and highly visible monuments have fallen. As the greatest architectural achievement of early medieval Ireland, the Irish Round Tower warrants the same level of attention as has been lavished on the necropolis of the Boyne Valley, or the monastic foundations of the late medieval period. The results of such scrutiny are liable to be as revealing and as important.

This study is confined to the visible architectural remains of the towers, which in many cases have survived the original church buildings which they served. The fact that towers have lingered on long after the monasteries have disappeared has orphaned them from the environment in which they need to be seen. Like the great stone effigies of Easter Island, Irish Round Towers present a remote and implacable appearance to the world. This book is an attempt to breathe some life into the silent stones.

fig. 1: Location Map of Round Towers
The location of church sites with Round Towers follows the general distribution pattern of early medieval monasteries, with a greater number of tower sites, both surviving and vanished, east of the Shannon, and a more sparse distribution towards the west. The north-west and south-west have the least number of sites.

INTRODUCTION

' *A cup of tea, at dawn, while standing shivering in the west wind, the isle of saints still hiding from the sun in the morning mist: here on this island, then, live the only people in Europe that never set out to conquer, although they were conquered several times, by Danes, Normans, Englishmen — all they sent out was priests, monks, missionaries who, by way of this strange detour via Ireland, brought the spirit of Thebaic asceticism to Europe; here, more than a thousand years ago, so far from the centre of things, as if it had slipped way out into the Atlantic, lay the glowing heart of Europe.* '*

Heinrich Böll, *Irish Journal*, 1957

The Round Towers of Ireland are ecclesiastical bell-towers, referred to in the Irish Annals as *cloicteach* (bell house), and were built between the 10th and 12th centuries primarily as the church belfries of early medieval monasteries. They also functioned as repositories for church treasures, places of refuge for members of the community, security lookouts, as physical landmarks for the location of a monastic settlement, and as buildings designed to emphasise the prestige of the monastery and its local aristocratic patron.

The seventy-three ecclesiastical towers of which some remnant still stands, complete or in ruins, are among the primary works of Irish medieval antiquity (**fig. 1**). Their uniqueness and enigmatic character had been sufficiently recognised by the 18th century, so that no image of epic Ireland could be considered complete without its representative Round Tower. Vincent Waldré's ceiling painting in the great hall of Dublin Castle, *Henry II meeting the Irish leaders* (1795), has its tower, as does Daniel Maclise's major history painting in the National Gallery of Ireland, *The Marriage of Strongbow and Eva* (1854), which celebrates the consummation of the Norman invasion of Ireland. Throughout the 19th century, and well into the 20th century, the Round Tower, often accompanied by Hibernia with her harp and wolfhound, came to represent an essential symbol and icon of Irish culture.

Revivalist Round Towers, of which rather more are standing than the original medieval examples, were mostly built during the widespread enthusiasm for all things Celtic which followed the Gaelic Revival of the late 19th century. They are found in ecclesiastical, political and private contexts, as church bell-towers, political monuments and private memorials and bear little close resemblance to the original towers, except in their general outline, and when seen from a distance. The degree to which the revivalists' designers varied the proportions and details is in staggering contrast to the ubiquitous presence of the latter-day Round Towers as catch-all symbols of Irish identity, found in all parts of Ireland, and can be the source of some confusion to those interested in the subject.

The use of the Round Towers became ubiquitous and, quite soon after it had been embraced by antiquarians and artists, it made the conceptual leap from graphic image to three-dimensional architecture, with replicas which were seen as representing the essence of Irishness, filling a void in Irish cultural identity with the image of one of the most imaginative creations of the Celtic past.

When the Wexfordmen who fell in the Boer War were to be remembered by a monument, a Round Tower was erected at Ferrycarrig (1851); likewise when Daniel O'Connell, the dominant Irish politician of the early 19th century, was commemorated at Glasnevin cemetery in Dublin (1869), the symbol chosen was a Round Tower. The nadir in this progress was reached at the Louisiana Purchase Exposition in St Louis (1904), where the Irish section was represented by a half-life-size arrangement of Irish architectural masterpieces, with a Round Tower standing next to the 18th-century Dublin Parliament House. University College Cork's Honan Chapel (1916), the applied-arts masterpiece of the Celtic Revival movement, has its token Round Tower – as thin and emasculated as a toothpick.

What could be the final act of the Round Tower's 18th- to 20th-century resurgence as a cultural symbol (although it may be premature to predict the demise of this vigorous image from the national aesthetic repertoire), is the erection in 1998 of a replica Round Tower at Messines in Belgium (equidistant from Ypres and Armentières), as a memorial to the Irish dead from both present-day political regions of the island, and all denominations, in the battlefields of the First World War. The conviction that a Round Tower might be an appropriate symbol of political harmony and reconciliation for the 21st century seems to be possible only by ignoring the savagery of the centuries during which the towers were built. The early medieval towers' relevance in their original liturgical, architectural or political role is not illuminated by repeated misappropriation of this individual building-form for the purposes of personal glory, as in Glasnevin, or war memorials, as in Ferrycarrig, and now Messines. A further irony in the evolution of this most recent tower is that it was constructed with stone taken from the Mullingar workhouse, whereby an authentic historical artefact has been dismembered in order to create a bogus one, the symbolism of which is confused and inappropriate. Whatever it represented in its original context, the Round Tower never symbolised religious or political harmony – nor for that matter, poverty of the imagination as its most recent usage implies.

The O'Connell memorial in Glasnevin was originally designed by the antiquarian George Petrie, who in 1833 wrote the first important scientific study of Irish Round Towers. This was published in 1845 as *Ecclesiastical architecture of Ireland anterior to the Norman invasion,* a book which stripped away the mystique and whimsy which had, up to that date, surrounded the Round Towers, and firmly established their purpose and dating as ecclesiastical bell-towers of the early medieval Christian period. After Petrie's landmark publication, Victorian technology came to the aid of the subject and Lord Dunraven's posthumous volumes of photographs of antiquities, *Notes on Irish architecture* (1875), further helped to dispel the mists by presenting the towers without the aid of 'improved', inaccurate or romanticised drawings (a crime of which even the great Petrie was guilty). Margaret Stokes, who posthumously published Lord Dunraven's work, produced the last significant work of the 19th century on Round Towers, in her *Early Christian architecture in Ireland* (1878), in which she assembled the literary and architectural evidence in an exemplary manner. Harold Leask, architect and Inspector of National Monuments, who, in his *Irish Churches and Monastic Buildings* (1955), deals authoritatively with the entire period during which the towers were built, surprisingly side-stepped the issue by devoting more space to those towers which were attached to churches, and are thereby, the least typical examples, and satisfying himself with comments on a single freestanding example. During the 20th century only a single publication, George Lennox Barrow's *The Round Towers of Ireland* (1979), as well as a pamphlet by the same author, have been added to the very small number of books dealing exclusively with Round Towers. Barrow's treatment of the subject combines exhaustive documentation along with the unsubstantiated proposal that the towers originate some centuries earlier than the evidence suggests, and his definition of a Round Tower is confined narrowly to the freestanding examples.

There is a curious and inexplicable contradiction between the centrality of the Round Tower as the supreme architectural achievement of the great age of Irish medieval monasticism, and latterly a symbol of Irish identity, and the paucity of studies devoted to the subject. If the 19th-century philosopher Friedrich von Schelling's observation that 'architecture in general is frozen music' can be taken as more than a facetious quip, then the Round Towers, scattered across the landscape of Ireland, may be seen as an inspired series of rising and falling arpeggios, composed like the Gothic Cathedrals which followed them, to the greater glory of God, attempting, by their soaring form, to unite the worlds of the human and the divine.

The present study looks at the towers in the wider context of European architecture and examines in detail all the surviving evidence, from towers of which no more than the foundations survive, to those that are in near perfect condition. The development of the Round Tower is carefully charted and a typology proposed, which if not provable, at least establishes a framework within which the majority of the towers can be considered. All the towers have been examined, drawn and photographed by the author, and instructions provided for the traveller who is intent on visiting these monuments. This is primarily an architectural study; the Round Towers have been the subject of far too much intrusive and ill-informed digging and correspondingly little archaeological excavation, to make a comprehensive archaeological evaluation possible at this time.

It may seem a trifle far-fetched that the shade of Helen of Troy, the *femme fatale* of Homer's *Iliad,* should be invoked as an epigraph in a book concerned with the ecclesiastical architecture of medieval Ireland, but Ireland too had its Helen, who played a significant if unconscious role in defining the fate and future of her people, as the impulsive Helen had done. Ireland's Helen also had a brief but central part to play in the history of Round Towers, or rather in their demise. The *Annals of the Four Masters* relate that in the year 1152, Dervorgilla O'Melaghlin, wife of Tiernan O'Rourke, King of Breifne, was abducted by Dermot MacMurrough, King of Leinster, 'with her cattle and furniture'. The *Annals of Clonmacnoise* relate that MacMurrough 'kept her for a long space to satisfy his insatiable, carnal and adulterous lust'. Whether it was the beautiful Dervorgilla or her real-estate which attracted MacMurrough, the effect of this drama on the fields of Connaught was that it led to the ejection of the King of Leinster from his domain. MacMurrough subsequently appealed for aid to Henry II in Aquitaine, the result of which was the eventual arrival in Ireland, in 1167, of a force of Norman Welsh barons who became the vanguard of successive waves of Norman adventurers. This influx culminated with the arrival of a large force in 1171, led by Henry II.

With the Norman conquest came the end of the autonomy of the native Irish church and the rise in influence of the Continental monastic orders, Cistercians and Augustinians, who were already established in Ireland, and whose highly structured ideas of religious community life and church architecture were the antithesis of the organic native tradition. Within a century of the initial Norman foray at Baginbun, Co. Wexford, the authority of the new civic and religious dispensation had so altered ecclesiastical taste that Round Towers, for over 250 years the most characteristic structures of the Irish church, were built no more.

Forty-seven of the surviving Round Towers are indeed topless towers, and as regards their relationship to the ruins of Troy, or Illium as it was to the Greeks, their debt to the architectonic heritage of the eastern Mediterranean is manifest in their dependence on archaic building principles which were first brought to perfection in that region two millennia earlier.

The monastic architecture of early medieval Ireland represents a forgotten golden age in European architecture, the church buildings of which are as precisely defined and stylised as the

ARDMORE Growth and change in the composition of an early medieval monastic enclosure can be studied at Ardmore where the bivallate enclosure is still partially intact. The well-preserved earthen outer ring is on the left side of the picture with, in the centre, the roadway following the line of an inner rampart. To the right of the Round Tower is the diminutive St Declan's Tomb, possibly the tomb-shrine of the saint, re-roofed in the 18th century. On the left is the 12th – 13th century church known as the cathedral, with its extended chancel. (Photo 1972)

temples of classical Greece. The signature of this remarkable period is the Round Tower, a form which is both unique to Ireland and without identified precursors elsewhere. The towers are a defining yet enigmatic feature of the landscape and have been the inspiration of many wild and fanciful theories since they were first commented upon by antiquarians during the 17th century. Suggestions about their origin have ranged from pagan phallic symbols to Scythian fire temples. The most perfect of these elegant circular buildings rises to nearly 35 metres of delicately tapering stonework, crowned by a conical cap, and can be seen from a great distance, indicating the location of an ecclesiastical site to the travellers and pilgrims of almost a thousand years ago.

Surviving Round Towers are widely distributed throughout the island. They are sited in twenty-eight of the thirty-two counties, the bulk of them located north of the Dingle Peninsula and south of Lough Neagh (**fig. 1**). They represent the larger part of the over one hundred towers, known from manuscript and other documentary sources, to have existed. Archaeological excavations have established the existence of a few previously unrecorded towers, and the discovery of others is to be expected. A small diaspora of Irish-style Round Towers is found outside Ireland, three in Scotland and one on the Isle of Man, but these are late examples and derivative of the originals and of Irish church influence. Of the seventy-three standing towers, some are mere stubs or foundations, but the majority are substantially intact; amongst these, forty towers are in association with surviving ecclesiastical settlements, and sited in some of the most beautiful and historic landscapes of the country, such as Ardmore, Devenish, Cashel, Clonmacnoise and Glendalough: eight towers are located on islands. Four-fifths of the towers may be visited within an hour's journey of a few central points, Dublin, Galway, Kilkenny and Mallow; the remaining fifth in Ulster are more widely distributed, but are roughly equidistant from Dungannon.

An attraction of the subject is its contained nature, a small corpus of unique monuments, in most cases beautifully sited; on the negative side is the sparseness of documentation and the fact that the Round Tower has become a cliché of Irish cultural nationalism through the repetitiveness of its form. Yet Round Towers retain their fascination, despite neglect and suffering a fall from grace as icons of monastic Ireland. It is important to view the towers, not only as isolated artefacts of early medieval Ireland, but also as an integral unit of historically complex ecclesiastical sites, where the tower has often survived successive waves of church building and lives on, deprived of its original context, and accompanied by anything from a Gothic cathedral to County Council offices or a handball-alley.

A certain tunnel vision is required in order to confront a single category of historic building, and not to engage with the wider ecclesiastical and architectural context in which Round Towers originated and are now found. These are vast subjects with an even vaster literature, most aspects of which have already been well covered, although archaeologically, the early medieval period has attracted far less scrutiny and funding than earlier and later periods of the Irish past. Of the seventy-three sites included here, only a disappointingly small number have both a Round Tower and a correspondingly early church which may be associated with the period during which the tower was built. Oratories and churches were susceptible to changes in ecclesiastical taste, and their history is one of gradually increasing dimensions and plan-complexity, between the original single-cell buildings and those with separate nave and chancel, sacristy, belfry or porch. There appear not to have been any alterations to the liturgical requirements of a *cloicteach* from the inception of the building type to its decline and disappearance, a phenomenon rare in terms of ecclesiastical architecture.

A disturbing factor which affects Round Towers and early monastic sites generally is the quite recent threat of gradually encroaching changes in land-usage, either in the form of farm buildings, factories, Heritage Centres with their attendant coach parks, or the voraciously expanding graveyards which are now seen, to increasingly disastrous effect, in such primary sites as Clonmacnoise and Glendalough. In many cases the decision to allow inappropriate land use on the boundaries of monastic enclosures constitute one of the most catastrophic blunders of present-day planning authorities. In the light of the growth in demand for funerary monuments and their visually intrusive nature, the expansion of monastic graveyards still in use needs to be relocated some distance away from the historic sites, before these become submerged in late-20th-century memorials. The fact that this process of encroachment on historic sites is prevalent throughout Ireland should be a cause for widespread concern. All of these important sites need to be protected from unnecessary disturbance by a *cordon sanitaire*. It seems that the rights of the present generations to bury their relatives in hallowed ground under catafalques of surpassing vulgarity has been allowed to totally override the need to preserve the most beautiful, historic and sacred sites which the island of Ireland possesses.

GLENDALOUGH I, CO. WICKLOW The distinctive cone-capped form of the Round Tower rises above the tree tops at Glendalough, announcing the presence of St Kevin's monastery, as it did for pilgrims almost a thousand years ago.

IRELAND DURING THE EARLY MEDIEVAL PERIOD

THE MEDIEVAL LANDSCAPE

During the five hundred years between 432 AD, the date traditionally ascribed to the beginning of Patrick's mission in Ireland (although this date is anything but confirmed), and 950, when the first documentary mention of a Round Tower (Slane) is found in the *Chronicum Scotorum*, one of the manuscript sources of the Irish annals, physical changes to the appearance of the Irish landscape were gradual rather than dramatic. The countryside had undergone a fairly seamless elision from the Iron Age (*c.* 300 BC – *c.* 400 AD), to the early medieval period (*c.* 400 – *c.* 1200), and would continue to change in a similarly undramatic manner.

The landscape, originally heavily concealed by tree cover during the Neolithic period and the Bronze Age, had been considerably opened up by clearance, to maintain a mixed-farming self-sufficiency and barter economy of cattle husbandry and tillage, as well as for domestic settlement. The pre-pottery material culture of the society depended almost exclusively on timber and animal products. Pollen diagrams for the period from the 1st through to the 6th century show a fall in tree-pollen and a rise in cereal-pollens, indicating a transfer of land usage from natural forest to cultivation. This phenomenon began to accelerate during the 4th and 5th centuries, and it is probable that the introduction of the iron coulter plough from Roman Britain, which ultimately replaced the less powerful and limited ard plough, facilitated the opening up of wider areas of previously uncultivatable land for tillage. Land in the drumlin belt (with much heavier soil), which forms the southern borderlands of Ulster, came into settlement use around the 5th century.

Bogs and wetlands abounded, yet across them could be seen the extensive man-made trackways or *tochers*, such as that excavated and preserved at Corlea Bog, Co. Longford (147 BC), which made possible easier communication between settlements during the Iron Age and medieval period. They are also evidence of organised communal activity. Major river arteries like the Shannon (bridged at Clonmacnoise in the late 8th century), coastal navigation and the great cross-country trackways, the *Slige Dála, Mór, Chualann* and *Midluachra*, contributed towards some sense of unity in what was essentially an island of distinct and only superficially connected regions. The degree of gradually increasing settlement had become widespread by the 10th century. A man-made landscape of open land with enclosed occupation sites, many of which still survive, had become characteristic at the end of a very extended period of over 1000 years of independence from serious foreign intervention. Although this independence was threatened by Viking raids and later settlement, it was not terminated until the Norman invasion of the 12th century.

Some 80,000 medieval settlement sites survive throughout the island, from craft and industrial sites and water-driven grain mills, to an enormously wide array of habitation sites, ecclesiastical and defensive enclosures (**fig. 2**). There doubtless were many more, of which 18th-century land clearances and more recent farming methods have eliminated all trace. Early field patterns, among the most vulnerable features of the historic landscape, survive in occasional clusters of small enclosures, associated with ringforts and other settlement sites. Even more vulnerable are unenclosed habitation sites for which no physical evidence remains above ground. The survival of post-and-wattle dwellings in the water-logged soil of Viking Dublin and Waterford is evidence of what may have existed elsewhere.

The Ireland of the centuries immediately prior to, and following, the coming of Christianity, display a remarkable unity in certain significant aspects. Most importantly, and unlike in Britain, its population spoke a single language, Irish, and was governed by a codified, if varying, system of laws. This legal system was without any form of central administration, but depended on consensus and the authority of *brehons*, specialist legal scholars, who were maintained by local magnates. Political unity, however, was non-existent, and the provincial divisions were, as they are now, with four rather than the original five provinces. Each of these was controlled by an uneasy alliance of some 150 petty and principal dynasties, most of whom claimed kingship over relatively small *tuatha* or territories. Beneath the ruling strata of local lords, bonds of kinship, which derived from four generations descended from a common ancestor, were the binding community structure.

Warfare and raiding between rival local leaders seems to have been a perennial theme of the times, although perhaps not as endemic as texts like the *Táin Bó Culailnge*, or the annalists' comments would suggest. Population figures (500,000 possibly) can only be speculated upon, but these cannot have been so great as to put a serious strain on the agricultural capacity of the island to provide an adequate living for all its inhabitants; famine years, and years of plenty, as a result of bad or good harvests, and other natural calamities are recorded by the annalists. Land, and trade in its produce, was the basis of the economy there was no native coinage until this was first struck by Sitric, King of Norse Dublin, in 997. In a society in which all status was hierarchical and bound by ties of kinship, full legal status was dependent on landownership, and the

fig. 2: The Medieval Landscape
Ringfort distribution, on the banks of the River Suir in Co. Tipperary, gives an accurate impression of the intensity of occupation during the medieval era, although the existing settlements are not necessarily contemporary. Closely related pairs and clusters of ramparted enclosures were generally occupied simultaneously by the same kinship group. The univallate smaller domestic and agricultural enclosures contrast with the scale of Cashel, originally the seat of the Eoganachta kings of Munster, and later an important ecclesiastical site, and Rath na Drinne at Lalorslot, an exceptionally fine quadrivallate fort.

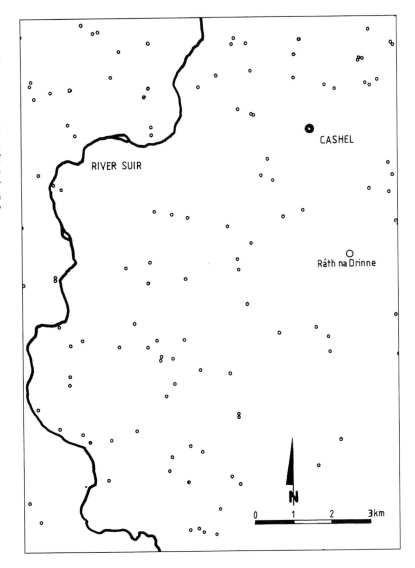

landless tenant-farmer remained the serf or client of a lord or strong-farmer. Wealth was calculated in cattle herds, and patronage by gifts of cattle bound the lower strata to those above them.

IRON AGE ANTECEDENTS: c. 300 BC – c. 400 AD

Domestic or residential remains have proved elusive from the Iron Age, the era which preceded and includes the coming of Christianity to Ireland. Indeed, the first centuries of the Christian period are sometimes referred to as the late Iron Age, but no archaeological evidence of change during this period survives. Little of its built structures have been identified, beyond the impressive and variously dated dry-stone defensive fortresses, the Grianán of Aileach (**fig. 3**)

GRIANÁN OF AILEACH, CO. DONEGAL
The Iron Age fortress of the Grianán displays some of the essential design elements of the Round Tower – circular – plan, battered walls, lintelled doorway with inclined jambs. Drystone masonry technique imposed height limitations on its construction.

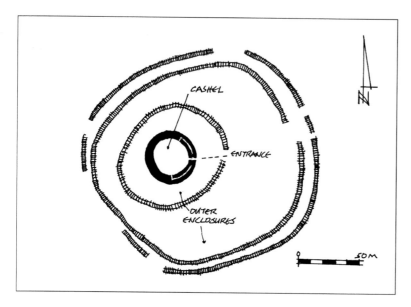

fig. 3: GRIANÁN OF AILEACH
The Grianán, a dramatically sited drystone cashel on a summit overlooking Loughs Foyle and Swilly, was a royal site of the Northern Uí Néill, and was occupied from at least the 5th to 12th centuries. A concentric series of earthen embankments surround the cashel, the single entrance to which is, as is conventional with ringforts, from the east. Souterain-like narrow passageways are enclosed in the body of the wall on either side of the entrance. The Grianán was destroyed in 676 by the Southern Uí Neill, again in 1101 by the King of Munster, and 'restored' in the late 19th century.

GRIANÁN OF AILEACH
The structural principles of the entrance doorway of the Grianán were adopted by the early church builders, and subsequently used, virtually without change, in the Round Towers.

in Donegal and Dun Aenghus on Inishmore in the Aran Islands, which are in a distant manner, the lineal ancestors of the Irish Round Towers: here the characteristic circular battered wall and lintelled entrance with inclined jambs makes its first appearance in Ireland. Enigmatic stone effigies, such as those on Boa Island in Fermanagh, and *La Tène* art form decoration on aristocratic horse trappings, weaponry and other objects such as the 'Cork Horns' or the 'Petrie Crown', are generally confined to the north of the country, and are characteristic of a period of great importance in defining certain aspects of the Irish-built environment, which were to remain influential to as late as the 12th century.

It is into the Ireland of this obscure period that Christianity first penetrated from late Roman Britain, some half-a-century or more before the coming of Patrick in the 5th century. The *Chronicle* of Prosper of Aquitane in Gaul (modern France) records for the year 431, *'To the Irish believing in Christ, Palladius, having been ordained by Pope Celestine, is sent as first bishop'*. The location of these communities, their size and structure is not known, although the east and south coastal regions are most likely to have first been influenced by Christian ideas. For that matter, there is no means of establishing whether these early Christians were isolated individuals, families or communities, although by the time of Palladius' arrival, large Christian communities must have existed to warrant papal awareness, and the dispatch of a bishop. There is no reason to suppose that, initially, the converts were persons of high status: the reverse may have been the case – Christian slaves brought from Britain, like Patrick – or returned immigrants, from the Irish settlements in Wales and the west coast of Britain, or people involved in trading.

Patrick, who came without any official prompting, but inspired by his vision, appears to have concentrated on the northern half of the island, although he is associated by legend with sites as far south as Cashel in Munster. Certainly, all significant and early associations with him are in the northern region of the island, in north Connaught, Ulster and north Leinster. The picture which Patrick gives of his progress around the country, accompanied by a group of paid young notables, is a far cry from the folklore and hagiographical image of the saint, heroically jousting with kings and pagan clergy in dramatic set-piece scenes directed by Cecil B. de Mille: the social protocols of the period seem to have demanded a more pragmatic response. There is no reason to doubt Patrick's very unvarnished account of his struggle with 5th-century Iron Age society. His *Confessio* (pre-493, the probable date of his death), is in marked contrast to such texts as Julius Caesar's *De Bello Gallico* and other later official histories of the Roman world, and is a unique document in that it is the autobiography of an ordinary Roman citizen, alone and unloved among the barbarians, beyond the protection or reach of the *Pax Romana*. The age of 'the work of Angels' was not to come for a further few hundred years.

LATE AND POST– ROMAN BRITAIN: 3rd CENTURY – 6th CENTURY

Contacts between Roman Britain (56 BC – 407 AD) and Ireland had never been on an organised level, and the failure of the legions to invade Ireland means that Ireland never became part of the Roman Empire. Nonetheless, much of what was new in the pre-Christian era, as well as during the early centuries of Christianity, must have come to Ireland through trade and travel between the neighbouring islands, and later, through involvement with the Irish settlements in Britain.

Ogham, the primitive Irish form of memorial inscription, possibly pre-Christian in origin, and the earliest Irish epigraphic material, has its origin in an adaptation of the Latin script; keys to its interpretation are found in the 15th-century *Book of Ballymote* and other manuscripts. Ogham stones in the Irish areas of Wales carry bilingual inscriptions, in ogham and Latin, the Latin written in the same bizarre, up one side and down the other format. Some of the Irish ogham inscriptions mention Irish-named sons of Roman-named fathers. Similarly, millifiori glass-working, ornamental metalwork, iron technology and advances in agricultural practice, all of which came into use in Ireland during the early medieval period, have their origins in the technologically advanced culture of the regions which had come under Roman influence. That Christianity should have followed the same route and also been a vehicle for many of these new ideas in writing, agriculture, technology and art is merely a simple fact of geography. The highly developed manufacturing skills of the late Roman world, honed on the consumer society of Republican and Imperial Rome with its one million or more inhabitants, influenced Ireland in many ways, even if hardly at all in terms of architectural style.

No Roman occupation sites have been found in Ireland, although there is enough artefactual evidence to substantiate a Roman trade presence; burials are the principal source of finds. A number of hoards of Roman silver have been recovered, but these might have been booty taken by Irish pirates, acting against the vulnerable settlements in the south of England in the years before or after the legions were withdrawn. Greater interest in the relationship of Roman Britain to Iron Age Ireland is liable to lead in the future to a more thorough scrutiny of possible evidence for contacts.

DOMESTIC, POLITICAL AND RELIGIOUS SETTLEMENT: 5th CENTURY – 13th CENTURY
Agricultural settlement throughout the early medieval period remained dispersed and sporadic, with circular earthen ramparts liberally distributed on the open areas of grassland. These beautiful and secure earthen grass-covered ringforts would have been the most familiar and characteristic feature of the man-made landscape: they contained the domestic homesteads and cattle enclosures, the centres of political power and the monastic settlements.

Wood was the essential and pervasive all-purpose material before the 8th century, and all structures, both public and private, were timber-built, employing either post-and-wattle or timber joinery. Prior to the construction of stone churches, and long after they became common, wood or wattle remained the characteristic material of all Irish settlements, with the exception of those on the west coast where stone was more readily available, and timber more scarce. Other than some imported ceramics, virtually everything required for the material needs of a settlement, from drinking and cooking vessels, to larger storage containers for liquids, as well as all domestic, farming and military equipment, depended heavily on wood, as did the entire range of architectural demands, from churches to the construction of boats, *crannógs*, or the creation of a trackway.

Excavation of ringforts and other enclosed sites (Garranes, Co. Cork; Deer Park Farms, Co. Antrim) have shed much light on the wide scope of activities which took place within them, and emphasised the degree to which self-sufficiency was the norm. This would have been equally true of both religious and secular settlement. By the close of the early medieval period an impressively wide range of skills were available for domestic, military and ecclesiastical clients. Many of these were practised in individual enclosures by community members, while other more complex and highly skilled techniques were probably only available from specialists, either resident under patronage at a particular place, or as itinerant craftsmen. Craft skills included carpentry, cooperage, boat-building and lathe-turning; smelting and foundry metalwork in iron, copper and silver were involved in the production of church plate, as well as in dress-ornaments and weaponry; decorative glass-working was also allied to metalwork. Leathercraft was important for shoes, clothes, equestrian equipment, manuscript materials and book satchels; bone carving provided tools, domestic and cosmetic utensils; wool and linen were spun, woven and dyed for fabric manufacture. In this impressive range of available crafts, as items from the archaeological record and museum collections amply demonstrate, technological skill-levels were in no way inferior to those practised in the great population centres of the then known world.

A curious anomaly of the early medieval period in Ireland, other than in Ulster, is that it was an aceramic society. The virtual absence of ceramics, other than imported wares, emphasises the population's total reliance on timber products. Irish 'souterrain ware' does not appear before the 7th century and finds so far have been confined to the north-eastern coastal region, its use never having been generally available or commonplace. Before the 12th century, Ireland's lack of development in this field was in complete contradiction to the widespread availability of ceramics in the lands of the Fertile Crescent and Mediterranean basin, and latterly in the territories of the Roman Empire. Evidence for the absence of direct Roman involvement in Ireland is nowhere more obvious than in the dearth of ceramics (an archaic trait) and in the survival of archaic mannerisms in architecture.

Political power during the early medieval era remained fluid, with a host of petty-kings held in some state of dependence on the main provincial dynasties: the Eoganachta Kings based in Munster, and the Uí Néill in Meath and in Ulster. The extended families of husbandry and grazier farmers occupied the enclosed homesteads or ringforts which gave shelter to wattle houses and livestock. Lower-status members of the extended family community probably lived in unenclosed house-site settlements. Richer individuals, local leaders, and ritual centres were an expansion of the principle of the single circular rampart, although people of high status did not necessarily live in multivallate ringforts. Here, the single ring was expanded to two or three great concentric rings

NENDRUM, CO. DOWN At Nendrum little remains of the Round Tower and church, yet its site is among the most evocative of all surviving early medieval monastic settlements.

fig. 4: NENDRUM MONASTIC ENCLOSURE
The location of Nendrum, on an island offshore from the western side of Strangford Lough, provided it with maximum security as well as ease of access, while the Round Tower ensured visibility over an extensive hinterland. The plan of the well-preserved trivallate cashel indicates the same approach to the organisation of domestic and ritual enclosure as is found in the political and defensive plan of the Grianán of Aileach.

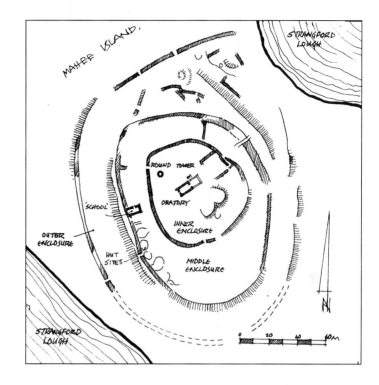

fig. 5: NENDRUM, CO. DOWN
The monastery, strategically positioned on high ground at the junction of two branches of the Lough, was surrounded by abundant resources for fishing and good agricultural land. Within the trivallate cashel, the church, tower and monastic graveyard occupied the inner enclosure, with domestic and craft quarters located in the outer rings.

of earthen ramparts topped by palisades. The form of the great royal or ritual centre of Emain Macha (Armagh), although late Bronze and Iron Age, differs only in scale from the humblest of enclosures, and the nature of the buildings which they contained were constructionally no different, merely larger and more complex in plan.

The univallate or single-ring enclosure is the most common, with multivallate sites probably being constructed for reasons of local prestige. The terminology which historically was used to describe these curvilinear enclosures – *dún*, *caiseal*, *cathair*, *ráth* and *lios* – may be divided into high-status enclosures called *dún*; stone-built enclosures (usually in the poor soil regions of the west coast) called *caiseal* or *cathair*; *ráth* for commonplace univallate earthen enclosures, and *lios* for the land contained within a rampart. Countless Irish topographical place names are derived from these settlement terms, as in Dundalk, Cashel, Cahir, Rathcormac and Lismore.

Free farmers, clients of the local lord, most probably occupied the single *ráths*. The bondsmen, at the bottom of the social order, occupied unenclosed sites. Within the circular enclosures the dwellings were of wattle and thatch, with souterrains excavated beneath the ground to provide food storage, shelter, or as a sally-port under the fortifications. It is probable that, allied to the practicality of the circular enclosure, was some concept of the cosmological significance of the form.

A further settlement variant are *crannógs*, artificial islands constructed in the shallows of the lakelands of the midlands and north, and following the same principles as the ringforts and cashels; a circular palisade enclosing a few wattle dwellings. The excavation of the waterlogged sites of *crannógs* has proved exceptionally fruitful (Ballinderry, Co. Offaly; Lagore, Co. Meath), with an even higher percentage of finds including ornamental metalwork objects, iron and timber, agricultural and domestic utensils, than from ringfort sites, prompting the understanding that they may be the dwellings of high status individuals, but this evidence may be circumstantial. The sites of over 1,200 *crannógs* have so far been identified.

The tyranny of the circle as a planning concept lasted longer in Ireland than anywhere else in Europe, from the late Neolithic to the late medieval period. The use of the motif changed from funerary to ritual to domestic, military and ecclesiastical, over an enormously lengthy period, yet maintained a central focus as a, possibly restrictive, architectural form throughout fundamental changes in the social organisation and religious beliefs of the peoples of the island. The power and practicality of all adaptations of concentric circles endowed them with versatility and quite extraordinary powers of survival. This became the dominant shape of all early medieval settlements, the domestic and political adapted to ecclesiastical needs without any significant change. At Nendrum, on Mahee Island (**figs. 4 & 5**) on the north-east side of Strangford Lough, the early medieval monastic site has remained virtually untouched by anything beyond the ravages of time. A trivallate cashel on the lough's shore contains not only a church with a later extension, but also a Round Tower, a monastic graveyard, domestic dwellings, craft workshops and possibly, a school. Nendrum is a ruin but the essentials are all here. Along the shore of Strangford Lough the monastery site overlooked the water and, on the cleared land, against a backdrop of trees, grazed the community's cattle. Standing sentinel, the only vertical element in a natural landscape was the Round Tower. On a clear day it would have been visible from many kilometres away, a sign to the pilgrim of the direction to be taken, and of the status of the settlement. From a distance, all earthen ramparted enclosures must have looked the same: the Round Tower, never found outside a monastic enclosure, defined an ecclesiastical context.

Monasteries, which were founded on land granted by local magnates, were ruled principally by members of the same families, to whom the abbacy became a family inheritance, passing from generation to generation within the close kinship of a few related names. It is a characteristic of Irish founder-saint's biographies that they are either of noble birth or closely related to the ruling families of their region.

The Church which developed in Ireland differed in its development from that in Gaul, and the diocesan and parochial structure common to the remainder of the European Christian world which were influenced by Rome. In Ireland an episcopal system existed in parallel with the monastic one, but it is the latter which dominated in the number of its settlements, and the widespread ties which attached smaller monasteries to more powerful ones. The monastic community became the essence of the early Irish Church.

From possibly the 5th century, and certainly from the 7th century through to the 12th century, there is an extraordinary physical cohesion in Irish monastic settlement, the evidence for which is dramatically visible in many parts of Ireland (Kildare, Kells) even today. The form and extent of these settlements lasted virtually unchanged, from their inception to the new era of civic and religious rule, which followed the Norman Conquest. In the externally undisturbed world of the island of Ireland, on the very periphery of Europe, and in most respects totally independent of it, the conservative planning concepts of an insular society showed considerable vigour in adapting and absorbing Christian usage, rather than being overcome by it. The aspects of Iron Age social order, such as ideas of agricultural settlement and architecture, were carried right through the timespan of the Roman Empire, the European Dark Ages, and the advent of medieval artistic style, without ever showing the need to significantly change. Only when the Irish Church and native kingship were confronted by better organised and more sophisticated religious ideas, more adept military forces, and more advanced civic order, did the old forms begin to capitulate and adapt to radical outside influences.

The evidence for such a continuity, which spans the changes in artistic style from *La Tène* through the early medieval world, which produced in the 9th century, the *Book of Kells*, is in the field of what can loosely be called architecture and town planning. The monastic cities of Clonmacnoise, Kildare, and similar settlements, in so far as their planning can be evaluated, remained from their foundation to their absorption by the late medieval world of Continental ecclesiastical order and politics, organic rather than structured.

fig. 6: ARMAGH, CO. ARMAGH
The longevity of circular monastic enclosures is demonstrated by this detail of a roofless Gothic chapel on the hill to the south-east of Armagh Cathedral, from Richard Bartlett's early 17th-century map which gives a bird's-eye view of the hill. The cartographer was murdered by the local people because 'they would not have their country discovered'.

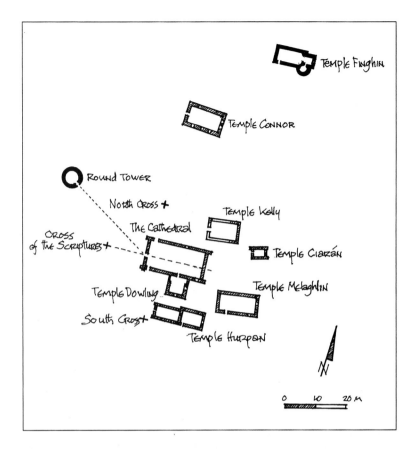

fig. 7: CLONMACNOISE, CO. OFFALY
The dispersed arrangement of the churches at Clonmacnoise is characteristic of all multi-church early medieval monasteries. A number of distinct oratories are loosely grouped around the cathedral, the principal church, all of which share the same orientation. The cathedral is the building for which the Round Tower was constructed, and the tower doorway is oriented towards its west doorway, establishing a direct relationship between *cloicteach* and church ritual. The three great scripture crosses are arranged in a cruciform manner around the cathedral. Temple Finghín, the only church of Clonmacnoise to have a separate chancel, also has an engaged Round Tower.

Unlike in Continental Europe, where the traditions of church building were directly influenced by the surviving monumental achievements of the Roman world, in Ireland churches were small, even minute at times, and a multiplicity of small single-cell buildings in an enclosure took the place of the Continental concentration on individual large-scale and liturgically adaptable buildings. In all the ecclesiastical settlements where numbers of churches survive, the common denominator is the presence of half-a-dozen stone church buildings, all similarly west-east oriented, yet without further relationship. The arrangement of the churches of Clonmacnoise (**fig. 7**), Glendalough or Inis Cealtra is like that of half-a-dozen cars left behind in a field after a race-meeting, all roughly oriented the same way, yet unco-ordinated to a central plan. Of the timber buildings which stood around or between the stone churches, no trace remains above ground. The absence of a planned approach derived from the classical tradition is evident in this diverseness.

During the 8th century and lasting into the 10th century, the *Céli Dé*, or Culdee movement of Church reform, had a wide influence on Irish monasticism, which, through a stress on study and anchorite principles, resulted in considerable literary activity, both secular and clerical, and it was during this

CLONMACNOISE, CO. OFFALY Clonmacnoise was one of the great ecclesiastical centres of early medieval Ireland, and to pilgrims and travellers using the major inland waterway of the Shannon, its many churches and pair of Round Towers must have been a magnificent sight. Here, the tower of Clonmacnoise II, Temple Finghín, is seen with the river as its backdrop.

KILDARE, CO. KILDARE Despite alterations to its top, and the ravages of time, Kildare, standing at almost 33 metres high, is among the most impressive of the complete but capless towers. It is one of the few to which there is still internal access.

figs. 8a-b: ECCLESIASTICAL ENCLOSURES
Many Irish urban centres, which originally came into being as Norman townships, preserve at their core the skeletal remains of the early medieval monasteries around which they developed. The present-day street plans of (a) Kildare, Co. Kildare, and (b) Kells, Co. Meath, eloquently demonstrate the former presence of bivallate ecclesiastical enclosures. In both towns the form of the inner enclosure is in part preserved by the line of the churchyard wall, while the concentric layout of the outer enclosure is represented by the orientation of the streets, the routes of which were laid down before the earthen banks had totally disappeared. Both sites have well-preserved towers, but the churches which they served have been replaced by a succession of later buildings. Kildare tower was positioned to the north-west of the west doorway of the church, while Kells was to the south-west.

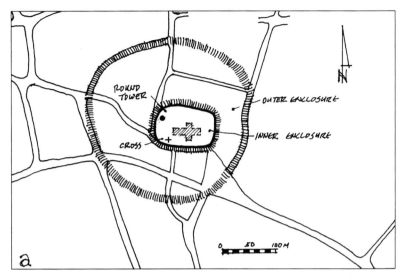

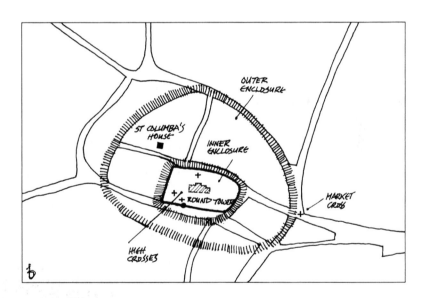

period that some of the greatest surviving manuscript treasures were created. It is at the latter end of the period, the early 10th century, that Round Towers make a first appearance in the ecclesiastical landscape. Church renewal continued throughout the 11th century, led by Malachy of Armagh, who was instrumental in introducing continental monastic orders to Ireland.

PROTO-URBAN SETTLEMENT: 9th CENTURY – 12th CENTURY

In the present-day city of Armagh (**fig. 6**), and in the towns of Kells and Kildare (**fig. 8a-b**), the historic church complex which is at the centre of modern built-up development represents the original presence of early Christian monastic enclosure. These survivals are eloquent testaments to the continuity of both Christian monastic settlement and pre-Christian ideas of enclosure. Armagh, bishopric of Patrick, is still the primal ecclesiastical see of Ireland, present-day seat of its Catholic and Protestant archbishoprics. From the air the street-plan surrounding Armagh Cathedral is startling in the clarity of its concentric layout, the outline of a circular enclosure is clearly preserved in the orientation of the curvilinear streets; the embankments dictated the shape of the town plan which evolved in the post-Norman urban expansion of the site.

Such palimpsest enclosures, whether in urban or rural locations, often reflect both the respect and the sense of apartness which their shape preserves. In many centres throughout Ireland, such as Armagh, Kells and Kildare, little in essence changed after their foundation in the 6th and 7th centuries (by the followers of Patrick), when the essential element of a sub-rectangular enclosure was adapted from contemporary domestic settlement types, and their diameter was expanded by the addition of further ramparts. The original timber churches were, by the 10th century, being replaced by stone-built structures, and as communities expanded in wealth and reputation, further churches were added, the principal church was frequently enlarged and a Round Tower was later added to the complex. Other buildings in the enclosure were domestic, educational and for craft purposes; many of them continued to be of timber or wattle construction. The plan and reconstruction of Nendrum shows the dominant presence which the Round Tower would have occupied in the monastic complex, both in terms of its physical presence as the most visible architectural element, and in the singularity of its appearance in the small-scale and low-level architecture of the enclosure.

Clonmacnoise and Kildare were regarded as monastic cities in their time and referred to as such. They had gathered around them, both within and outside the enclosure, all the support personnel necessary for the various craft and agricultural activities of the community. These activities required many specialists, including those providing skins for the scriptorium, precious metals, smelting and casting of ornamental metalwork, as well as building craftsmen, artists and sculptors for the High Crosses. It is obvious that a very considerable and active lay-community must have been involved in such proto-urban settlement. Nonetheless, from what is known to have remained, organisation appears dispersed rather than structured in a specific manner.

The essentially aclassical layout remained unchanged until the advent of the

Cistercians, who, at Mellifont (1142), produced the first example of a symmetrically planned complex in Ireland, a complex in which all the functions of the community are reflected in the layout of co-ordinated buildings. All aspects of church ritual, even the physical circulation of the monks and lay-brothers, were ordered in a precisely disciplined manner. The aesthetic mind-set of the Irish Church, infatuated with the curvilinear as a motif, which had also inherited much from its Iron Age predecessors, and had adapted the uncompromising Christian rectangle to its ecclesiastical needs, finally succumbed to the greater rectangular world of 12th-century Europe. The skeleton of Celtic concentricity was evidently respected by even the new dispensation of Continental monasticism, and the civic organisation of the Anglo-Norman authorities. The Anglo-Norman chartered boroughs of Kells and Kildare, towns with a defined civic identity, maintained the ramparts of the older church at their core. Even more remarkably, like a multiple-exposed negative, they still do.

Within a fifty-year span the 1,500 year long ordinances of Iron-Age planning which had moulded the Irish world, and which had never advanced further than the creation of unplanned proto-urban settlements, was overcome and subsumed by the feudal environment of chartered towns. Before this happened another cultural group, seafaring Scandinavians from Norway (*Fin-gall* – fair foreigners) and Denmark (*Dubh-gall* – dark foreigners) had introduced fresh ideas into the rather enclosed world of Irish society. It was not to be a welcome intrusion, although, ultimately, its fruits were many, not least of which is a spattering of Viking place-names and family names, right around the coastline – Fingall is still the name of the Dublin county borough, north of the Liffey, while Doyle is a common family name.

THE VIKING AGE: 9th CENTURY – 12th CENTURY

No group involved in Irish affairs has ever received such a bad press as the Vikings; the management of their Irish excursions proved to be a public-relations disaster! Viking presence in Ireland occurred in two separate waves. The initial period, which followed the first sea-borne attack on Rathlin Island off the Antrim coast in 795, culminated in the establishment in 841 of a *long phoirt* (boat harbour) and permanent base, possibly near Islandbridge on the River Liffey, west of Dublin Bay. The location of the settlement, other than burials, the grave goods from which are in the National Museum of Ireland, has not yet been established. The settlement survived until 902, after which the Vikings were temporarily dislodged by the kings of Brega and Leinster. The Norse reputation for ferocity and the pillaging and burning of monasteries became established during their initial phase of occupation, although their contribution to raiding monasteries and the taking of slaves, cattle and valuables were not significantly worse than that of the Irish themselves. A fundamental difference seems to have been in their not observing the concept of sanctuary which was associated with monasteries, although the Irish themselves also frequently abused the concept.

The second and more significant period of Viking presence begins in 917, with the founding of *Dyfflin* (from the Irish *dubh-linn* – a black pool, a topographical feature on the south bank of the river) on the Liffey, centred on where Christ Church Cathedral (a Viking foundation) now stands, and ends with the Norman occupation of the city in 1172, after which the Vikings disappear as a separate cultural group. Viking settlements became the origins of many Irish coastal towns, as is reflected in the Old Norse source of the names of Waterford (*Vethrafjöthr*), Wexford (*Veigsfjörthr*), Limerick (*Hlymreke*) and many other places on the eastern seaboard, as well as more scattered locations in the north and west of the island.

In the second phase of Dublin occupation is found the evolution of an urban trading community which became Ireland's first true town, about which a great deal is now known from excavations. Metalwork, leatherwork, carpentry and shipbuilding were all practised in *Dyfflin*, and formed a basis for trade not only within Ireland, but also with both Scandinavia and Continental Europe. The *Ringerike* and *Urnes* graphic-art styles, which the Vikings brought to Ireland, significantly influenced native ideas of design. As the foreigners intermarried, became Christianised and integrated into the Irish polity, they became by the mid-11th century, as Hiberno-Norse, merely another element in the dynastic struggles of restless monarchs and ambitious regional lords. The Battle of Clontarf, fought on the north shore of Dublin Bay in 1014, was retrospectively elevated to the status of a great national victory of the Irish over the Norse. Since the kingdom of *Dyfflin* remained Norse for a further 150 years, the extravagant claims that the foreigners were totally routed is manifestly untrue, although it did weaken the military strength and independence of the Dublin Vikings. The Irish forces were aided by the Norse of Limerick, while the Dublin Norse fought in alliance with the Irish of Leinster. Brian Boru, High King and leader of the Irish, was actually the father-in-law of Sitric, Christian king of Viking *Dyfflin*.

Extensive and highly successful excavations of Norse Dublin (1960-86) were carried out by the National Museum of Ireland, which uncovered the street-plan and house-types of the 10th – 13th century city, and recovered a rich array of artefacts which cast light on the domestic life, crafts and trades of the settlement. The abundant artefactual materials recovered are on display in the Viking Rooms at the National Museum of Ireland, Dublin. The form of urban development found in Dublin is not paralleled by that in the Celtic society of the island as a whole. Dyfflin is a medieval town in embryo, composed of narrow streets lined with house-plots of uniform size, each with rectangular wattle buildings, houses, stores and privies. The planning is ordered in a new way, which was ultimately to become the structure of all late medieval towns. It is a complete break with the Irish idea of multiple organic enclosures and dispersed settlement.

Round Towers and the Vikings appear to have become a species of transgenus Siamese twins: you cannot have one without the other. Nothing could be further from the case, and there is little evidence for supporting the theory of a relationship between the arrival of marauding Norse and Danes, and the construction by Irish monks of these ecclesiastical bell-towers. The dates of the initial raids, from the late 8th century to the early 9th century, seem like

LUSK, CO. DUBLIN The distinctive pencil-form of the Round Tower (extreme left) is muted at Lusk by the late medieval addition of a belfry with circular turrets at three corners, the tower making up the fourth. It is one of the masterpieces of Irish tower building.

compelling evidence for a connection, but this is merely coincidence.

The boundaries of *Dyfflinarskiri*, the shire of *Dyfflin*, the area under Norse control, a territory which varied in its extent, can only be charted by the survival of Viking topographical names on the east coast, north and south of Dublin, and in its hinterland. It certainly stretched inland to the upper reaches of the River Liffey at Leixlip (*Lax-hlaup* – salmon leap in Old Norse), and to the south of Wicklow (*Vikingalo* – Viking's lough), more than that is difficult to ascertain.

Within what was the territory of *Dyfflinasrskiri*, the Round Towers of Clondalkin, Lusk, Rathmichael and Swords still stand, while another (St Michael le Pole, a short distance to the south-west of the walls of Viking Dublin) was demolished in the 19th century. While all of these are probably early towers, 10th – 11th century, their presence does not make a great deal of sense if the territory is considered as excluding Irish monastic activity and they differ in no respect from those built in other regions, unthreatened by Viking presence. Within a century of the re-establishment of the Vikings on the River Liffey in 917, they had become a Christian community.

KINGS IN CONFLICT: 11th CENTURY – 12th CENTURY

The centuries which lead inexorably towards outside intervention in Irish political affairs, and spell the end of the extraordinarily extended span of Irish self-rule – in itself unique in European terms – is a period which is ominously and increasingly warlike. It is difficult not to see the period as suffering from too many Napoleons, without a fortunately faraway Campagna or Russian Steppes to be conquered. Moscows there were in plenty: determined invasions into distant provinces were rapidly followed by crushing defeats. The provincial regional antagonisms which were an ancient heritage, yet which in the earlier centuries appear to have been modulated by some accepted concept of the rules of war, expanded during the Viking Age. It is possible that the situation was exacerbated by Viking ruthlessness, and that in their hit-and-run military tactics, the local lords found a new model for warfare. Certainly, the use of naval fleets to carry war into enemy territory is a Viking contribution to the native repertoire in military tactics and mayhem.

If Irish High Kingship had proved elusive in the past it was to remain so until the concept ceased to have any meaningful existence, when a different dynasty and a foreign prince had seized the ultimate plum in Irish power politics. O'Brien of Munster, O'Conor of Connaght, Mac Loughlin of Ulster and MacMurrough of Leinster struggled for total power in ruthless rotation. The annalist's phrase 'High King with opposition', is a wry acknowledgement of the vanities of the status quo: each claimant to the High Kingship almost achieved total dominance. The Irish kings and their followers appear to have been looking the other way, concentrating on their internecine conflicts, and as a result were collectively mugged from behind before they could grasp the enormity of what had occurred.

Dermot MacMurrough (1110-72), was King of Leinster from 1126 and over-lord of the Dublin Hiberno-Norse. He was only one among the many disputing warlords of the 12th century. At his base in Ferns he endowed a church which carries one of the last and most eccentric Round Towers. He found himself banished from his kingdom in 1166, and felt that the neighbouring monarch, Henry II of England, in consequence of Henry's use of the Dublin Viking naval fleet the previous year, owed him a favour. The debt was paid and Dermot returned in 1167, to be followed in 1169 by Richard de Clare, second Earl of Pembroke, with a small mercenary force of Welsh Norman barons, a further complement to the indigenous population of ruthless adventurers, skilled in the art of war. Richard Stanyhurst, in *Holinshed's Chronicles* (1577), with acerbic brevity encapsulated what followed:

At the creek of Bagganbun
Ireland was lost and wun!

THE NORMAN CONQUEST: 12th CENTURY – 13th CENTURY

Following the introduction of the Continental monastic orders of Cistercians and Augustinians, and the spread of Anglo-Norman rule, church building expanded at a rapid rate, both numerically and in the scale of the new establishments. In a country where the scale of the building tradition had remained virtually static for 500 years, and only began to develop following the introduction of the Romanesque in the 11th century, the sudden expansion in building must have been dramatic and overpowering to the native Church. In the fifty years since the foundation of Mellifont (1142, consecrated 1157), forty-three Cistercian foundations were built in such a widely distributed manner that their influence became the prevailing theme of the age.

These Cistercian foundations dwarf anything built in Ireland prior to their arrival. The imposition of rules of planning by the European monastic orders dynamically altered what was considered appropriate for an ecclesiastical complex, and although this did not bring an end to the native church-building tradition, its end was in sight. Paradoxically, the fate of the Round Towers was not (as with churches) to be outmoded and replaced by a Continental model, and they continued to maintain a parallel existence. There are only a small number of instances of incorporation, where a Round Tower co-existed on the same site as a Continental foundation, and became part of the new complex. On the Rock of Cashel the Round Tower became the bell-tower of the 13th-century cathedral, as an integral part of the complex, while at Kilmallock the remainder of a destroyed tower was incorporated into the Collegiate Church of SS Peter and Paul. In other instances (Armagh, Cloyne, Kildare, Kilkenny), the Round Tower remained in use throughout the medieval period, declining with, as in Kildare, the destruction of the cathedral and returning to use only with the many Anglican reconstructions of the 19th century.

TIMAHOE, CO. LAOIS Disguised by the vertical formality and decorated Romanesque doorway of this 12th-century tower at Timahoe are the underlying structural principles embodied in the cashel of the Grianán of Aileach, and practised by the monastic master masons with little modification for 300 years.

CHAPTER TWO

ARCHAIC ARCHITECTURE IN EUROPE, PRINCIPLES AND PARALLELS

'Vernacular architecture does not go through fashion cycles. It is nearly immutable, indeed, unimprovable, since it serves its purpose to perfection.'

Bernard Rudofsky, *Architecture without Architects*, 1965

The subject of this brief chapter is an unanswered and probably unanswerable question; why does a society, metaphorically speaking, independently discover the wheel? The achievements of archaic architecture in Europe are well known and, at least in the area of the eastern Mediterranean and the Greek mainland, well documented. From the earliest sites where architecturally ambitious structures appear, like the Neolithic aceramic settlement of Khirokitia in Cyprus, with its circular flat-roofed dwellings, to the still-lived-in *trulli* of Apulia in southern Italy, attempts to span open spaces with beams, corbels and, more latterly, vaults and domes, are the very bones of the progress of European architecture from 5000 BC. Architecture is as much a mirror of the progress of basic material needs, to provide security and shelter, as it is the parallel record of intellectual aspirations and structural discoveries.

The walled city of Mycenae is perched on a hillside in the rugged landscape west of Athens. It was, according to the *Iliad*, from Mycenae that Agamemnon led the Greek expedition against Troy, after Paris, son of King Priam, had carried off Helen, the wife of King Menelaus of Sparta, to Troy. In one of the legendary acts of early archaeology, Mycenae was revealed by Heinrich Schliemann in 1876, when he excavated the Royal Graves. Mycenae has among its surviving buildings a comprehensive library of archaic architectural forms, which, despite the separation in time and geography, are worth examining for the parallels which they share with the Irish context. This is not a case of direct influence, but of rediscovery of long-established European building methods. Harold Leask, in the first volume of his *Irish Churches and Monastic Buildings* (1955), remarks on the connection but without coming to any conclusion. He observes:

> *Though a connection has not been proved between the tholoi of the eastern Mediterranean and the corbel-built huts of southern Italy, the Adriatic coasts, France, Spain and Portugal,*

where they are fairly numerous in treeless and stony areas,
it is tempting to trace the Irish clocháns to the same ultimate
origin by way of the western Mediterranean.

It is helpful to understand the defining structural characteristics of the earliest Irish Christian architecture in stone. The monastery on Skellig Michael has
many of them: drystone buildings, circular in external plan and round or rectangular internally, with corbelled roofs; rectangular buildings with corbelled
roofs; trabeate doorways with inclined jambs and cyclopean masonry. When
the Irish began to build churches in stone, initially in the 8th century and more
widely in the 9th and 10th centuries, this was the architectural repertoire which
they had at their disposal, inherited from the Iron Age, and hardly deviated
from until after the onslaught of the Romanesque world-view brought them
into line with the progress of ideas elsewhere. The enigma of Irish architectural
development is in the reliance on out-dated rather than available contemporary
technology and style.

DEVENISH I, CO. FERMANAGH
At Devenish the interior of the cap shows
concentric courses of masonry, with a
cap-stone placed on the apex, to close the
interior cone. Devenish has an internal
cornice, as well as an external one.

The most famous building of Mycenae is the tholos tomb, the *Treasury of
Atreus* (*c.* 1325 BC), constructed on a circular plan in a pit excavated into the
ground, which was subsequently filled to enclose and cover the building. The
roof (only visible from within) is a perfect and beautifully corbelled structure,
indistinguishable in section from a north-south cut through the 11th – 12th-
century Gallarus Oratory (**fig. 9**). In both buildings each course of masonry
slightly overhangs that below, to create an inwardly-inclined wall surface.
Looking up into the apex of the Treasury's dome one could be excused for
attributing it to the same hand as the internal dome of the cap of the Devenish
Round Tower. The equally famous Lion Gate in the Citadel of Mycenae has
close structural parallels with the entrance to a number of Round Towers, such
as at Monasterboice. The double recessed bands around the entrance door of
the Treasury of Atreus closely resemble the doorcase of Aghowle Church; the
cyclopean masonry of the Citadel resembles that of Temple MacDuagh. From
the inclined jambs of the entrance to the fortress of the Grianán of Aileach
(4th century), to the even more inclined orders of the doorcase on the
Timahoe Round Tower (mid-11th century), or the similar detailing of the
entrance of Clonfert Cathedral (1200), there is a clear line of influence and
tradition, a way of doing things which was not to be improved upon.

The civilisation of Mycenae led on to the greatest architecture of the ancient
world, the imaginative wealth of classical Greece. What might have happened in
Ireland can only be, rather fruitlessly, speculated upon. The insular and archaic
architecture of Ireland was possessed of such style, vigour and sense of form
that, if it had continued to flourish undisturbed, the results might have been
remarkable. Only a single church building of great worth, Cormac's Chapel
(Cashel), was built in the final years of the barbaric splendour of Irish architectural individuality. If stripped of its Romanesque applied decoration, it expresses a pure geometry and sculptural aesthetic so different from the European
monastic architecture which supplanted and now surrounds it, that the sense of
volumes is closer to what can be understood of its timber predecessors than

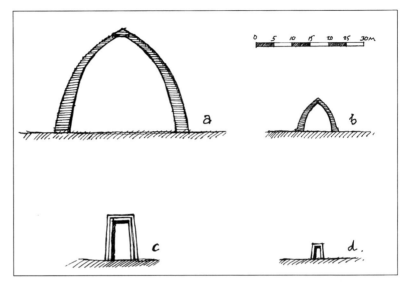

fig. 9 a-d: ARCHAIC ARCHITECTURE
Archaic architectural elements, which first found significant expression in Mycenean Greece, survive in the buildings of medieval Ireland. The drystone corbelled dome of (a) the great tholos tomb of the Treasury of Atreus at Mycenae, shares structural principles with (b) Gallarus Oratory. In both cases the walls are constructed of horizontal courses which override each other, rising to an inverted-boat-shaped section. Doorways from the same periods display similar features, with the main doorway of (c) the Treasury and (d) St Mary's Church, Glendalough, both having inclined jambs.

it is to Glastonbury or the Carolingian world.

The significance of these parallels is that they remain no more than parallels; there can be no question of direct influence of ideas carried across millennia. The time gap which separates the architecture of the Mycenean Age (1600 – 1120 BC) and the stone buildings of early medieval Ireland (800 – 1200 AD) is vast. What is of interest is the manner in which the native builders remained for many centuries impervious to the most obviously adjacent source of architectural influence, late Roman and Anglo-Saxon Britain, and Carolingian France and Germany, yet with considerable verve and imagination, reinvented for their own purpose the primary building principles of a bygone age. By the time tower-building began in Ireland, the Anglo-Saxon architecture of Britain could have provided an alternative mode to that which was ultimately adopted.

The Irish attitude to urban planning and their infatuation with the ubiquitous and eminently adaptable concentric circle, which became a catch-all for any exigency, either in curvilinear or sub-rectangular variations, is in total harmony with the archaic building approach of the stone structures. All that can be said, architecturally, to have penetrated from without, is the Christian requirement of a rectangular church building, and particularly germane to this book, the principle without which the building of Round Towers would have been impossible, lime mortared stone, or as it began, Roman cement.

Vitruvius, writing in Rome in 100 AD, in the second of his *Ten Books on Architecture*, remarks:

> *There is also a kind of powder which from natural causes produces*
> *astonishing results. This substance, when mixed with lime and rubble,*
> *not only lends strength to buildings of other kinds, but even when piers*
> *of it are constructed in the sea, they set hard under water.*

The discovery of rigidly binding mortars (lime and aggregates), which became the core principle of all Roman building, was clearly available centuries later, whether from the Carolingian Empire or more plausibly from early medieval Britain, to make Round Tower building a structural possibility.

Staigue Fort in Kerry, the Grianán of Aileach in Donegal, and Dun Aenghus on Inishmore, all date from the late Iron Age or pre-Christian early medieval period; their precise dating has not so far been clarified by excavation, although the Grianán was probably in occupation throughout the early medieval era. Excepting Dun Aenghus, the rampart of which is cut by a precipitous cliff, both Staigue and the Grianán are circular, drystone fortresses with high battered walls, the central enclosure entered through a trabeate doorway with inclined jambs. The building tradition which these structures represent was carried into the Christian world and became the kernel from which Round Towers evolved. The lines of the Grianán, projected into the air, become those of a Round Tower. The imaginative leap generated by the sight of a Continental prototype, allied to new liturgical requirements, unleashed the possibilities inherent in the Iron Age fortresses of the west coast. Add lime mortar and, *presto!*

A parallel can be drawn, or a relationship seen, between the Irish tradition of building in the round and the Irish Round Tower. The corbelled chamber of Newgrange (3000 BC), in itself a more primitive ancestor of Mycenae, has been cited as an ancient and plausible ancestor for Irish building practice. Closer, in time and space, are the innumerable earthen ringforts, dry-stone-walled cashels and beehive huts. These constitute more formidable evidence of a tradition of thinking in the round, and knowledge of the principle of corbelling. Ringforts were occupied over an extended period which may have lasted for centuries; excavations suggest a 300-year occupation span as typical.

Thus, Iron Age concepts of planning, archaic architectural principles, surviving Roman technology and Christian ecclesiastical purpose were combined to form a synthesis in the early 10th century, which allowed the Irish Round Tower, one of the great flights of the Irish imagination, to be born. Before the coming of Patrick, and for centuries after his passing, virtually everything (with the exception of Christian churches) contributed by the human hand to the forming of the Irish landscape was roughly circular in plan: huts, forts, domestic, royal and ritual enclosures and finally, striking a vibrant note in this green Moon-landscape, the extraordinary verticality of the circular towers. It must have been a truly remarkable spectacle, a supreme example of a vernacular architectural tradition which had discovered for itself a form which was practical, beautiful and infinitely adaptable, being driven by the inspiration of a new belief system to create towers in the air.

CHAPTER THREE

EARLY MEDIEVAL TOWERS OUTSIDE IRELAND

'A cloicteach of fire was seen in the air over Ros-Deala, on the Sunday of the festival of George, [23 April] for the space of five hours; innumerable black birds passing into and out of it, and one large bird in the middle of it; and the little birds went under his wings when they went into the cloicteach.'

Annals of the Four Masters for the year 1054

There is no archaeological evidence to substantiate the idea that timber predecessors of the stone-constructed Irish Round Tower existed, nor is there any textual evidence to lend support to such a proposition, yet their existence is probable. It is possible that shorter timber towers pre-date the stone ones, but in the absence of any proof, this is a matter for speculation. Where then did the idea of such vertical architecture come from? The alternatives are that the concept generated within Ireland, answering the ecclesiastical requirements of the monastic church, or that it is an adaptation of similar ideas which were to be found elsewhere in the known world of Europe and the Near East. In the total absence of a high-rise building tradition within Iron Age or early medieval Ireland, the inspiration must be sought elsewhere (**fig. 10**).

Among the earliest credible claimants to there being an outside source for the inspiration of the Irish Round Towers is the 9th-century *Plan of St Gall*, which originated at the island monastery of St Reichenau on Lake Constance (the parchment manuscript now in the library of St Gallen, Switzerland, is dated to *c.* 820). This ambitious drawing, which is the earliest architectural manuscript of the early medieval period, preserves an ideal monastic layout. Paired, round, turret-like buildings, with internal spiral staircases, flank the western end of the basilican church, and are connected to the porch of the church by short enclosed corridors. Since the plan was either not carried out as envisaged, or never completed, it is unknown what height the planners proposed for these towers. In imaginative present-day reconstructions of the plan, the circular turrets have been interpreted as resembling Irish Round Towers, but this conception may be possible only with the vision of hindsight (**fig. 11a**). However, the information derived from the plan which pre-dates, by more than a century, the earliest reference to an Irish Round Tower, is that circular buildings with internal stairs were considered as an adjunct to the church, and positioned at its western end, offset to the north-west and south-west (as

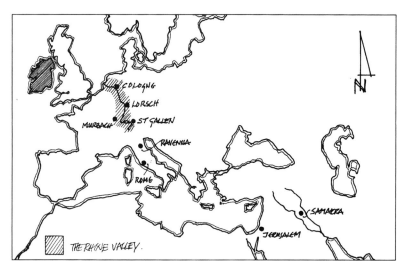

Left: fig. 10 EUROPE IN THE EARLY MEDIEVAL PERIOD
Pilgrimage routes from Ireland would have brought both lay and clerical pilgrims into close contact with the most important building projects of the period. Although the evidence for connections is more in essence than in detail, the source of much which was new in Irish Christian architecture must have come from Romanesque Britain and Europe. Along the Rhine valley are grouped Continental monasteries with significant Irish connections.

Irish towers are also positioned). Whether or not the turrets of the St Gaul manuscript were inspired by existing features on vanished 8th- and 9th-century buildings has yet to proved; on this factor hinges their relevance to the Irish Round Towers.

With the rise of Islam during the 7th through to the 9th centuries in Saudi Arabia and the lands of the eastern Mediterranean, the demands of a new religion generated new architectural forms. The earliest mosques were vast rectangular open courtyards, oriented towards Mecca (as Christian churches were towards Jerusalem), with, at the centre of the shorter south-eastern side, a minaret or tower from which the call to prayer was announced by a muezzin. The earliest surviving examples are not like those with which a Western reader will be more familiar; the Syrian, Turkish and Egyptian minarets, with internal stairs, a number of balconies and steeply pointed roof, dating from the 12th century and later. These early examples were ziggurat-like brick towers, with a spiralling external access ramp and a small platform at the top. The literary evidence suggests that minarets were being built from the 7th century, although none of these early towers survive. The Islamic towers are related in function to the Irish towers, since both are high-rise buildings and devoted to announcing the hours of community prayer. However, these Islamic towers otherwise bear no physical resemblance to their Irish counterparts, beyond being an alternative approach to achieving height, but are relevant in that they certainly pre-date, by a century or more, their Irish equivalents.

Among the most important surviving early minarets is that attached to the Omayyad Great Mosque of Samarra, 848 – 852 AD (in modern Iraq), known as Manáret al-Malwíya (the spiral minaret). It stands 53 metres high, and is composed of a 3 metre high rectangular podium on which is based the spiral-ramped tower, its ramp ascending anti-clockwise (**fig. 11b**). It was built by the Caliph al-Mutawakkil who ruled from 847. As the Spanish-Jewish traveller Benjamin of Tudela (d. 1173) saw the ramped ziggurat of Khorsabad (800 BC)

Right: fig. 11 a-f
EARLY MEDIEVAL TOWERS OUTSIDE IRELAND
The emergence of the Irish Round Tower was progressively influenced by architectural developments in the known Christian world of the Mediterranean Basin and Northern Europe during the 9th – 12th centuries. Developments ranging from the architecture of early Islam to that of Italian and Carolingian church building led to an extraordinary proliferation of ecclesiastical tower building. This is the context to which the Irish towers belong: (a) Reconstruction of the Plan of St Gall; (b) Minaret of the Great Mosque of Samarra; (c) Campanile of the Cathedral, Ravenna; (d) St Pantaleon, Cologne; (e) St Cyriakus, Gernrode; (f) St Riquier, Centula Abbey Church (after Conant).

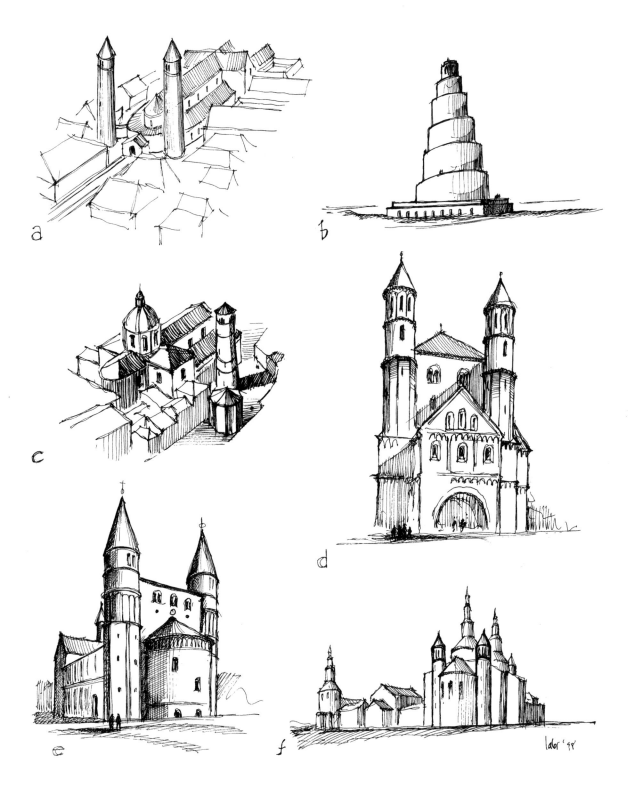

a

b

c

d

e

f

still standing in the 12th century, it can be assumed that this provided the inspiration for the 9th-century tower of Samarra, from which all other early minarets are derived. If their origin is not derived from Europe, then their influence may have travelled to Europe.

Owing to lack of connecting evidence, it is difficult to substantiate whether the Omayyad and Abbasid minarets in the early Islamic world of the Near East can be considered as forerunners of the ecclesiastical bell-towers in northern and southern Europe. It must, nonetheless, be considered as a possibility, even if a tenuous one. As contemporaneous structures, generated by the requirements of evolving Islam, they represent important examples in early medieval architecture of 'height for hire', a new ecclesiastical building type, which was to become as synonymous with Islamic culture as 'westwork' church towers were to be identified with north European Christian building, and are at least tentative claimants to being the origin of medieval ecclesiastical towers.

The minute scale and peculiarities associated with the buildings of the Irish Church, which did not produce its first stone church before the early 8th century, and where church building in stone did not become commonplace until possibly the 10th century, is difficult to accommodate to the parallel existence of monumental church buildings in Continental Europe and the Near East, planned on the grand scale, and dating from the 5th century onwards. The period of Round Tower building, at its broadest extent, corresponds roughly with the Middle Byzantine Period (843-1251, the Second Byzantine Golden Age), when the greatest achievements of Christian ecclesiastical and civil architecture were those of the Byzantine world. The Great Church of Hagia Sophia (532) was already standing, as it still today triumphantly dominates the skyline of Istanbul, throughout the entire early medieval period in Ireland. Its fantastic interior space, spanned by one of the greatest domes ever built (30 metres in diameter, 53 metres high), could have contained three-quarters of the entire number of Round Towers under its majestic roof. Seventy-five Round Towers could have occupied the oval nave covered by the central dome and its flanking hemi-domes. This is proof, if any were needed, of the vast difference in scale between what was being constructed in early medieval Ireland and what was available as contemporary exemplars in the Christian world.

The achievement of Irish medieval tower building retains its uniqueness on the edge of the civilised world, but the fact that almost the entire corpus of its towers could be contained within the nave of a contemporary church elsewhere reduces the achievement to one of singularity, rather than size. The wealth of architecture, church plate, ecclesiastical objects, fine art and manuscripts produced in Byzantium and within the territory of the Eastern Orthodox Church, fuelled the creative imagination of the western church throughout the period.

The great basilican churches of S. Apollinare Nuovo (5th – 6th centuries) and S. Apollinare in Classe (6th century) at Ravenna, and S. Lorenzo fuori le Mura in Rome (7th century), all have freestanding campanile, which although later than the foundation of the churches, perform the same function as the Irish towers.

The bell-tower of Ursiana Cathedral in Ravenna stands 38 metres high and has a base diameter of over 8 metres (**fig. 11c**). While in appearance it differs considerably from the Irish examples, the principle is identical: a freestanding round, slender, multi–storey ecclesiastical belfry, with rudimentary windows in the drum, substantial windows at the top floor, and with a pitched roof which rises to an apex. This description will do equally well for either Italian or Irish towers, only the details are different. The siting, however, of this Ravenna campanile is quite different, placed as it is on the north-east corner, rather than offset from the west front. St Peter's in Rome had the earliest recorded campanile, built in the mid-8th century and rectangular in plan.

The architecture of the Carolingian Empire, which covered most of modern France, Germany and the Netherlands between the 8th and 10th centuries, is likewise on a massive scale which dwarfs Irish building endeavours. The revival of Roman classicism, promoted by the court of Charlemagne, became a bridge between the architecture of the eastern and western Roman worlds, and the development of the Romanesque in north-western Europe. Substantial churches were built from the 8th century in France and Germany during the early Carolingian period. In Germany, among many similar examples, St Pantaleon, Cologne (966), has paired west towers (**fig. 11d**), and St Cyriakus, Gernrode (961), has paired east towers (**fig. 11e**). The presence of Italian church towers clearly establishes the principle of circular belfries as an established form, from the period when the Irish towers were first built. The Carolingian church towers demonstrate the prevalence of west front towers, even if these are all engaged examples. The destroyed 9th-century French abbey church of St Riquier, Centula, had similar east-end towers (**fig. 11f**).

In summary, the options seem to be as follows. If the *cloicteach* was not an indigenous Irish invention, which in a country with no tradition of any type of tall buildings, is improbable, then from where did it derive? The fact that the Irish church in the 6th century adopted its ideas of monasticism from Egypt and Syria does not establish a like connection for its architecture during the 9th and 10th centuries. For the Irish church to absorb concepts of ecclesiastical architecture from the Middle East, where the earliest minarets were probably built by Christian craftsmen during the 9th century, is not impossible, but would depend on there being some established connection between the Euphrates region and Ireland. Alternatively, it is more plausible that the source of inspiration was either the campanile of Ravenna and Rome, the engaged towers of the Rhineland, or some similar unidentified or vanished exemplar, which there is far more reason to believe would have been familiar to Irish pilgrims and clergy, travelling the fairly well-worn routes to northern Europe and Italy. Geography, religious and cultural affiliations, allied to probability, certainly favour the influence of the Rhineland and Italy over Samarra. The source for the origins of freestanding ecclesiastical belfries is firstly most probably northern Italy, with Carolingian northern Europe at a later stage providing stylistic options for the further development of the idea in Ireland. Nonetheless, the virtually simultaneous erection of similarly motivated architecture, at opposite ends of the early medieval world, is an intriguing parallel.

A distinctive feature of both Carolingian and later Romanesque church

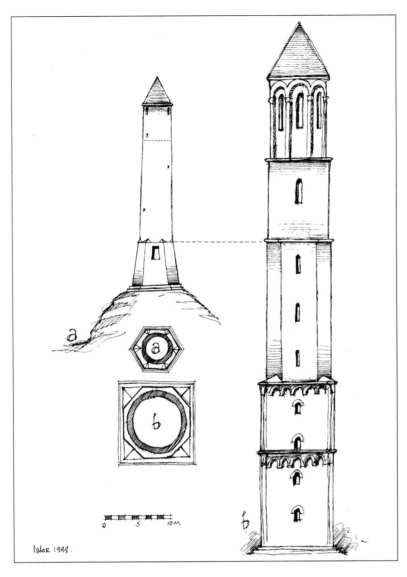

fig. 12 a-b
COMPARATIVE DETAILS OF KINNEIGH AND ST PANTALEON, COLOGNE
A comparison of the plans of (a) Kinneigh Round Tower, and that of one of the engaged westwork towers of (b) St Pantaleon, shows the influence of Continental architecture on Irish building practice. In St Pantaleon, the graduation from rectangle through octagon to circle and cone is paralleled in a simplified manner at Kinneigh, where the progression is from hexagon to circle to cone. Considerable differences of scale and detailing do not obscure the essential geometrical development of both towers.

KINNEIGH, CO. CORK
Kinneigh's hexagonal base is without precedent in Irish architecture and is evidence of direct influence from Continental building practice.

architecture of the Rhineland (and latterly in Britain) is the prominent display of western paired towers and monumental decorated portals, known as 'westwork' and symbolising the power of the civil, regal or ecclesiastical authority under which individual churches prospered. In the open-plan combination of the Irish church, with a Round Tower projected to the north or south-west at a distance from the west doorway, with an intervening open space (the platea or forecourt) defined by a High Cross with its bas-relief scriptural panels, and sometimes the site of the founder-saint or patron's burial place can be seen as an intellectually brilliant deconstruction of the 'westwork' idea of Continental church architecture. All the elements are there, dispersed and reassembled in a manner appropriate to a society with no dependence on, or experience of, classical planning tradition, nor of monumental building practices, yet liturgically satisfying to local demands. This Irish 'westwork' depends for its coherence on an imaginative leap in which the individual elements exist independently, united under the sky by the enveloping concept of the *civitas dei*, the city of God – without its walls.

The fact that specific Round Tower details, the plan at Kinneigh (12th century) and the decorated second-floor window at Timahoe (12th century), can be traced directly or indirectly to Rhineland originals, Cologne (**fig. 12b**) and Lorsch (**fig. 13a**), not more than 100 kilometres apart, suggests that the Carolingian, Ottonian and Hohenstaufen church architecture of the Rhineland may be where the inspiration for the Irish Round Tower actually began. Furthermore, the fact that both these towers are late, even if not contemporary examples, lends further strength to the possibility that there could be architectural connections with a region known for its strong Irish monastic connections over a lengthy period. Correspondingly close parallels are not found in either Italy or Britain, although triangular-headed window features of Anglo–Saxon church towers (Barton–on–Humber, Earls Barton, [**fig. 13c**] Sompting), in the south of England, which resemble other Irish tower details, may be their immediate source, and themselves also derived from Rhenish origins. Early medieval church builders in Ireland and elsewhere in western Europe were not, except in rare instances, motivated by a search for originality, but in copying and emulating existing forms for their symbolic and liturgical content.

The significance of the parallels in **fig. 12a-b** is that the influence which the westwork towers of St Pantaleon, or some similar building, had on Kinneigh is that the information must have been carried to Ireland by an Irish monk, trained in Germany, rather than a German monk who travelled to Ireland. This can be seen in the manner by which the polygonal element in Cologne is adapted to Irish building norms. No German mason is likely to have favoured a battered wall for the base, which was a purely local manner of building in Ireland, and an archaic survival. The Rhenish octagon is reduced to a hexagon, and the drum placed upon it without the use of a graduating cornice to allow for the change of planes. The characteristic corner squinches in Cologne, which allow for the change from rectangle to octagon, are employed in Kinneigh to convert the hexagon to a circle. A comparison of both plans is fairly convincing: they are a product of the same intellectual and structural understanding, but the Irish example is less ambitious. By stripping away the embellishments of the Rhenish tower (more complex plan-form, pilasters, cornices and arcading), the process leads directly to the Irish example. The four axial windows on the bell-floor of Irish towers are paralleled in the windows of St Pantaleon in Cologne. In the bell-floor of the Cologne tower the number of windows is increased to eight. The Irish roof cone also follows the Rhenish example.

In **fig. 13a-c** the connection is more immediately obvious with, in the Torhalle of the abbey of Lorsch (early 9th century), round-headed windows framed by a triangular-headed arcade. This is composed of classical pilasters

fig.13 a-c: COMPARATIVE DETAILS OF LORSCH, TIMAHOE AND EARLS BARTON
The facade of the Torhalle (gatehouse) of (a) Lorsch Abbey in the Rhineland, has a gabled window arcade composed of classical pilasters framing the windows. At (b) Timahoe, the second floor window displays remarkably similar detailing, although its mannerisms are characteristic of the Irish Romanesque. The Anglo-Saxon window from (c) Earls Barton, Northamptonshire, also derives from the same source, but is more basic in its detailing.

TIMAHOE, CO. LAOIS
New ideas in architectural style were imported from Romanesque Britain and Europe. The second floor window at Timahoe shows the direct influence of foreign examples.

with capitals and bases, surmounted by tangential gables. The Timahoe window, the only decorated one in any Round Tower, closely follows Lorsch, with a reduction in scale and the substitution of local elements, human-head capitals and paired-spool bases (an Anglo-Saxon import). The frame surrounds, as in Lorsch, a round-headed window. Such substantial relationships between both a mid-period and a late Round Tower to the same region of the Rhineland argues strongly for a Rhenish origin for the Irish Round Tower. The Lorsch Torhalle (entrance porch to a vanished monastery) is the finest surviving Carolingian exterior, and its survival emphasises a difficulty in tracing Irish tower origins – the small number of unaltered Continental buildings which have survived from the 10th century and earlier.

Kinneigh might be, depending on how the evidence is interpreted, a mid-period or late tower although its late date is most probable, is a case of the path not followed; its hexagonal base was either too demanding for local building practice, or did not appeal for other reasons. Liturgical or theological reasons may also be an explanation for the failure to pursue the hexagon. In the language of Continental church architecture, geometric form had symbolic significance: the square symbolised the world; the circle the divine; the octagon, eternity. The octagon, which finds its way from the Byzantine S. Vitale, Ravenna (526), to the Islamic Dome of the Rock in Jerusalem (691), admired and converted into a church by the crusaders, to Charlemagne's Palatine Chapel in Aachen (798), illustrates the manner in which the spread of forms which were both complex and symbolic travelled widely from their source, over an extended time-span. In the context of symbolic form the hexagon, which seems in Ireland to be unique to Kinneigh, bears a close resemblance to the mandorla, the almond-shaped aureole which commonly enclosed the Christ-figure in early medieval church westwork sculptural decoration, as well as in mosaics, murals and manuscripts.

It seems probable that at some date during the early 10th century the inspiration for the Irish Round Tower was brought to Ireland from the Rhineland. The fact that the two examples given here are respectively an intellectual understanding and a stylistic parallel makes them difficult to dismiss in art-historical terms. These Continental connections have been established with late and eccentric Irish towers rather than more typical representatives, emphasising the fact that towers lacking eccentric details are architecturally anonymous. In terms of geography, there is no logical reason why the church architecture of Britain should not have been the springboard for Irish building endeavours, as it certainly was during the flowering of Romanesque church decoration. However, the geometry of early English churches provides no adequate parallel for the Round Tower, which seems to have its source purely in the concepts of the continental mainland. The round flint-built church towers of East Anglia (which date from the 11th century) provide another significant contemporary parallel, and their lime-mortar structure connects them closely in technological terms to the Irish towers. In spirit, however, they seem to relate more to Saxon rectangular bell-towers, and are neither tall nor freestanding.

A consideration which requires stressing regarding the Irish towers is that they are remarkable in a non-urban landscape of miniature architecture; placed in a Byzantine, Italian or Carolingian urban context, they would appear neither so tall nor so extraordinary. They represent the scale and concepts of monumental European architecture, erected in the middle of a field! The Irish genius was in adapting the indigenous archaic architectural principles to a new ecclesiastical requirement.

fig. 14: LITTLE SAXHAM, SUSSEX
The geographically closest round ecclesiastical bell-towers of the early medieval period are those found in the south-east of England, but they neither pre-date nor resemble the Irish tower, nor are they freestanding.

GLENDALOUGH II, CO. WICKLOW During the 12th century the cone-capped bell-towers, which had been freestanding structures since first introduced 250 years earlier, were adapted as embellishments for church buildings. Glendalough II, St Kevin's Church, is the most substantial survival of this new usage.

CHAPTER FOUR

DEFINITION AND TYPOLOGY

‘ *It is not in its size or form that the Irish tower is so singular, but in its isolation.* ’

Margaret Stokes, *Early Christian Architecture in Ireland*, 1878

The number of Round Towers now standing is generally given as sixty-five, although seventy-three will be found in the inventory. The increase in number is not caused by eight further towers being discovered, but by the conviction that an inclusive rather than an excluding definition of what constitutes a Round Tower is both correct and necessary for the proper evaluation of the subject. The definition used here to identify an orthodox or standard Round Tower is of a freestanding tall and circular tapered ecclesiastical bell-tower, with or without a conical roof, constructed of stone, with the use of lime mortar as its structural principle, and built in the early medieval period, between the 10th and 12th centuries.

Round Towers may be, as are the majority of those which survive, freestanding, or alternatively engaged, that is attached to a building. The terminology used here is that applied to the most essential of all architectural forms, the Greek classical column: they are either freestanding or engaged. A classical column is no less a column for being attached to a wall. With Round Towers it should be the same – freestanding or engaged. Unfortunately, few of the latter survive intact (Clonmacnoise II, Glendalough II), but the existence of these two, and the known former existence of other vanished examples, establishes the need for their inclusion in the corpus (**fig. 15**). A third subdivision can be added of attached towers where (unlike Glendalough II, St Kevin's Church, sites in which the tower is integral), the tower has been included by the addition of a further unit or cell to the building, not contained within the original external wall of the structure, such as Glendalough III, Trinity Church, where a second chancel-like extension has been added to the west end to form the podium of an attached Round Tower.

The existence of a fourth category of towers is tentatively proposed, that of the half-sized tower. A significant number of towers stand no higher than 10 metres and may never have been much taller. The probability that the tower at

Tory stood no more than 15 metres high when complete raises the consideration that some of the short towers may always have been so, dictated by the economics of the community, the demands of the local topography or other considerations, such as the perceived hinterland of individual towers. In sites of extreme elevation, such as Ardpatrick, Co. Limerick, only ostentation or conspicuous wealth would have called for a full-height tower of around 30 metres.

As all towers are to some degree atypical, to eliminate the most eccentric from the inventory is to seriously diminish the wealth of the subject and to impose limitations which are historically invalid. In the later centuries of their construction, the concept of the Round Tower, so pleasing to the eye and definitive of a prestigious ecclesiastical context, had been adapted and expanded to embrace new possibilities and greater experimentation. In Glendalough's three towers (which are respectively, freestanding, engaged and attached), can be found a library and typology of Irish Round Tower types, all located within a single important monastic site. Eccentricity is of central importance in the study of Round Towers, for it is only by being able to relate the eccentric details of some towers to other datable buildings that the entire corpus of towers may be more definitely dated. Towers which display no architectural details, or which tend towards stylistic anonymity remain enigmatic, outside the scope of a developing typology or chronology. Towers devoid of architectural features – doors, windows, external decoration – have nothing beyond the quality of their masonry to relate them to other contemporary buildings.

Round Towers are pure geometry and aesthetically appeal to the eye in the manner of all shapes which are beautiful in their simplicity. The body of the standard tower is of a slightly tapering tube, its diameter diminishing upwards only sufficiently to maintain the stability of the structure. The cap, which concludes the tower, is a cone, separated from the drum by a slightly projecting cornice which repeats the definition of the circular offsets at the base; it could not be more simple. Le Corbusier, in one of the pioneering texts of the modern movement in architecture, *Towards a New Architecture* (1923), observed that '*Profile and contour are the touchstone of the architect*'. If profile and contour are the very essence of the beauty of form which Round Towers achieved, their medieval master masons knew this well.

The architectural features of Round Towers may be divided into constants and variables, although even the constants cannot be regarded as absolutes, but they are more or less to be relied upon. The constants are the circular form, the entrance door positioned well above external ground floor level, the four axially placed windows below the conical cap. The character of the doorway and the windows of the drum are the variables, and their design, number and distribution differ enormously from those towers with well-lit floors to others with almost no internal lighting. Height is a further variable, as are external or internal decoration, style and quality of masonry.

Although the surviving corpus of towers is sufficiently numerous for generalised observations on most aspects of tower building to be plausible, the fact that local or regional variants depend for their identification on specific geographic bodies of information, casts the reliability of anything beyond an

fig. 15 a-e: ENGAGED TOWERS

In the development of the engaged tower no standard solution emerged; each example appears to be an independent variant on the problem of how to combine an oratory with a tower to produce a hybrid architectural form. Towers positioned at both western and eastern ends, as well as apsidally, indicate the experimental nature of these buildings.

(a) Glendalough III, Trinity Church
(b) Glendalough II, St Kevin's Church
(c) Kilmacnessan
(d) Clonmacnoise II, Temple Finghin
(e) Cashel, Cormac's Chapel with cap of
  South Tower restored

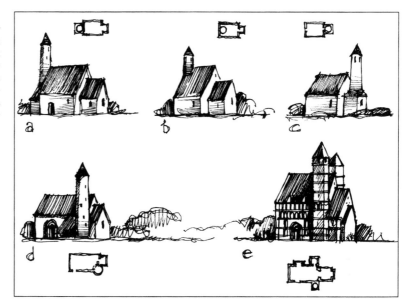

CORMAC'S CHAPEL, CASHEL, CO. TIPPERARY

The chapel, built by King Cormac MacCarthy, and finished in 1134, has a pair of transeptal rectangular towers, the only other ecclesiastical towers to be built within the 10th – 12th-century time frame of the Round Towers.

57

overview into some doubt. Similarly, the discovery over the course of the last 120 years of three additional towers, St Mullins (1880), Liathmore (1969), Devenish II (1970), although they are widely separated and fail to affect in any way the general pattern of distribution, does suggest that those areas of the country, with appropriate ecclesiastical sites yet lacking towers, may not always have been so. The north-west (Donegal and Sligo), west (Mayo and Connemara west of the Corrib) and south-west (Cork and Kerry), are virtually without towers, yet the presence of towers on specific isolated sites in all these regions demonstrate the probability that others may have existed which have not survived nor received mention in the literature.

CONFRONTING THE ARCH

A considerable part of the later history of the development of the Round Tower is the story of the Irish medieval masons' struggle with the concept of the arch. This difficulty, a product of the fact that Ireland never came under Roman rule, meant that the native masons lacked the immediate evidence of Roman buildings from which to learn this most basic structural principle of Late Antique, Carolingian and Romanesque architecture. A measure of the degree of isolation in which Ireland existed, from the arrival of Christianity to the Norman invasion, is the fact that it took until the 12th century for correctly constructed arches to become a commonplace of Irish building practice. A small number of correctly constructed arches are found in earlier churches but this use is untypical. The structural principle of the Romanesque round arch went through a wide range of tentative approaches and unhappy contortions before the idea became understood and subsequently mastered although, almost to the end of the Romanesque, archaic features were still inherent in Irish church building practice (Clonfert Cathedral). Unfortunately, by the late 12th century, the era that the round arch had been adopted and mastered (Ardmore, Dromiskin, Timahoe), the building of towers had come to an end.

Many of these timid approaches suggest that this new structural principle failed to gain acceptance among practitioners of what was a very conservative building tradition. Generations of practice had made Irish masons sufficiently experienced in the method of spanning openings with corbels or a lintel, that when they initially became familiar with the appearance of arches, it was evidently first merely considered as a decorative feature. The widespread development of tower entrances in which the apparent arch is, in fact, only a modified lintel represents the transitional phase between those towers with trabeate entrances, and the small number of towers which have a true arch as the doorhead. Even when the idea of the true arch had become part of the building repertoire, the structural principle of the space to be spanned being bridged by a specific number of equal wedge-shaped units or voussoirs, seems to have been a long time in achieving acceptance. Dummy-arches and proto-arches for a lengthy period occupy the place of an intellectually conscious understanding of this means of spanning openings.

Lintels into which an arch has been cut (Kilree) show, by the manner in which they have cracked, that cutting away the soffit of a lintel was in fact weakening the load-bearing capacity of the lintel which had, on average, 25 metres of stonework above it. This was not an approach with a future, and other than stylistically, no improvement on a solid lintel.

Another significant area of development is in the treatment of the masonry which surrounds the door-opening. In early and more rudimentary examples, the only distinguishing features are the sill and the treatment of the doorhead. At a more advanced stage the idea of articulating the doorframe by using contrasting masonry, large quoins or a pseudo-architrave, developed the idea of a distinctive doorcase which served to emphasise the entrance and contributed to the beauty of the tower. When the masonry was fresh, such distinctions were more dramatically apparent than they are today. The polychrome effect of the red sandstone doorcase and window jambs, combined with limestone masonry at Dysert Oengusa, would have made this tower particularly distinguished and reflected the interest in colour as well as form to be found in many 11th- and 12th-century English and Continental Romanesque buildings. Even when towers were rendered in limewash or lime plaster, the distinctive design of the doorcast would still have been apparent as it would not have been covered.

In perusing a typology based on doorcase styles, the number has to be restricted to towers in which this feature survives (the doorcase is missing on 22 towers, and only a single engaged tower, Clonmacnoise II, has a conventional entrance). Other stylistic factors, such as the quality of the masonry, manner of cutting and finishing of the stonework, window details and general decorative features, can also contribute towards bringing more towers into a typology, but here the evidence is even more sparse. The doorcase is the most consistently surviving architectural element on which a system can be based.

It is tempting to propose dates to parallel the typology. By simply dividing the timespan between Slane (950) and Annadown (1238), then it probably developed over a protracted period. While it is not plausible to suggest that such a linear chronology should be adopted, it does provide a tentative framework within which some individual Round Towers, not datable by any other means, can be situated. As the majority of the surviving and architecturally identifiable towers stylistically date from the 11th and 12th centuries, the number of examples which can safely be attributed to the 10th century are extremely few. Within the sixteen stages, indicated here, it is unlikely that, with a few minor and problematic instances, it will be found necessary to move a tower more than a single step forward or back.

TYPOLOGY

Establishing a Round Tower typology must precede any attempt at a chronology. Fortunately, the architectural features (46 doorcases, 260 windows) on which any analysis can be based are sufficiently well represented for some observations to be possible (**fig. 16**). The typology presented is based on entrance door types, and moves from corbelled through lintelled and round headed towards Romanesque, with various regressions and culs-de-sac. It cannot be claimed that the Round Towers developed in such a defined linear manner, yet it is probable that the broad outline of this typology will stand the test of more precise dating methods. In general, external window details follow the broad thrust of the arrangement, with lintelled openings (170) preceding triangular-headed ones (60), but there is less consistency here. Decorative elements are confined, with the exception of vestigial architrave details, to the later stages, and are insufficient in number to help in expanding the basic direction of development.

COMMENTARY ON THE TYPOLOGY

The development of the door-opening can be envisaged as follows: the first step (1) in spanning the gap is extremely crude: a short lintel is supported by corbels on both sides; a better solution would have been a larger stone, as seen in (2), where the simple lintel spans the narrow door-opening. In (3), the form of the opening is better defined, with attention devoted to the masonry of the jambs, with large and well-proportioned lintel and sill stones. Development is continued in (4), by placing a relieving triangle above the lintel; this spreads the load of the superstructure, as does the archaic feature of inclined doorjambs, a standard element from the beginning. At this stage, the introduction of contrasting stone and the use of well-formed large quoins served to establish the idea of a distinctive doorcase as an individual entity, which was to become the principal architectural feature of most Round Towers. In (5), a substantial lintel has been established as the ideal structural answer, here adapted to resemble the inner curve of an arch, by cutting away the soffit of the stone, and adding a decorative band to suggest the outer arc of an arch. At (6), the simulated arch is enhanced by a well-defined doorcase, complete with the archaic feature of inward-inclined jambs characteristic of most Irish early medieval buildings. The move towards a round arch is advanced in (7), by extending the architrave-like band to surround the opening. The arch is still merely a cut-away lintel. Another step is taken in (8): what appear to be a regression to corbels is further advanced in getting rid of the large lintel, in favour of something approaching the scale of voussoirs. With the exception of (1), all the above examples have a square-shouldered external doorhead, while those below are round-shouldered; this represents a fundamental shift of emphasis in the appearance of the doorcase and a fundamental characteristic of the appearance of the majority of surviving examples is that they display some variant of the round-headed doorway. The lintel undergoes a final contortion in (9), where the cut-away soffit is mirrored by a cut-away extrados. This is still only a monolithic lintel contrived to look like an arch. In (10), despite the significant appearance of an arch composed of voussoirs, there is no attempt to define a concentric extrados, the outline of which is clumsily detailed with the upper sides of the voussoirs merely being treated as building blocks and adapted to the courses. The true arch makes its appearance as a three-voussoir type (11), with the intrados and extrados cleanly defined, yet the central stone of the arch is flattened by the course above, making this form short of a fully expressed arch. In (12), the tripartite arch has the keystone expressed; some examples show the keystone projecting above the line of the extrados. By (13), a well-cut radial-voussoir arch appears where the extrados and intrados are concentric,

Right: fig. 16 SCHEMATIC ROUND TOWER DOOR TYPOLOGY
The typology indicated here is derived from a study of surviving tower door types. The examples shown are characteristic of the generality of the towers and demonstrate a pattern of development which can be divided into two main phases, the lintelled and the arched. The stages might be expanded to contain even further details, or reduced to more basic principles, but these steps do represent a logical progression from the archaic towards the architectural sophistication of international Romanesque. The weakest link in the typology is the first example, Scattery, which may be the earliest tower, although its eccentric doorhead can also be interpreted as a proto-arch, which would place it later in the sequence.

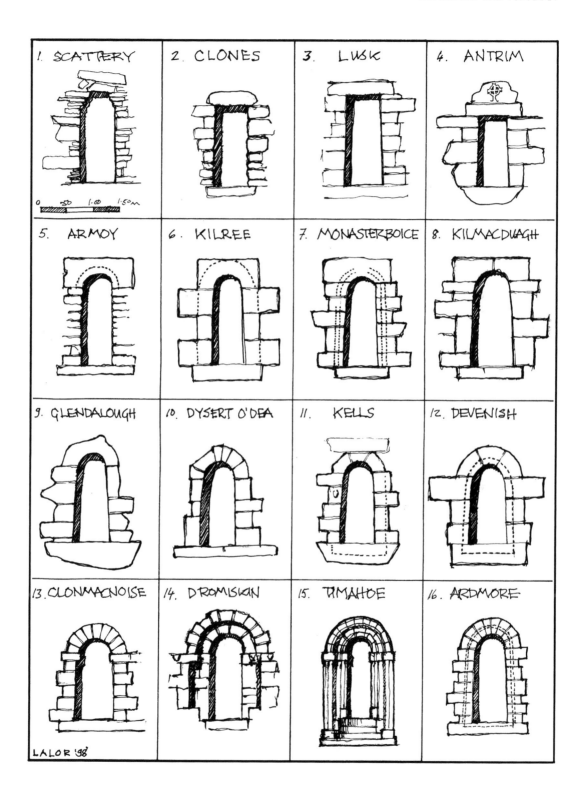

Swords, Co. Dublin

Clondalkin, Co. Dublin

DOORS: SWORDS, CLONDALKIN, ARMOY, TAGHADOE

If the Round Tower developed at all, and in essence, its form shows no radical variations over a 250-year span, its progress can be charted in the subtle modulations of the doorway. In these four examples, the passage from simple lintelled opening through articulated doorcase with contrasting stone to rudimentary arch cut from a lintel and, lastly, a true arch, is clearly seen.

Armoy, Co. Antrim

Taghadoe, Co. Kildare

WINDOWS: ANTRIM, ROSCREA, MONASTERBOICE, BALLA

Tower windows display parallel development to the doors, although the emphasis differs. The stylistic changes run from lintelled examples to triangular-headed, with the occasional modification such as the round-headed window at Balla.

Antrim, Co. Antrim

Roscrea, Co. Tipperary

Monasterboice, Co. Louth

Balla, Co. Mayo

and the arch finally achieved a clear identity and the impost-block from which it springs appears for the first time. At (14), the Romanesque with orders expresses itself as an accomplished example of the international style. The jambs are vertical but the voussoirs of the inner arch are still irregular. At (15) is a more elaborate version of the above yet the archaic Irish habit of inclined door-jambs is maintained. Finally (16), where, for the first time, the entire door-design is integrated into the structure of the building, with a well-formed arched doorhead and a continuous roll moulding surrounding the arch and jambs. A true synthesis of forms has now been achieved, yet the archaic inclined jambs survived to the end of the tower's development.

Unfortunately, the window details are less responsive to analysis than the doorcases, although windows are far more numerous than doors. They may be divided into lintelled, triangular-headed and round-headed, of which the first group make up the greater number. The triangular-headed windows seem to derive directly from examples found in the 9th-century Rhenish (Torhalle, Lorsch) and 10th-century Anglo-Saxon (Earls Barton, Northamptonshire and

63

Barton-on-Humber, Lincolnshire) church belfries, or vanished Irish timber buildings, which themselves are no doubt based on earlier Continental skeuomorphic timber window designs, emphasising the early supremacy in Continental Europe, Ireland and Britain, of timber over stone.

CHRONOLOGY

There is no precise or provable manner of establishing a chronology for the building of Round Towers. Very few have been scientifically excavated and, although many were dug out during the 19th century, little can be gleaned from these pre-stratigraphic investigations which would cast light on their dating. Investigations into the carbon-dating of medieval building mortar, which is currently taking place, are not liable to produce sufficient data to further the quest for a precise dating, although a much more promising and precise method, dendrochronology or tree-ring dating, could provide the answer to the problem, if oak putlock timbers were found in situ in the tower walls. Stylistic evidence can only be used in a speculative manner, but it does at least form an extensive and coherent body of evidence.

The only definite evidence for dating the towers occurs at what is close to the end of the period of tower building, when a few examples with clearly identifiable 12th-century stylistic details establish a date before which all other towers lacking such details were most probably built. By placing the range of true Romanesque arches earlier than the developed and decorated ones, the proto-arches before the true arches, lintelled openings earlier again, and possibly the use of corbelled techniques at the beginning, it is possible in reverse order, to map out a tentative chronology. There are four principal phases into which the development of Round Towers can be divided, based on this structural and stylistic evidence. The difficulty encountered is in determining the order of what lies between that which is evidently of an early date and what can be confirmed as of a later date.

Masonry styles have also been used as a guide to chronology, but this approach also has problems. While towers which exhibit fine ashlar masonry can be assumed as being late, and those with crude rubble construction early, there are far too many contradictions to this approach to use it as more than representing additional evidence; 12th-century according to its door-development, Tory is constructed of extremely rough and early-looking masonry. More significantly, masons' techniques have been studied and the cutting and finishing of the stonework can be divided into two styles, which roughly belong to before and after the introduction of the high Romanesque style of decoration in the early 11th century. These differences are related to tooling, the manner in which a stone mason 'closes' the surface of the stone. Hammer dressing, which leaves the stone surface with a very slightly pocked finish, is the common form of masonry finish on all early Irish church buildings up to and including the early Romanesque period. After that the second style, of short diagonal axe strokes, was introduced and appears, mostly, to be confined to the fine ashlar masonry of the later Romanesque buildings with decorated doorways. Clonmacnoise I, begun in 1124, is of diagonally axed masonry.

TOWERS: ANTRIM, KILMACDUAGH, GLENDALOUGH I, RATTOO

The innate conservatism of Irish medieval building practice allowed for little change, and, where a new idea, such as the Round Tower, had been introduced, its form, once accepted, became a ubiquitous presence. These four examples, one from each of the provinces – Ulster, Connacht, Leinster and Munster – indicate uniformity despite wide geographic distribution.

Antrim, Co. Antrim

Kilmacduagh, Co. Galway

Glendalough I, Co. Wicklow

Rattoo, Co. Kerry

COPING WITH LIME MORTAR

The essential difference between Greek and Roman architecture is that the former is an architecture of load-bearing walls, pillars and lintels, whereas the latter is the domain of the plastic. Greek temples are products of the rigidity of materials, while the architecture of the Roman world exploits the idea of materials as pliable and capable of being bent to new requirements. The construction of walls composed of outer skins of brickwork or marble, filled with builders' rubble and lime mortar has obvious advantages of speed, strength, economy and malleability. The development of the arch, vault, dome and curved walls was facilitated by Roman virtuoso building methods using *opus caementicium*, the Latin term for the structural use of lime mortar. As early as 200 BC 'concrete' domes are known (Stabian Baths, Pompeii).

It is this knowledge, which survived the European Dark Ages, and resurfaced in early medieval Ireland before the 10th century, that enabled the Round Towers to be built. Without the binding strength of lime mortar their wonderfully plastic form would have been neither conceivable nor attainable. The Round Tower is a perfect example of the genius of Roman engineering, being practiced many centuries after the collapse of the Empire in an island which never experienced the discipline and order of their rule.

Whilst working on the excavation of the Omayyad early Muslim palaces of 8th-century Jerusalem, buildings which were erected to provide accommodation for the Caliph el-Walid and his court, and centred on the *Haram el-Sharif* (the distant sanctuary), the third holiest shrine of Islam, one of the most impressive aspects of their construction was the durability and strength of the walls and foundations, all built with Roman lime-mortar techniques. The foundations were of rubble 'mass-concrete', poured between timber form-work which had left its imprint on the foundations as eloquently as present-day poured concrete, or the rush matting form-work of Irish late medieval vaults. The walls were of fine ashlar construction, bound by an iron-like mass of poured rubble and lime mortar which, where the masonry had been robbed, stood without support, as the core of an Irish Round Tower will do (Nendrum). Other than not being round, these walls were indistinguishable from those of an ashlar-built Irish Round Tower. Here, kept alive in the eastern Roman Empire and practiced under Muslim rule by Byzantine Christian masons, is an example of the constructive technique which alone made the Round Towers possible. It only required a single master-craftsman or monastic mason to travel from the Eastern Mediterranean to Britain or Ireland to transfer the technology, which once understood, is easily mastered. The source may, more plausibly, have come from much closer to home: Carolingian Gaul, Anglo-Saxon Britain or any part of the post-Roman world. Geographically, Anglo-Saxon Britain is the most likely source.

CHAPTER FIVE

THE ANATOMY OF AN IRISH ROUND TOWER

' *For which of you, intending to build a tower, sitteth not down first, and counteth the cost, whether he have sufficient to finish it ?* '

Luke, chapter 14, verse 28

Round Towers are about height. This is perhaps the only indisputable fact which can be stated concerning the Irish Round Tower: that they were built to achieve an aural and visual presence at a considerable elevation above the ground. The definitive answer as to the various uses of the towers is that they were built as bell-towers and, by their presence acquired further functions that may have led to some minor modifications in their design. Since *cloicteach* and campanile are equivalent and contemporary terms for bell-tower, there should be no mystery in the concept of the northern or southern European church belfry from the Carolingian Rhineland or elsewhere, being translated in Ireland into something different; an Irish solution to the local requirements of ecclesiastical ritual and politics.

What was built to achieve a specific function as a belfry could certainly be adapted to serve other purposes. While timber buildings were commonplace, stone structures were few and therefore more highly valued. Whatever subsidiary functions towers may have served, other than of acting as a *cloicteach* or campanile to summon brethren from the fields or to remind them of the hours of the day required for prayer, were secondary to the guiding principle of establishing a platform for bell-ringing above the tree-line. There are also other possible tower functions: as repositories for monastic treasures, as security for community members, as a lookout, and as monuments of monastic presence and prestige. Looking at each of these alternatives in turn, and considering the documentary evidence of the surviving textual references, it can be substantiated that the towers did indeed have secondary uses (**fig. 17**).

TOWERS AS REPOSITORIES FOR MONASTIC TREASURES

We gather from the annals that in a number of tower burnings, which occurred during attack by the Irish or the Vikings, that bells, books and crosiers were among the treasures destroyed. The towers would have doubtless provided the most secure location in a monastery for the safe-keeping of the church treasures: relics of the founder, manuscripts and church plate. From the early 10th century tower building coincides with the end of the most productive period in the production of ecclesiastical ornamental metalwork and illuminated gospel books; they had plenty of treasures which required security from both warlike neighbours and rival monasteries. As the existence of larger-than-normal windows on the second floor of some towers suggests a special function for that level, this was most probably the Treasury. The objects stored in towers were probably kept in purpose-made leather satchels, some of which have survived. These would have been suspended from stone corbels or wooden pegs in the walls, or in more permanent timber furniture, such as the shelved bookcase shown in the Northumbrian illuminated manuscript, the *Codex Amiatinus* (c. 8th century). Monasteries with extensive libraries must have possessed similar purpose-made furniture.

Of all the tower details which appear relevant in establishing their range of functions, the gradually rising height of the entrance door must be of considerable significance. The mortared fabric of Round Towers, with an entrance, on average 2 to 4 metres from the ground, could provide admirable safety for portable or manuscript treasures; from theft, damp or rodent damage. The doorway of Kilmacduagh, the highest of those to survive, is 9 metres above ground level, a height at which neither convenience nor speed of access can be a serious consideration.

Round Towers could certainly function as a place of security for the valuables of the community, and it is as the Treasury of the monastery that they may have had the most important of their secondary roles. No tower possesses any form of permanent external access, nor is their evidence for timber platform or ladders in any semi-permanent state. The annals record three instances of towers being burned with their treasures. It has been suggested that the elevated doorway of a Round Tower might, in times of pilgrimage, be used as a visible and secure position from which to display a revered shrine, probably that of the founder. Although this proposition cannot be substantiated it is certainly plausible. The Round Tower, as monastic Treasury, would be an appropriately secure position from which to display to a crowd of pilgrims vulnerable monastic treasures or relics, as the churches were generally too small for this purpose.

TOWERS AS PLACES OF SECURITY FOR COMMUNITY MEMBERS

Round Towers have long been associated with the threat of Viking raids and seen as the point of refuge for the community. Of all the possible explanations for their construction this one has the least substance in terms of their original planning. The towers were never conceived as defensive or military architecture; they are, in fact, indefensible to any serious-minded enemy intent on destruction. The access ladder could not easily in most cases (or in Kilmacduagh, at all, unless it was of rope, which sounds implausible) be withdrawn into the interior, on account of the low height of the internal floors (**fig. 17**). This fundamental point contributes to the impracticality of the towers as

Right: fig. 17 TIMAHOE, Co. LAOIS
In the external elevation, internal profile section, cross-section and plans of Timahoe are assembled all the significant features of most Round Towers, although individual examples differ in detail and emphasis. Whether access was from a groundfast timber structure or by a simple ladder is unknown, as is the precise method of internal access Timahoe demonstrates both principal methods of floor support, offsets and corbel, and external base offsets with shallow foundations. The entrance is conventional in its position, although unusual in the degree of its decoration. Whatever the actual location of the ladders and trapdoors, they left little internal floor space within the tower. The bell floor typically has four axially-placed windows, splaying inwards, and positioned just above the timber floor level.

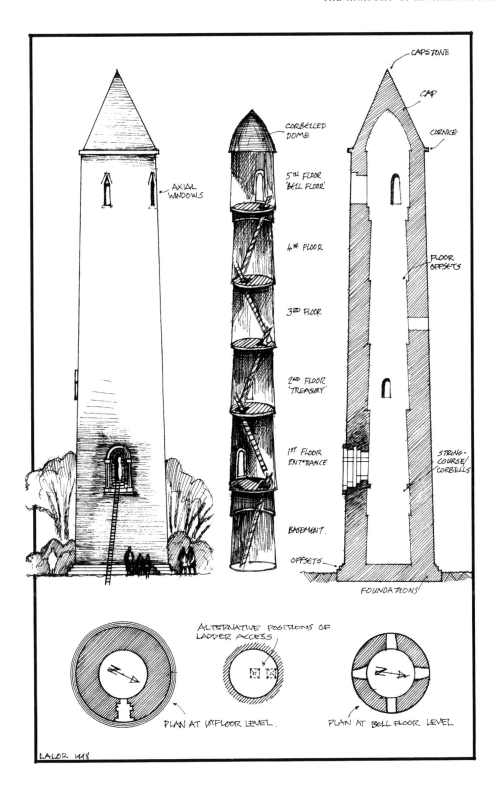

CAPSTONE

CAP

CORNICE

CORBELLED DOME

5TH FLOOR 'BELL FLOOR'

4TH FLOOR

FLOOR OFFSETS

3RD FLOOR

2ND FLOOR 'TREASURY'

AXIAL WINDOWS

STRING-COURSE CORBELLS

1ST FLOOR ENTRANCE

BASEMENT

OFFSETS

FOUNDATIONS

ALTERNATIVE POSITIONS OF LADDER ACCESS

PLAN AT 1ST FLOOR LEVEL.

PLAN AT BELL FLOOR LEVEL

LALOR 1998

places of safe retreat. Even the last to be built, during the 12th century, display, among the modifications or embellishments to their design, no tendency (after over 200 years of practice) to adapt them for defensive purposes; rather the opposite. Some towers have a window positioned directly above the entrance, a most basic consideration from the point of view of repelling attackers, but these vary both in size and level, and there is no consistency whatsoever about this feature. In fact, the window apertures are in general so narrow and ill-placed as to inhibit any effective use being made of them in order to hurl rocks on those besieging the tower, a fact which presupposes that the towers had been previously stocked with ammunition.

Curiously enough, earlier commentators on the subject display considerable enthusiasm for the idea that these towers were built for defence, and state that the windows are admirably suited to throwing missiles on the enemy. Nothing could be further from the evidence and this possibility has to be entirely discounted. Rattoo, a complete tower and a good exemplar for all test cases, has a single small fourth-floor window in the drum, directly above the entrance, through which only a skilled gymnast could manage to drop anything on attackers threatening the entrance: the batter of the tower wall would further inhibit the efficiency of defence from the windows.

Although it is known from the annals that towers did become places of refuge, this frequently led to the death of those taking shelter, either by asphyxiation or being burnt alive by those outside. The timber door of a tower, positioned at the rear of the door passage, could with little effort be set on fire. From that point the interior of the tower, with only timber furnishings, would act as a chimney, with appalling consequences for those trapped. The fact that such catastrophes are recorded has little bearing on the purpose for which Round Towers were originally built. The two recorded instances of kings being killed in Round Towers (the King of Tara in 1076 and the King of Fir Mhanach in 1176), suggests that towers, like churches, were regarded as places of sanctuary, even though this concept was frequently violated. The annals record six instances of large numbers of people dying in deliberate tower conflagrations. Margaret Stokes, in her *Early Christian Architecture in Ireland* (1878), makes the astonishing proposal that in times of danger, a tower could provide safety for up to eighty people, a situation as grotesque as the Black Hole of Calcutta! With minimal light, no availability of fresh water, no sanitation and no means for the occupants to defend themselves or escape, the tower refuge can have been little more than a vertical prison and a horrible place in which to face being burnt to death.

TOWERS AS A LOOKOUT

The idea that Round Towers had a role as lookout places demands consideration. The time required to ascend from external ground level to the bell-floor is not more than two minutes, a factor which could be of enormous importance to a community in danger. Likewise, a hand-bell rung from the bell-floor can be heard quite clearly, with a favourable wind direction, for over a mile away and possibly even further.

LUSK, CO. DUBLIN
The view from the bell-floor window at Lusk gave the community members a distant, and uninterrupted, prospect of the surrounding countryside. In the foreground the view is now obscured by the roof-parapet of the late medieval belfry.

KILMACDUAGH, CO. GALWAY
If 'form follows function', then the tower's central purpose was a concern with achieving maximum height for bell-ringing and visibility; security and the storage of valuables were secondary uses, of which security was the least sustainable. Annalistic references relate the deaths of numerous clergy, besieged and burnt in their towers.

From the bell-floor it is possible to see a distance of some miles, depending on the local topography, but the orientation of the usual four windows towards the cardinal points has much more to do with the bell-ringing liturgical ritual, and with creating a conceptual cross-form, than with any relationship to topography or geography. From the point of observation alone, with its rigidly oriented windows, the bell-floor is severely limited by the depth of the embrasures and the narrowness of the windows. Towers, which continued in use throughout the medieval period, such as Castledermot, Kilkenny and Kildare, were adapted as lookouts by the removal of the conical cap which was replaced by a parapeted flat roof (some later towers may have been completed in this manner; Kilmacduagh, which retains its cap, has six bell-floor windows). In their altered state a more strategic survey of the local landscape might be easily made. This was clearly difficult from the very limited window orientation of a conventional tower. Even late towers (Ardmore, Devenish) show no inclination to develop the observation potential of the bell-floor, although a few examples have more than four windows. There are no supporting annalistic references.

TOWERS AS BUILDINGS OF PRESTIGE

This is the aspect of tower-building which has hitherto received the least attention and may, in fact, hold the key to their attractiveness to early medieval church circles, and their increasing numbers, particularly over the later centuries of their construction. The enormous investment of resources required by a rural church or civil community, whichever was funding the project, in order to create these monuments, defines them as not merely functional bell-towers but essentially buildings of prestige and local aristocratic patronage. If the entire assemblage of the west portal of the church, Round Tower, High Cross and prestigious burial area can be identified as deriving from the Continental tradition of church westwork, the focal monument of the complex is the Round Tower.

The presence of a Round Tower in the landscape, whether that of a west-coast island, midlands plain or east-coast valley, defined by its monumentality the spiritual territory of the ecclesiastical compound and enhanced the reputation of the local king as religious patron, as much as that of the individual monastery. In the heightened atmosphere of the 12th-century religious revival, the towers acquire added significance which is both ascetic and political and, by their dramatic and soaring verticality, established an element in the Irish landscape which was without parallel even in the royal enclosures. The late proliferation of Round Tower sub-species, the engaged and attached variants, as well as the eccentric un-tapered and anomalous forms, emphasises the significance which the cone-capped towers had achieved within the language of Irish early medieval architecture as a means of enhancing existing ecclesiastical building types. The annals for 1124 record the completion of the tower of Clonmacnoise by the king and abbot, a measure of its significance, and a direct link between tower-building and royal patronage.

In a man-made landscape of earthen ramparted enclosures of univallate, bivallate and trivallate ringforts, the only distinguishing feature between a monastic enclosure and a civil one was the internal stone architecture of the former. Prior to the Normans there was no Irish civil equivalent of ecclesiastical buildings in stone. A tower, 30 metres high, would enable a monastic settlement to be distinguished from the neighbouring domestic enclosures, even at a considerable distance. The towers rose above the earthen ramparts and the enclosing tree-lines like permanent smoke-signals, proudly proclaiming an ecclesiastical location to the local world of patrons, pilgrims, rivals and, with unfortunate consequences, also attracting the attention of enemies, whether Irish or Norse.

EARLY CHURCH BUILDINGS

All early church buildings in Ireland were of wood, for which there is now archaeological evidence, and timber churches continued in use as late as the 12th century. The earliest annalistic reference to a stone church, or more precisely, to a place-name which records the presence of a stone church, is to Duleek in the 8th century (*damliac* is the old Irish word for a stone church), but references to stone churches do not become commonplace until the 11th century. The earliest stone church, at Armagh, was not built before the late 8th century. Archaic buildings, like Gallarus Oratory, are likely to be considerably later than the 7th to 9th centuries as originally proposed. The Romanesque arched window in the east gable of Gallarus can hardly be earlier than the late-11th century. Similar internally arched and splayed windows are also found in Balla and the north tower of Cormac's Chapel. The progress of influence is therefore liable to be from the east coast westwards, as the church building of Anglo-Saxon Britain, itself derived from late Roman and Carolingian examples, began to affect building style in the most distant areas of Ireland. Church-building in stone must have been sufficiently advanced by the 10th century for the development of the first Round Towers to take place.

Since the towers are entirely attendant to the churches, the development of

CASTLEDERMOT, CO. KILDARE
The few Round Towers which are eccentric in their location emphasise the normal location for the tower, to the north-west or south-west of the west entrance of the church. Castledermot, unusually, stands on the north-east side of the current church which may not occupy the position of the original.

the latter in stone is likely to have been well-established before the towers. There is no evidence for a simultaneous progress. Timber towers were possibly developed before stone examples but, in the absence of archaeological evidence for their existence, this must remain an open question. Churches with ante or projecting side walls or date from the 10th century and later, and many of these must represent the church-buildings with which the Round Towers were originally associated. The absence of epigraphic evidence in stone and a paucity of archaeological information has continued to make the dating of early Irish stone churches a difficult subject. The more firmly they can be dated, the easier it will become to establish a corresponding chronology for the towers. In the vacuum of reliably dated churches, the towers must attempt to speak for themselves. At the many tower sites where the church for which the tower was built has entirely vanished, or been replaced by a succession of buildings, medieval, 18th and 19th century, the only information, other than the occasional annalistic reference, must be derived from the surviving masonry. Within the fairly rigid style of the Round Tower, and over the centuries of their construction, while the form remains constant, considerable modulations of design and decoration occurred.

Early medieval Irish churches were as minimally provided with windows as is conceivably possible. They could hardly have had less internal light. This factor is difficult to appreciate in what are now roofless buildings, and even in roofed ones (Gallarus, Temple Macdara), lacking their original solid doors, they are still brighter than was the case when in use. Similarly, excavated examples of timber or wattle dwellings, from before and after the 9th and 10th centuries, probably did not have windows, the doorway providing all the light which was required. Add to that the Irish dependence on the sub-rectangular and circular as ideal plan-forms for all circumstances and it is hardly surprising that the Round Tower was the product of a fusion of plan conservatism, lack of dependence on light and the functional requirements of the bell-tower. Unlike churches, which are obliged by their function to be oriented towards the east, the bell-tower has no such definition, merely requiring height to fulfil its purpose. The western bell-tower of All Saints Church, Earls Barton (*c*. 935), and that of Sompting Church (*c*. 950) reflect the presence of timber belfries as their predecessors. Sompting, with its pyramidal roof on a square plan (probably derived from Rhenish or other Continental examples), is conceptually not too far removed from an Irish Round Tower; it is playing with a parallel approach to the same problem. The triangular-headed window slits of Irish towers are also a familiar detail and are found in many Anglo-Saxon towers. The question should not be why did Irish monastic masons produce the Round Tower but, rather, is not the Round Tower the most consistent and logical product of their concepts of building?

TOWER ANATOMY

The towers discussed are the freestanding examples rather than the engaged or attached variety. Because the latter are, in most instances, supported by some form of rectangular church building or extension and lack a conventional

73

entrance, they do not correspond to the same general format, although they all maintain a similarity of design and detail and would have been more or less identically constructed.

SITING

Because Round Towers were never built independently of ecclesiastical enclosures, although many have survived without them, their siting is dependent on the prior existence of the church settlements which decided, from the early 10th century and subsequently, to build the towers. The siting and orientation of the Round Tower within an ecclesiastical enclosure was established by the position of the church to which the tower was attendant and secondary. Stone churches are merely fire-resistant replacements for their timer predecessors.

By Christian convention all church buildings were aligned east to west, the altar-end facing Jerusalem with the entrance from the west. Planning the orientation of the church was not an exact science, being based on local observation, and most churches are some degrees off the cardinal points (even multi-church sites show perplexing variations in orientation). With a few exceptions (e.g. Castledermot), the Round Tower was placed to the right or left of the entrance, that is to the north-west or south-west, more frequently the former, with the tower doorway facing the west door of the church. The distance from tower to west entrance could vary considerably, as can be seen in Inis Cealtra and Glendalough I.

The principal church is generally located centrally within the inner enclosure. Looking at bi- or multi-vallate settlement-plans of monasteries where enough information survives, the plans tend to have a fried-egg or moving-target appearance, the inner enclosure wandering arbitrarily within the more concentric larger ramparts, as is demonstrated by Nendrum (**figs. 4 & 5**), Kells, Kildare (**fig. 8a-b**) and many other examples. The fact that the towers post-date the emergence of stone-built churches ties down their dating to the period from when the first annalist's references occur by the mid-10th century, although the first, and virtually all the references, record not the building of towers but their damage or destruction by fire or natural causes.

PLANNING AND CONSTRUCTION

The precision with which the finest examples of the towers are built clearly states the involvement of a master mason, presumably a monk who had observed building techniques in either Anglo-Saxon Britain or the Carolingian Rhineland. It is possible, from what is known of medieval building practice, and from the study of medieval building methods outside Ireland, to describe how a tower was constructed.

Adomnán, Abbot of Iona in the late 7th century, biographer of and successor to Columba, gives in his *De locis sanctis*, which deals with an inventory of sites in the Holy Land associated with Christ, an interesting insight into the visual accomplishments of learned men of the day. Arculf, a Gaulish bishop, whose observation Adomnán is recounting, drew him a little sketch of the Church of the Holy Sepulchre, that he might better understand what was being

TORY, CO. DONEGAL
The tube-like interiors of all towers are only broken by the floor offsets, corbels or, in this instance at Tory, the projecting remains of a corbel-domed floor, a feature found in only a few instances.

TOWER BASES: TIMAHOE AND AGHAVILLER
Tower foundations are wider than the above-ground structure, with a number of graduated steps, known as offsets, used to accommodate the difference in dimension between the circular foundation and tower as at, above, Timahoe Co. Laois. Below, Aghaviller, Co. Kilkenny, is an eccentric example, because it has a rectangular foundation.

described. The master mason in charge of the building of a Round Tower might equally, as masons have always done, scribed a door or other detail on a slate or some such convenient surface in order that his building team would properly understand his intentions.

The Lodgebooks of Villard de Honnecourt (fl. *c.* 1225, Bibliothèque Nationale, Paris) considerably post-date the 10th-century origins of the Round Tower, although they indicate the degree to which early medieval building practice had become a highly skilled profession. The manner of de Honnecourt's building plans, sketches and studies of proportion would be familiar to any practising architect or master mason from Near Eastern antiquity to the present day. The identities of many of the principal master masons working in early medieval Europe are known.

Laying out a circle with string from a centre-point can have presented no problem to native masons; in a land littered with ringforts and sub-circular enclosures of all kinds, they clearly had abundant practice (although the wobbly circumference of some ringforts are not the best recommendation of this skill). To begin building, all that was required was a round doughnut-like foundation trench or circular hole, to be excavated in the ground to the depth required, and the ring-form or solid circular mortared stone foundation constructed within this. Two previously unknown towers which exist only as foundations were excavated during the 1970s (Devenish II 1970, Liathmore 1969-70). The foundations of Liathmore went to a depth of 2.6 metres, which is quite deep for a Round Tower, less than a metre being more typical. Tower foundations may be based on bedrock, or whatever soil conditions, including the disturbed soil of early graveyards, the masons encountered. When the rough foundation reached ground level, it needed to be brought to a relatively flat surface and the precise centre of the built circle carefully marked. Internal clay, plastered or stone floors at this level have been found in numerous towers excavated during the 19th century: Clones *c.* 1840, Kilkenny in 1847, and Kilmacduagh in 1878. This point would become the datum from which, with the use of a plumb-line, all vertical measurements were accurately calculated, from the base to the completion of the tower. Horizontal measurements for the circumference were also calculated from the same datum-line.

From the top of the circular foundations (rectangular in two instances, Aghaviller, Kilree) offsets were created which, like concentric steps, occupy the space between the outer circle of the below-ground masonry and the line intended for the wall-surface of the tower. The initial courses of wall masonry (1 metre – 1.15 metres thick) required no scaffolding but, as soon as the wall had risen above a metre high, a timber groundfast scaffold was erected around the outside of the structure, with some of the horizontal beams, at right angles to the wall-surface, allowed to penetrate around 30cm – 50cm (or sometimes to penetrate right through it if a movable scaffolding was required) into the masonry in what are known as putlock holes. Evidence for external scaffolding is confirmed by the presence of putlock holes evenly spaced and over a number of courses of masonry on some towers (Cashel, Fertagh, Roscam). The fact that they are not visible over the entire surface of all towers may be explained by the holes being plugged with stone when no longer required, and also by the fact that the external scaffolding may have been tied to the wall through the window apertures, and not to the wall, except in occasional places. Scaffolding which embraces a circular building derives stability from its interlocked shape. Close studies of the construction of early medieval Anglo-Saxon church towers, with walls of shuttered flint and mortar rubble, have revealed considerable information on the scaffolding techniques used by masons in post-Roman Britain. The same systems were evidently available in Ireland for tower building, although a similarly exacting scrutiny of Irish tower masonry has yet to be achieved.

The wall as it rose was constructed of an outer and inner surface, with the space between the faces filled with a rubble and mortar mix, capable of binding together both faces. The internal and external stonework had the vertical and horizontal joints trimmed by masons at the site and laid by the building team on the scaffolding. Only when a certain number of courses were in place would the 'closing' of the surface be attempted, by hammer-finishing or chiselling the stonework both to the curve and to the batter.

One or more hoists would have been installed as beams set through the masonry, and were allowed to project out beyond the scaffolding. These were necessary in order to raise the stone and rubble material. The dimensions of the large ashlars on some towers (Dysert O'Dea 2 metres; Kilmacduagh 2.5 metres) could not have been managed otherwise. All lighter materials were raised on ladders by hand, in timber or leather buckets.

With the scaffolding in place, maintaining a uniform angle of batter is likely to have presented the greatest difficulty in the building of a tower. It is probable that a timber template, angled to the precise batter required, was used to check and maintain the uniformity of the angle by rotating it around the circumference of the wall. As the height increased, the datum could frequently be re-established on each floor level. It is probable that the internal floor-carpentry was completed as the tower rose, enabling the datum to be transferred upwards with each floor. In those towers (Clondalkin, Glendalough) where there are no floor offsets or corbels, and the floors were carried by alternately oriented pairs of wooden beams, this timber-work was set into the masonry as the wall rose. In the timber-dependent culture of early medieval Ireland, carpenters are likely to have been amongst the foremost craftsmen of the period, and the now totally vanished interior woodwork of the towers would have been skilfully installed and finished.

By using a revolving trammel or beam-compass attached to the datum point on each floor-level, the uniformity of surface and batter could be effectively monitored. Internally, the successive storeys are stacked upon each other like a series of inverted buckets (**fig. 18**), the wall rising at an internal batter from one floor-level, setting back to provide support for the next floor, and then contracting again (external and internal batter are only the same in towers without offsets). This pattern was not always pursued consistently (Ardmore, Kilmacduagh). The doorcase and windows were installed as each appropriate level was reached, as were the bell-floor windows. The suggestion that the

PUTLOCK HOLES: CASHEL AND ROSCAM
The rudiments of building technology hardly changed between the 1st and 10th centuries, when tower construction began. Putlock holes used to support and fix timber scaffolding can be seen on some towers, although the system adopted varied considerably, with irregular putlock holes above, at Cashel, Co. Tipperary, and regular ones below, at Roscam, Co. Galway.

fig. 18: **TOWER INTERNAL PROFILES**

With the exception of Ardmore, Kinneigh and Timahoe, all the freestanding towers have a sheer and unencumbered external profile. Internally, however, they differ widely, having variants on the 'stacked bucket' or 'celery stick' profile, displaying phasing which, where it exists, can sometimes be interpreted as building stages.

Ardmore's internal offsets (a) are unrelated to the external string courses, and are interspersed with floor levels, supported on beams. Clondalkin (b) is sheer internally, while Devenish (c) and Kilmacduagh (d) are typical of the inverted stacked bucket outline, with the occasional anomaly, as in the corbelling of Devenish's bell-floor (after Barrow).

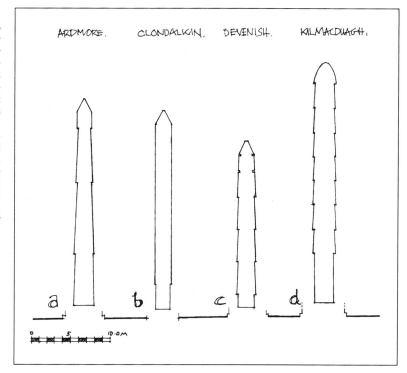

doorcases – where the masonry differs from that of the tower wall – might have been inserted later, are to be discounted. There is no structural justification for such a proposal. In fact the doorcase could have been constructed freestanding on the sill-level of the wall, and then the surrounding wall built to enclose it. More probably they rose together, the horizontal wall surface being used to manoeuvre in the large ashlars of the doorhead.

As to how long a tower took to construct, this can be estimated from a study of the scaffolding lifts – the number of times a groundfast or dismantleable scaffold was raised, as indicated by the number of putlock levels. The scaffolding might be either of a dismantleable type, raised at each level, or a fixed scaffold, covering the entire building. The latter obviously uses far more timber, but is more likely to have been employed in the building of a Round Tower. At Roscam the putlock levels are on average 1.1 metres above each other, and this division most probably indicates work levels. In a 30 metre high tower, this allows for roughly 28 lifts. If each lift represents a week's work, a tower might be built in seven or eight months on average. This allows two days for a team of masons to raise the circular wall 1.1 metres high and approximately five days for the lime mortar core to set before the next rise might be commenced. Sagging or buckling of the wall-surface was liable to occur if the superstructure was added before the course below had set, and may account for surface irregularities in a few towers (Scattery, Killala). The time-scale suggested here presupposes that doorcase and window features were already cut and prepared for installation. A team of at least six masons would be needed to accomplish the work: four on the scaffold, two or more on the ground, with other apprentices to mix mortar and work the hoists, and an adequate labour-force to transport the stone from a quarry where a further team was employed to extract the necessary material. Ashlar masonry would require considerably more time to construct.

While engaged in archaeological reconstruction work with local Arab stone-masons in the Middle East, it was possible to observe the capacity of a traditionally trained, elderly master mason, aided by two assistants, to move and raise metre-high ashlars considerable distances. Using only ropes and wooden ramps, timber levers, wedges and log-rollers, this was a living example of the almost leisured manner in which a skilled and confident building team could have tackled the task of lifting and inserting the monolithic lintels and other major stones used in tower construction.

Another challenge in the building of a tower is the consideration of the cap. Like the stonework for the curved and battered walls, the cone masonry was prepared, course by course, at ground level and finished in situ. It is probable that once the corbelled roof had been constructed above the external cornice from which it springs (Devenish I, has an internal cornice), then a timber template or formwork was erected outside in order to establish and control the angle of the cone. The importance of maintaining the uniformity of the cap's profile would have required some means of monitoring the angle from all sides, and probably moving the template around to check it. The external apex of the cone should, as long as there had been no deviation from the centre, be directly above the original datum point, up to 35 metres below. There is no reason why this precision could not have been within the consummate skill of the masons involved. The fine-chiselling of the batter was, most probably, finished as the scaffolding was being taken down. This was the first opportunity for the masons to see, unencumbered, the external surface of the tower, and to eliminate blemishes.

It is easy enough to imagine how the masons were directed. What should not be underestimated is their skill in maintaining over more than 30 metres a precise and beautifully even surface, simultaneously worked to a horizontal curve as well as to a vertical batter. In complete towers the superlative quality of the masonry gives the tower a space-rocket-like sheer finish, despite the weathering of over 800 years (Ardmore, Devenish, Glendalough, Kilmacduagh, Rattoo).

MASONS AND MASONRY

The possibility is that the masons responsible for directing the construction of Round Towers were, at least in the initial years, Irish monks or craftsmen trained in the Rhineland or Britain, rather than foreign masons brought to Ireland for the purpose. This can be inferred from the fact that archaic features inherent in Irish-building practice are found in the towers which, having no contemporary continental parallels, would not have been introduced from outside in the early medieval period. The base of Kinneigh is classically Rhenish in its form, except for the pronounced batter, which is the Irish contribution to

DEVENISH I, CO. FERMANAGH
Round Tower masonry reached its peak during the 12th century when the last of the towers were being built. Here, at the internal threshold of the entrance door to Devenish I, vertical, horizontal and jog-gled joints, a well-maintained curve, and the diagonal-axed finishing of the stonework, are all characteristic of the best work of the period.

MASONRY: DRUMBO, DRUMLANE AND MAGHERA

The quality of masonry was dictated by the geology of the region and also by economics. Three Ulster towers demonstrate the manner in which available stone was used by skilled masons to the same purpose, with the partly-hewn blocks of Drumbo and the field-stones of Maghera in contrast to the diagonally tooled ashlars of Drumlane. The mortared core of the wall, sandwiched between outer and inner skins of masonry, gave the structures their strength, irrespective of the type of stone used, or the standard of the masonry.

Drumbo, Co. Down

Drumlane, Co. Cavan

Maghera, Co. Down

the design of the structure (**fig. 12a-b**).

There are enormous variations in the style and quality of masonry in the towers, ranging from the rounded sea-worn boulders (Tory), to the sleek perfection of fine coursed ashlars (Ardmore, Clonmacnoise I & II, Devenish I). The photographs of masonry styles from individual towers demonstrate the wide variety of finishes, from stonework as rough as that of Iron Age Dun Aenghus to work as accomplished as in a 13th-century Cistercian abbey. Dating is not an explanation for such differences. It has in the past been assumed that the earlier towers are more crudely built while the latest display more accomplished masonry, but there are sufficient variations to suggest that these criteria cannot be relied upon. Geographic location, type and availability of stone, economics and local patronage are far more significant factors, and probably the dominant ones, which contribute to explaining such differences.

Even in good quality masonry, anomalies are widespread, such as the peculiar habit of, in coursed masonry, allowing the horizontal lines of the stonework to dip and deviate from the horizontal, as can be seen below the doorway of Dysert O'Dea. Another mannerism is the use of courses of varying height, where courses of general regularity are interrupted by one of slim dimensions (Clonmacnoise I, Roscrea). Quite frequently the lines of the courses have been allowed to sag or rise over the doorway, a phenomenon more understandably found in Anglo-Saxon poured-flint wall building.

Masonry finishes found in Round Towers may be described as follows, although while the listing is presented in order of development, individual styles can be contemporary: unwrought stone, seaworn boulders, field stones, quarry-bedded rough stone; hammer-dressed or pocked stone which has been dressed by hammering to a finely scalloped surface finish; diagonally axed or comb-finished stone; ashlar stonework which displays diagonal marking from an axed finish, generally considered to date from the arrival of the Romanesque in the early 12th century. The best ashlar stone-work displays horizontal coursing, vertical joints and the use of joggle-jointing.

FOUNDATIONS

It is surprising that such tall and ambitious structures as Round Towers, varying in height from *c.* 15 metres (Tory) to 20 metres, to a possible 35 metres (Fertagh), should have such shallow foundations, and that these are frequently not based on rock but are merely sunk in the subsoil. Depth of foundation can be as little as 60 centimetres below ground level. This shallowness of foundation is presumably the cause of a number of standing towers (Kilmacduagh, Lusk, Timahoe) listing visibly off the perpendicular, and most probably contributed to the unexplained collapse of others, as is related in the annals. Despite these examples of subsidence, the builders clearly displayed a justifiable confidence in the capacity of the shallow foundations to carry such an enormous load.

This is generally a drum of solid rough masonry, with or without mortar. A significant variant on this general picture are the rectangular stone pad foundations, constructed from cyclopean masonry such as at Kilree and Aghaviller, or those towers which are directly based on visible bedrock such as at Cloyne, and Kinneigh.

BATTER

A significant consideration in the structural stability, as well as the visual attraction of Round Towers, is the batter or inwardly inclined angle of the wall which varies from 1:3 to 1:75. By building in this manner any tendency towards instability was significantly counteracted although not prevented. Even in cases where there has been subsidence, and a tower's foundations have allowed movement in the tower (see the Leaning Tower of Kilmacduagh), the tower wall has not generally deviated beyond the vertical. A conical cap, rather than the late medieval variant of castellated top, contributed to this stability.

Aesthetically the batter and the cone, which is its ideal and logical conclusion, combined with a proportion of diameter to height of, on average, 1:5, give the towers a near-perfect outline. A glance at the reconstructed section of Timahoe (**fig. 17**), and at the four celery-stick-like internal profiles of Ardmore, Clondalkin, Devenish I and Kilmacduagh (**fig. 18**), will show more clearly than a similar treatment of their external outlines that there is no uniformity in the internal construction of the towers, however similar they may appear from the outside.

BASEMENT

If the tower basement had a specific function (other than to elevate the entrance) this is not now obvious. Whether the entrance floors were of wood or of stone, the access was probably as in Kinneigh, through a central square opening in the floor, which could be closed with a wooden trapdoor. Two towers have a small horizontal pipe-like rectangular passage running right through the basement wall (Glendalough, Kilmacduagh). It is difficult to determine their function but they could possibly be a drain or air-vent. One tower basement has a window (Balla) which would have provided a minimal light source for the interior. The height of basements can vary considerably, from being the same as the average floors, to less than half their height. In numerous cases the internal stonework of the basement is very roughly finished, suggesting that this floor was not generally intended for use.

FIRST FLOOR, THE ENTRANCE PASSAGE AND THE DOORCASE

The entrance floor is not distinguished from those in the drum, other than having an access opening, and obviously being much brighter internally. While most window embrasures are internally splayed, the doorway has parallel jambs, with the opening narrowing towards the top, more-or-less in line with the batter of the tower, or occasionally, a slight narrowing towards the internal wall. The doorhead may be corbelled, a lintel, a modified lintel into which an arch has been cut in the soffit, or an arch. More elaborate doors with Romanesque orders are found in the 12th century. While the decoration of the architrave is uncommon, there are half-a-dozen examples, all of which are different in emphasis. A rebate occurs at the internal jamb of some doors, with evidence for the hanging of the door which must always have been on the inside face of the door passage.

SECOND FLOOR, THE TREASURY

Six towers are distinguished from the body of Round Towers in having an exceptionally large window on the second floor, generally to the right or left of the entrance door, rarely above it. These windows – that in Roscrea is almost as large as the entrance door – provide the only satisfactory lighting to the drum-levels of the tower interiors and suggest a specific function for this particular floor level, more than that of merely another access floor. Of these six windows, four face east, irrespective of being to the right or left of the variously oriented doors. If any floor level can be proposed as the depository of the monastery's collection of relics, its treasury, its holding of the bell of the

LUSK, CO. DUBLIN
Internal corbels can be divided into those of structural and non-structural use, the former being principally employed as floor supports. This corbel at Lusk was most probably used as a hook on which to suspend leather satchels containing manuscripts or other valuables.

founder, church plate and manuscripts, then this floor clearly must be considered as the most plausible candidate. The extent of the monastic libraries should not be underestimated and a substantial collection of books might have required accommodation. Between the 7th and 12th centuries, the level of classical scholarship was evidently high; this could have been achieved only by the possession of large manuscript collections, which would have included extensive versions of Latin literature, grammars, ecclesiastical texts, Irish legends, annals and practical works of geography and history.

PRESENCE OF LINTELLED OR TRIANGULAR-HEADED 'TREASURY' SECOND FLOOR WINDOWS
Lintelled: Swords (E). Triangular-headed: Antrim (NExE), Devenish (NE), Inis Cealtra (N), Monasterboice (E), Roscrea (E), Timahoe (SExS).

PRESENCE OF INTERNAL DOMED OR CORBELLED SECOND FLOORS
Castledermot (below), Tory (above), Inis Cealtra, Meelick.

THIRD TO TOP FLOOR OF THE DRUM
Between the second floor and the bell-floor (it can be as few as one, or as many as four), the intermediate floors are undistinguished and lack features of any significance (**fig. 19**). Exceptions are floors which have corbels that are not structural, but were possibly used to suspend satchels containing valuables stored in the tower. Depending on the quantity of materials to be stored, all floors might have been used but there is no evidence for this.

Little is known about the interiors of Round Towers beyond what can be deduced from an examination of their empty masonry tubes which, when roofless, resemble nothing so much as factory chimneys, a tall empty cylinder, rising towards the distantly visible sky. Most have internal offsets in the walls, provided in order to support the floors. Evidence of stone floors, supported on corbels from the wall, are also found (Kinneigh) where the entrance floor is intact, with a central rectangular opening providing access to the basement. Towers with restored floors provide examples of how they may originally have been floored. Devenish is now provided with timber floors, each with a central opening, from which ladder access enables communication between the different floors. In Cloyne the arrangement is quite different, with the access trapdoor close to the wall surface, leaving much more floor-area available for storage or other uses. The latter solution is certainly the more practical.

INTERNAL LIGHTING, THE DRUM WINDOWS
All the early Christian churches and oratories of which we know (prior to the early 12th century) were characterised by the darkness of their interiors. Oil-lamps, tallow or beeswax candles could have been used during church services, at which a congregation of any size would have had to attend out-of-doors, many of the churches being far too small to admit more than a small number of people. The 12th-century Cormac's Chapel is the earliest church with a window anything larger than a narrow slit. With no tradition of large windows in the churches, it is probably not surprising that the Round Towers' interiors

INTERIORS: DEVENISH I, CO. FERMANAGH
Above: A floor corbel providing additional support for floorboards resting on a masonry offset. Tower floors are in some cases supported entirely by corbels, more normally by offsets.

Below: Other than the centrally placed floor opening in the stone entrance floor at Kinneigh, there is no proof for the precise positioning of access ladders between the floors. Here, in Devenish I, the restored ladders are near-vertical and centrally placed.

fig. 19: WINDOW ORIENTATION
Windows in the tower drum (a) are arranged in a clockwise or anti-clockwise manner, either as a result of being derived from the example of towers with internal spiral staircases, or for security reasons. Bell-floor windows (b) are oriented towards the cardinal points, although some towers have a greater number than the conventional four.

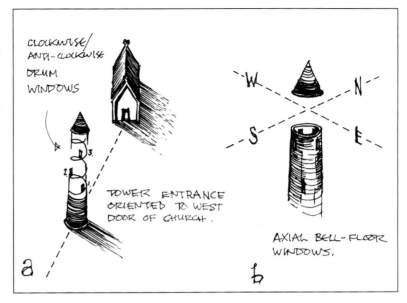

CLOCKWISE/
ANTI-CLOCKWISE
DRUM
WINDOWS

TOWER ENTRANCE
ORIENTED TO WEST
DOOR OF CHURCH.

AXIAL BELL-FLOOR
WINDOWS.

a

b

are so ill-lit. Unlike churches, where the planning was ordained by Christian ritual, and a window could be expected in the east gable for the altar, there were no similar criteria for bell-towers; their windows could occur where the masons chose to place them. The best-lit of them may have a small window on each floor, although there are enough examples in which only occasional floors have windows, to suggest that internal light was not a high priority. Rattoo has only a single window in the drum, leaving the second and third floors blind. While this is an extreme example, single unlit floors are commonplace. There is no evidence to suggest that the positioning of the windows was determined by external criteria, although, alternatively, no internal logic is obvious either. Their location seems to be defined by the position of the window on the second floor, from which the others ascend in a clockwise or anti-clockwise arrangement, as though based on the presence of a spiral staircase. It is unclear whether this is a skeuomorphic survival, a mannerism introduced by a mason familiar with spiral staircases in Continental bell-towers and maintained as a stylistic mannerism, or is a conscious attempt to distribute the observation capacity of the windows. The former seems more likely, as the size of early windows is so small as to have little utility other than as a light source. In Cloyne the five ascending windows rotate clockwise, south, west, north-east, south-east and south-west; in Ardmore three windows rotate clockwise, north, east, south, and in Devenish, three windows rotate anti-clockwise, north-east, north-west, south-east.

Whatever the external dimension and form, windows almost invariably splay inwards in order to better spread the available light. Most frequently, the windows are positioned slightly above the floor level, rather than higher up where the light might have been better distributed. It would, in general, have been possible to see out of the windows by sitting on the timber floor, although the view was severely restricted.

TOP WINDOWS, THE BELL-FLOOR

Although the orientation of the four top-floor windows often departs from the true cardinal points, it is probable that this is more due to the difficulty of establishing true north with precision, than to any intention otherwise on the part of the builders. The idea that the towers were used as lookout posts seems to be undermined by the fact that the windows are thus oriented, rather than paying any attention to the local topography. The fact that they represent, in plan, a Greek equal-armed cross would not have been lost on the builders in an age acutely conscious of the power of Christian symbolism. Glendalough I is a case in point. The bell-floor windows are off the cardinal points, although still placed axially. This deviation might be seen as adapting them to the approach down the valley from Laragh.

The practicality of ringing an iron hand-bell from the bell-floor windows is another consideration which is unresolved. At best, the floor-level windows in the deep embrasure of the wall do not make the idea of ringing a hand-bell from them particularly practical. Kilmacduagh, with six bell-floor windows, and which stands complete to its cap, is alone among towers with more than four windows at the top in being undoubtedly original. Other multi-windowed bell-floors (Kildare, Kilkenny, Tullaherin) appear to have been altered in the late medieval period or during the 18th century.

THE CAP

Although there are incomplete and 'unsatisfactory' caps to some towers (Donaghmore, Scattery), they are in essence a simple cone separated from the drum of the tower by a projecting cornice. Most of the existing caps have been repaired or completely rebuilt during the late 19th century, yet when partial evidence exists for missing caps (Fertagh), what remains confirms the probable accuracy of the restorations. Ardmore and Temple Finghin are unorthodox caps: the former is exceptionally steep, the later displays a unique herring-bone pattern in the external stonework, a feature found in 11th- and 12th-century buildings in Britain. Internally, the roof-cone is supported on a shallow corbelled dome, which can still be seen at close quarters in surviving complete towers such as at Clondalkin and Devenish. The dome is constructed of nine or more diminishing concentric courses, with the centre-point capped by a closing stone. Between the internal dome and the external apex, the cap is solid masonry.

ANOMALIES

Virtually all towers display anomalies which suggest the absence of a master-plan in their conception. Based on the fact that no two towers display all the same features, they appear to have been continually evolving, with each tower representing a fresh re-arrangement of the standard elements. The most recent or, equally, the nearest tower in a region could have provided the prototype for further developments.

CAPS: DEVENISH I, GLENDALOUGH II, AND CASHEL

At a height of, on average, 26 metres from the ground (the 13 complete free-standing examples range from 22.86 to 34 metres high), a maintenance-free roof for the Round Tower was a necessity. Like the form itself, the conical cap suited this role to perfection and was never improved upon. Three examples, Devenish I, Glendalough II and Cashel, although displaying minor differences of detail, are all essentially the same.

Devenish I, Co. Fermanagh

Glendalough II, Co. Wicklow

Cashel, Co. Tipperary

DECORATION

Decoration generally appears to be confined to late towers, principally those of the 12th century. Where the decoration is integral with the structure (Ardmore, Devenish, Donaghmore, Kells, Kildare, Rattoo, Timahoe), it helps to date those towers. Alternatively, where the decoration is not necessarily integral (the Sheela-na-Gig at Rattoo, the cross at Antrim), it is of less help in establishing the date of the tower. With the exception of Devenish, where the decoration is at cap level and is located on the face of the cornice where it forms a decorative frieze, all external embellishment is confined to the door-case of towers. Donaghmore is the most important of these on account of the crucifix and paired heads which decorate the doorcase. Timahoe is exceptional in the richness and well-preserved nature of its Romanesque door and window. The decorations at Ardmore are internal and confined to the corbels on a number of floors.

HEIGHT

In the 250-year timespan over which the Round Towers were built, height was established from the beginning, without any significant variation taking place over the period. Scattery, possibly the earliest standing tower, is 26 metres high, while Ardmore, possibly the last complete tower to be built is 29.2 metres, while others such as Kilkenny and Fertagh, which have lost their caps, could have stood as high as 35 metres. Kilmacduagh, at over 34 metres, is the tallest standing tower complete with cap.

DEVELOPMENT

The position of the entrance door to a Round Tower must to some tentative degree define the relative chronology of the towers, without it being possible to establish any truly reliable order. Ground floor entrances are presumed to be early (Castledermot, Scattery), while elevated doorways represent a later and definitive development. Kilmacduagh is an example of a Round Tower where the door is 9 metres from ground level, almost a third of the way up the tower. The gradual escalation in the height of the entrance is evidence of a changing attitude to their security, rather than to their function.

ARTICULATION

A common feature of many Round Towers is the use of different types and colours of stone for entrance doors and windows. This phenomenon has given rise to the idea that features of a different stone were later insertions into the towers. This understanding is a product of a failure to appreciate that the use of different types of stone in architecture is commonly employed in order to enhance the features of a building. The contrast between a limestone tower and its sandstone doorcase would have been far more pronounced when the stonework was fresh and a significant contribution to the beauty of the towers. When limewashing of the tower exterior masked the building stone, the door and window features would have remained uncovered. The use of different stone types for ashlar features can also depend on ease of cutting.

FIRE DAMAGE

Considering the frequent mention in the annals of assaults by fire upon the towers, it is surprising that more of the surviving ones do not exhibit extensive fire damage. The nature of the stone used would have made some far more susceptible than others to destruction by fire: towers of limestone would have been particularly vulnerable. Two towers where one can be fairly certain that their condition is as a result of fire damage are Aghagower (the doorcase) and Dysert O'Dea (the breach), where the fractured nature of particular parts of the stonework represent attempts in antiquity to destroy them or their contents and those unfortunately sheltering within.

THE LAST ROUND TOWERS

Which towers are the last ones? In any shortlist it is immediately obvious that the claimants to being the last towers to be built have little in common beyond an obvious departure from the norm, in so far as there ever really was a norm for Round Towers; eccentricity is their hallmark. Ardmore shows a sense of the

AGHAGOWER, CO. MAYO
The impregnability of the Round Towers in Irish popular legend contrasts starkly with the annalists' accounts and with the evidence. Aghagower's burnt doorcase is powerful testimony of the vulnerability of those seeking shelter, as well as of the buildings themselves.

FERNS, CO. WEXFORD
No other engaged or attached example of a drum-on-a-rectangle tower still stands, although there were doubtless numerous variants on this theme, of which a few survive at foundation level. Originally provided with a conical cap to the tower and steep roof to the church, Ferns would have related closely to Cormac's Chapel, Glendalough II and III.

impending Gothic revolution in its soaring attenuation, which represents the most radical and successful departure from the solidity of surviving complete towers. This change is based on a logical pursuit of the possible and an avoidance of the architectonic cul-de-sac represented by the collage approach of Timahoe, where two irreconcilable forms have been inappropriately combined, an approach for which there was little future. Every detail of Ardmore is harmonious. Such protrusions as there are do not scar the profile, the doorcase is elegant, the string-courses, which are unique and radical in their implications, are so proportioned and detailed as not to upset the profile. In an architectural form which was evolving over a 250-year period, Ardmore is the apogee.

Ferns is not generally considered to be a Round Tower at all, but what else could it be? It is not freestanding, does not have a significant batter and internally has a spiral staircase. Yet it was built at the latter end of the time-frame of the 10th – 12th centuries and must be considered within the corpus. It certainly is a product of the same building tradition and is among the last engaged towers to be built. It therefore deserves consideration among the last of the towers. What is most obvious about these three examples is how much they differ in design: Ardmore expresses refinement of the concept, Timahoe, an experimental attitude to the potential of the form, and Ferns a departure in the architectural direction of Cormac's Chapel.

They all stand at well-documented sites: Ardmore, clearly on the path of new ideas entering Ireland, while Ferns is one of the last throws of the native church-building tradition. They show that the vigour and versatility, which are the hallmarks of Round Towers, lasted until the very end of their development.

REDISCOVERY AND REVIVAL: 18th CENTURY – 19th CENTURY
During the Anglican rebuilding of parish churches during the 18th and 19th centuries, and particularly after the 1800 Act of Union and the availability of

the Board of First Fruits' funding for churches, many Round Towers were pressed into service, fitted with floors and ladders and used as belfries for Church of Ireland parish churches (Armoy, Castledermot, Clondalkin, Drumbo, Drumcliff, Kinneigh, Swords and numerous others). This led to the last considerable period of structural interference in the towers. After disestablishment in 1871, no more towers were returned to use, in parallel with the vesting of many of the more prominent in the Office of Public Works, the restoration of the caps, repairs to the fabric, and a general and much-needed programme of conservation. Under the Office of Public Works in the Republic of Ireland and the Department of the Environment in Northern Ireland, this conservation process has continued to the present. Lightning, always a greater enemy of Round Towers than warlike enemies or Norse raiders, has been rendered impotent by the installation of lightning conductors and this threat, which had so impressed the annalists, can be dismissed from the scene.

What is now required, most towers having been made safe from the annalists' 'thunderbolts', and all of them protected by legislation from ecclesiastical, private and public interference, is to see that the surviving Round Towers should be treated with more respect and their immediate environments be protected from insensitive change. There is still much more to be discovered.

CHAPTER SIX

MANUSCRIPT SOURCES
AND
MISSING TOWERS

' *A great storm happened on the nones of December, which tore off the Beannchopar [cap] of the cloicteach of Armagh, and caused great destruction of woods all over Ireland.* '

Annals of Ulster for the year 1121

THE LITERARY SOURCES

Irish annalistic references to Round Towers may be regarded as the primary sources of information on the subject, and, as early written records, they collectively provide a solid basis of information, even if these annotations are written in medieval 'telegramese'. The original annalist's notations, which from the late 6th century can be considered more reliable than for the earlier period, are the result of later editing of records contemporary with the events described. As the sole literary documentation it is inevitable that more reliance has been placed on them than is always warranted, yet the tower references are both so brief and explicit that the internal evidence which they contain harbours little room for misinterpretation. It is worth stressing that, however cryptic, the significance of the annalists' references can hardly be over-estimated. For the early medieval period they form an invaluable commentary on the towers and the uses to which they were put. Between them the annals contain sixty-two *cloicteach* references (noting twenty-three separate events, repeated with variations in different annals), all but one or two of which directly refer to events which took place in or at Round Towers.

Of the various sets of annals, the last to be written, *The Annals of the Four Masters* (AFM) (*Annála Rioghachta Eireann* or *Annals of the Kingdom of Ireland*) is the collection about which most is known. It was compiled from 1632 to 1636 by a number of scholars in the Franciscan friary of Bundrowse, probably located on the Leitrim and Donegal border, under the direction of Mícheál Ó Cléirigh. Written in Irish, the annals are based on manuscript copies of earlier compilations going back to the 6th century, most of which have not survived, and covering the period from the Flood to 1616. The original intention of the compilers was to publish this collection of Irish historic records in Louvain, since the 16th century a major centre of the Counter-Reformation, and the principal location for Irish language publishing during the 17th century. The purpose of the enterprise was an attempt to counter the negative version of Irish history produced by English chroniclers from Giraldus Cambrensis in the 12th century to Edmund Spenser in the 16th century. Ó Cléirigh's work was published in part in Louvain, but *The Annals of the Four Masters* did not finally appear in print until 1848-51, when a full text with an English translation was published in Dublin, edited by the Irish scholar John O'Donovan.

Other annals are the *Chronicum Scotorum (CS)*; *Annals of Clonmacnoise (AC)*; *Annals of Innisfallen (AI)*; *Annals of Lough Cé (ALC)*; *Annals of Tigernach (AT)*; *Annals of Ulster (AU)*, which, together with the *Miscellaneous Irish Annals (MIA)*, are compilations of annual records of events, reliably from the 7th century onwards. The earlier history – from the flood to the advent of Christianity – is a strictly legendary compilation, but from the early medieval period these records are, with some reservations, an accurate if occasionally confusing and contradictory inventory of the principal events of the particular time-span covered by each collection. The annals are one of the principal sources for early Irish history, dealing mainly with the reigns of kings, dynastic struggles, monastic foundations and personalities, as well as natural phenomena, catasstrophes, and unexplained wonders such as an entry for the year 1054 when '*a cloicteach of fire was seen in the sky*' at Rostalla, Co. Meath. Round Towers being struck by lightning or burned by marauding armies are among the events which attracted the annalists' attention.

To consider the Round Towers without the evidence of the annalistic references would mean there would be virtually no evidence at all to put flesh upon the bones of these precise and enigmatic structures. Significantly, the annals provide both a *terminus ante* and *post quem* for the towers – from the year 950 to 1232, although the vast body of the towers may have been built in the 11th and 12th centuries, rather than in the initial period. The small number of references are widely scattered across the pages of all the manuscripts: before and after there is only silence. Attempts to date the towers to earlier than the 10th century have been enthusiastically pursued, particularly with regard to giving them a very early date and associating them with the founding fathers of the Irish church, but these efforts are lacking in substance. In reality, the stone towers follow by almost two centuries the building in the 8th century of the earliest Irish stone churches, and attempts to place them before the 10th century are entirely without evidence.

Giraldus Cambrensis, in his *History and Topography of Ireland* (published and read at Oxford in 1188), makes a passing reference to Round Towers. In discussing folklore about the origins of Lough Neagh being caused by an overflowing magical well which drowned the sexually degenerate inhabitants of that region, he states:

> *There is some confirmation of this story in as much as fishermen of*
> *the lake clearly see under the waves in calm weather towers of churches*
> *which, as is usual in that country, are tall, slender and rounded.*
> *They frequently point them out to visitors who are amazed at the occurrence.*

Giraldus, who seems to have spent much of his time in Ireland having his leg pulled by the local wits, has nonetheless preserved the first tourist's account of public response to Round Towers from the early medieval period. The well-known words of Thomas Moore's 19th-century ballad, *Let Erin Remember the Days of Old*, are based on this passage from Giraldus:

> *On Lough Neagh's bank, as the fisherman strays,*
> *When the clear cold eve's declining,*
> *He sees the round tow'rs of other days,*
> *In the wave beneath him shining.*

Of the twenty-three towers to which there are annalistic references, three references are to the tower at Armagh which has since disappeared. All the annalist's references are given in full; some refer to existing towers, others to vanished examples, as fourteen of the twenty-three to which reference is made no longer exist. While it is most unsatisfactory to base conclusions related to existing structures on historic literary references to destroyed buildings, the fact that all the towers belong to a very specific type of building which share a common function and design, the totality of the literary references can be taken as reflecting on the function of all towers. The different sets of annals occasionally record the same event in variant entries for the same year; where parallel readings exist, only a single version is given.

ANNALISTIC REFERENCES

Dates are listed chronologically. The capital letters following each entry identify the particular annals, as shown on the previous page.

SLANE, Co. Meath (first literary reference to a Round Tower, now vanished)
950: *The belfry of Slaine was burned by the foreigners [the Vikings of Dublin], with its full of relics and distinguished persons, together with Caeineachair, Lector of Slaine, and the crosier of the patron saint, and a bell, the best of bells.* (AFM)

TUAMGRANEY, Co. Clare (vanished tower)
964: *Cormac Ua Cillin, of the Ui Fiachrach Aidhne, comarb of Ciaran and Coman, and comarb of Tuaim-greine, by whom the great church of Tuaim-greine, and its cloicteach, were constructed, sapiens et senex, et Episcopus, quievit in Christo.* (CS)

LOUTH, Co. Louth (vanished tower)
981: *There was such boysterous stormy winds this year that it fell down many turretts, and among the rest it fell down violently the steeple of Louth, and other steeples.* (AC)

ARMAGH, Co. Armagh (vanished tower)
995/6: *Ard-Macha was burned by lightning, both houses, damhlaig and cloicteach.*

and fidnad – a complete destruction such as occurred not in Erin before, and will not occur before doomsday. (AT)

DOWNPATRICK, Co. Down (vanished tower)
1015: *Dun-da-leathghlas was totally burned, with its Daimhliag (stone church), and Cloicteach by lightning.* (AFM)

ARMAGH, Co. Armagh (vanished tower)
1020: *Ard-Macha was burned, with all the fort, without saving any house within it, except the library only, and many houses were burned in the Trians, and the Daimhliag-mor (great stone church) was burned, and the Cloicteach, with its bells; and Daimhliag-na-Toe, and Daimhliag-an-Sabhaill; and the old preaching chair, and the chariot of the Abbots, and their books in the houses of the students, with much gold and other precious things.* (AFM)

CLONARD, Co. Meath (vanished tower)
1039: *The Cloicteach of Cluain-Iraid fell.* (AFM)

ROSCOMMON, Co. Roscommon (vanished tower)
1050: *Doire-Caelainne and the Cloicteach of Ros Comain were burned by the men of Breifne.* (AFM)

EMLY, Co. Tipperary (vanished tower)
1058: *Iarleach-Ibhair was totally burned, both Daimhliag and Cloicteach.* (AFM)

KELLS, Co. Meath (existing tower)
1076: *Murchad, son of Flann Ua Maeleachlainn, at the expiration of three days and three nights after his having assumed the supremacy of Teamhair (Tara), was treacherously killed in the Cloicteach of Ceannus, by the lord of Gaileanga, Amhlaeibh, the grandson of Maelan; and the latter was himself immediately slain in revenge, through the miracles of God and Colum-Cille, by Maelseachlainn, son of Conchobhar.* (AFM)

MONASTERBOICE, Co. Louth (existing tower)
1097: *The cloicteach of Mainistir, with its books and many treasures were burned.* (AFM)

TULLAHERIN, Co. Kilkenny (existing tower)
1121: *The cloicteach of Tealach-nInmainne in Osraighe was split by a thunderbolt and a stone flew from the cloicteach, which killed a student in the church.* (AFM)

ARMAGH, Co. Armagh (vanished tower)
1121: *A great wind-storm happened in the December of this year, which knocked off the conical cap of the cloicteach of Ard-Macha and caused great destruction of woods throughout Ireland.* (AFM)

CLONMACNOISE, Co. Offaly (existing tower)
1124: *The finishing of the cloicteach of Cluain-mic-Nois by Ua Maeloin, successor of Ciaran.* (AFM)

TRIM, Co. Meath (vanished tower)
1126/7: *A great hosting by Connor MacFergall O'Loughlinn, together with the people of the North of Ireland, to Meath; they burnt Trim, both cloicteach and church, and these full of people.* (AU)

DRUMBO, Co. Down (existing tower)
1130-1: *A hosting by Conchobhar son of Ardghar Mac Lochlainn along with Cinéal Eóghain and Cinéal Conaill and the Oirghialla into Ulaidh, and they plundered Druim Both, including cloicteach and oratory and books. The Uldaidh came to Cnoc Cluana to meet them in battle and the Ulaidh were defeated and slaughter inflicted on them.* (MIA)

CLONMACNOISE, Co. Offaly and ROSCREA, Co. Tipperary (existing towers)
1135: *Lightning struck off the head of the Cloicteach of Cluain-mic-Nois and pierced the cloicteach of Ros-Cre.* (AU)

DULEEK, Co. Meath (existing tower)
1147: *A thunderbolt fell this year upon the cloicteach of Daimhliag-Chianain and knocked off the beannchobhair (conical cap).* (AFM)

FERTAGH, Co. Kilkenny (existing tower)
1156: *Eochaidh Ua Cuinn, the chief master was burned in the cloicteach of Fearta.* (AFM)

TULLYARD, Co. Meath (vanished tower)
1171: *The cloicteach of Tealach-aird was burned by Tighearnan Ua Ruairc (Tiernan O'Ruairc), with its full of people in it.* (AFM)

DEVENISH, Co. Fermanagh (existing tower)
1176: *Domhnall son of Amhlaoibh Ó Maoil Ruaanaidh, king of Fir Manach, was burned by his own kinsmen in the cloicteach of Daimhinis.* (AU-MIA)

ARDBRACCAN, Co. Meath (vanished tower)
1181: *The steeple of Ardbreakean fell this yeare.* (AC)

ANNADOWN, Co. Galway (last mention of tower building, now vanished.).
1238: *The cloicteach of Enachduin was erected.* (AFM)

ROSSCARBERY, Co. Cork (vanished tower)
1285: *A very destructive wind this year, about the Feast of Brigid (Feb. 1); it blew down the bell tower of Ross Ailithir and caused much damage generally.* (AI)

LATE DOCUMENTATION

Following the cryptic annotations of the annalistic scribes which record the completion of Annadown in the early 13th century, there are a few passing mentions in the annals and other documents. After a leap of 400 years comes a much more extensive body of information, or rather documentation, in the form of the many drawings and engravings produced between the early 17th and late 19th centuries by antiquarians, artists and travellers. These valuable records are allied to speculation and learned commentary on the subject of the towers' origins, much of which is of questionable value.

This body of information ranges from representations which are startling in their inaccuracy to well observed and accurate renderings of the architecture of the Round Tower. Of particular importance are the drawings which record the appearance of towers which either have not survived (St Michael le Pole, Dublin; Downpatrick, Co. Down) or, equally importantly, those which have been repaired since the 18th century. Without this form of documentation it is exceptionally difficult to determine if what now survives is the unaltered work of the 10th to 12th centuries, a late medieval rebuilding, or a 19th- or 20th-century restoration. Problematic or eccentric towers which lack such representations, yet where it is known restoration work took place (Donaghmore), emphasise the vital significance of this form of documentary record. A prevailing difficulty with the majority of 17th- to 19th-century drawings of Round Towers is a tendency to represent them as being more slender and taller than was actually the case, a product of the prevailing aesthetic concepts of the Romantic movement which sought to emphasise the gulf between all natural and antique phenomena and human experience, and thereby making grander or more awe-inspiring natural or architectural wonders. This manner of approach has led to the heights of towers being vastly exaggerated in early drawings and descriptions.

A further category of documentary material is photographic and this represents the most valuable record available for the early pre-restoration appearance of the towers. Nineteenth-century photography overcomes the difficulties of bad draughtsmanship and aesthetic theorising to present the towers as they were, before the Office of Public Works, Church Commissioners and local landowners considered Round Towers to be important antiquities or curiosities which required conservation. There is something stark and raw about the towers before they were repointed and, in many cases, had their caps either repaired or totally replaced. The beauty of Glendalough I, probably the most well-known of all the towers, is significantly altered by the image of it in Lord Dunraven's photograph of 1870, in which it stands capless and with its unpointed masonry displaying the weathering of more than half a millennium.

The scope and content of this survey conducted in the last years of the 20th century is strictly defined by what exists. The number of towers dealt with could have been considerably expanded if all those whose existence is definitely known from literary or other evidence were included. The small number of almost complete towers which survived into the late 18th century, on which the information is quite credible, are a tempting category for inclusion.

ROSSERK, CO. MAYO
Late medieval masons excelled at spirited low-relief stone-carving, of which very many examples are to be found in the church complexes of the Continental monastic orders, on tombs and, often arbitrarily placed, as casual decorative pieces. This unique miniature carving at Rosserk Abbey is a lone voice from the past, the sole visual response to the aesthetic beauty of the Round Tower.

Schematic or more precise drawings exist for a number of the vanished towers, some of which can be relied upon as being adequate representations of the demolished buildings, whilst others are of secondary value, being more symbolic than actual renderings of a particular antiquity (Rosscarbery, Co. Cork). Local folklore concerning jumping towers, families of towers at a single site, towers never completed or of fabulous height, all appear to be late musings and do not cast any significant light on the subject. These accounts are usually rather more engaging than the annalists' terseness, yet it is in the latter's very brevity of language that one comes closest to the society which produced them.

Locations for which indisputable evidence exist of a Round Tower are listed below; there are numerous other sites where the evidence for a Round Tower is insubstantial, yet plausible. This group of known towers could be expanded by further information on the doubtful sites. The arrangement is by counties, as with the listing of existing towers. Adding the definite seventy-three towers to the known, but vanished, twenty-four examples, and allowing for further unknown towers to be excavated, as well as doubtful examples to be verified, a figure of more than a hundred towers is a perfectly reasonable hypothesis.

THE MISSING TOWERS

Vanished Round Towers may be divided into those known from annalistic or other documentary references, and those of which a drawing or engraving was made prior to their disappearance. The annalists' notations are as brief for those towers which have survived, as for the ones which did not last into the present, and are concerned more with the disasters which befell the building or their contents – burnings and lootings by the Irish or the Vikings, the occasional murder within a tower, and the ubiquitous 'thunderbolts' – than with the intrinsic interest of the buildings themselves which, remarkable sights though the towers must have been in the medieval period, did not excite any literary comment. In this sense the annals cast only a limited light on Round Towers, beyond confirming their presence at particular sites and elaborating on the function to which they were put.

Visual records are more tangible evidence for the towers and, other than the unique carving of a tower in the piscina of Rosserk Abbey, Co. Mayo (*c.* 1440), they were not drawn between 1440 and the early 17th century when a representation of Devenish I appears on a local estate map. In Sir James Ware's book there is a passable representation of Temple Finghin, although it is shown with a late medieval conical roof within a parapet, rather than correctly with its roof cone, and was not drawn by someone who had seen the original.

The missing towers are arranged by counties, the numbering follows on from the listed existing towers in the Inventory (chapter seven).

74. ARMAGH, Co. Armagh (annalistic reference 988 et seq.)
75. KELLISTOWN, Co. Carlow (possible visual record)
76. RATH BLAMAIC, Co. Clare (possible historical reference)
77. TUAMGRANEY, Co. Clare (annalistic reference 964)
78. CORK, Co. Cork (schematic representation on 17th-century church plate)

79. ROSSCARBERY, Co. Cork (annalistic reference 1285; schematic representation on 17th-century church muniments)

80. DERRY, Co. Derry (visual record; historical reference)

81. RAPHOE, Co. Donegal (historical reference)

82. DOWNPATRICK, Co. Down (annalistic reference 1015; visual record)

83. DUBLIN, Co. Dublin (visual record)

84. ANNADOWN, Co. Galway (annalistic reference 1238)

85. ARDFERT, Co. Kerry (historical reference and fragments on site)

86. TULLAMAINE, Co. Kilkenny (annalistic reference 1121)

87. AGHMACART, Co. Laois (annalistic reference 1156)

88. KILLESHIN, Co. Laois (historical reference)

89. LOUTH, Co. Louth (annalistic reference 981)

90. ARDBRACCAN, Co. Meath (annalistic reference 1181)

91. CLONARD, Co. Meath (annalistic reference 1039)

92. TULLYARD, Co. Meath (annalistic reference 1171)

93. SLANE, Co. Meath (annalistic reference 950)

94. TRIM, Co. Meath (annalistic reference 1127)

95. KILBARRY, Co. Roscommon (historical reference and fragment on site)

96. ROSCOMMON, Co. Roscommon (annalistic reference 1050)

97. EMLY, Co. Tipperary (annalistic reference 1058)

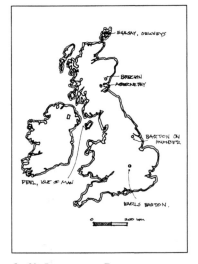

fig. 20: IRELAND AND BRITAIN
Of the four examples of Round Towers of Irish type which are to be found outside Ireland, one, Egilsay, is in Orkney, two others, Brechin and Abernethy, are located on the east coast of Scotland, and one is at Peel on the Isle of Man.

IRISH TOWERS ABROAD

Whether Round Towers can be considered as a purely Irish form of architecture must depend on whether or not there are similar buildings elsewhere, and if so, whether or not their number warrants consideration in the context of the Irish towers. Of the small number of contenders for consideration, less than half-a-dozen in all, which are scattered along the eastern and western seaboards of Scotland and Wales, only one is an indisputable Irish-style Round Tower, which if it were standing in a churchyard in Meath or Kerry would not appear out of place. This is the tower of Brechin in Angus, Scotland, and it closely resembles Donaghmore in the sculptural detail of the doorcase of which it is a superior version. This is a particularly beautiful example of a 12th-century Round Tower.

The tower in Abernethy, Perthshire, is also of Irish type, although inferior to Brechin in conception and detailing. St Patrick's Isle tower, at Peel harbour on the Isle of Man, is also Irish in sympathy, particularly in the treatment of the doorcase which, although more widely splayed than any Irish counterpart, is nonetheless closely related to Irish examples. At Egilsay, in Orkney, the church has an engaged tower projecting from the west gable which resembles an Irish tower in height, although its relationship on plan is closer to the East Anglian flint-built towers which are similarly placed.

With the exception of Brechin, none of these buildings can seriously be considered as significant influences on Irish early medieval tower building. None retains a conical cap, and as all appear late in terms of the door typology, cannot be considered as forerunners to the *cloicteach*, but as parallel developments or evidence of the influence of Irish building practice in adjacent territories.

CHAPTER SEVEN

INVENTORY

‘ *The belfry of Slaine was burned by the foreigners* with its full of relics and distinguished persons together with Caeineachair, Lector of Slaine, and the crosier of the patron saint, and a bell, the best of bells.* ’

Annals of The Four Masters for the year 950
[* the Dublin Vikings]

The purpose of this inventory is to document and record the seventy-three known Round Towers in a coherent and accessible fashion. The information covers the present-day appearance and location of the towers and their environment, with observations on any peculiarities or distinguishing features, followed by statistical details where these are obtainable. The counties are listed alphabetically, with the location of the individual towers presented alphabetically within each county. An advantage of a county-by-county over an alphabetical arrangement of individual sites is that it locates adjacent sites in closer textual order, allowing for ease of comparison. Included are all towers of which any vestige remains, however slight, and in a few instances, vanished towers, where the building to which the tower was attached has survived. Also included (although not numbered) in this inventory are (A) a single tower-in-effigy, Rosserk, Co. Mayo, the only known medieval representation of a Round Tower, and (B) Cormac's Chapel, Co. Tipperary, which was built within the time-frame of the Round Towers and has a pair of related rectangular towers.

At the three sites which have more than one tower (Clonmacnoise, Devenish, Glendalough), the towers are represented by the site-name followed by Roman numerals, which are allotted in order of conventionality (free-standing towers taking precedence over engaged examples; engaged over attached), rather than as a means of establishing a chronology.

A considerable difficulty which confronts anybody wishing to study Round Towers is access. A few examples, such as Fertagh, Tullaherin and Turlough, are hermetically sealed off from any internal scrutiny. In many other towers, although in theory access is possible, in practice they lack internal floors and ladders, thus close inspection of internal areas above the first floor is impossible, other than with field-glasses. Some towers have internal ladders, while a few have remnants of the many floors and ladders installed during the 19th century, now in ruins, and these are all either dangerous or inaccessible.

The findings of this book, are, in so far as was possible, based on direct observation in the years prior to 1999. As is the nature of any time-based study, the documentary photographs, all taken during 1997-98 (with the exception of Daphne D.C. Pochin Mould's aerial shots which are independently dated), were dependent on the local weather conditions. Some sites seemed to be forever lingering under a canopy of black clouds, irrespective of the time of day or year during which they were visited; others, conversely, were bathed in eternal sunshine, or might be caught unawares on a rare bright day. At times, the prevailing greyness of Round Towers, seen against a backdrop of a leaden sky, tended to deprive these wonderful structures of their sense of effortless grace, and reduce them to grim fortresses of rooks, admonishing relics in an empty landscape, more the creations of Industrial Revolution toil than religious inspiration.

As the emphasis of this study is with built remains rather than monastic legend, ecclesiastical tradition or local folklore, the wealth of extraneous information associated which most sites is not dealt with here. If the tower in question was mentioned in antiquity, the relevant reference is given in Chapter Six. In consideration of the fact that the bulk of literary references relate to vanished towers, all tower references are given in full, for the light which they cast on the corpus of Round Towers. Annalistic references to the site in general, to the succession of abbots, or to the number of times the settlement was destroyed by the Irish or the Vikings, are not included because these references bear only indirectly on the towers.

Much ink has been spilt by previous commentators on the question of human burials found beneath the foundations of Round Towers or, as in Kilkenny and elsewhere, half inside – half outside the walls, based on the consideration as to whether they represent pagan or Christian burials. What these burials undoubtedly do indicate is the prior existence of a graveyard or individual burials in an area subsequently chosen as the location of a tower; the orientation of the burial in a Christian manner (head facing east, and the absence of grave goods), or erratically, does not provide any significant information (regarding the towers), beyond the obvious fact of these being most probably Christian burials which may have, by centuries, preceded the 10th-century origins of tower building.

The criteria in locating a tower within an ecclesiastical enclosure depended entirely on the position of the west doorway of the principal church; whatever obstructions lay in its way were clearly not seen as prohibitive. The tower site was canted to the right or left to allow for ecclesiastical assembly or burials directly in front of the church entrance. From the mid-19th century, the interiors of many towers were 'excavated', often by absentee commentators, as in the case of Drumbo, where the supervisor was present only on the final day of the work. None of these probings within towers were conducted to any scientific standard and the value of the information gathered on these occasions is of extremely limited value.

The dimensions given are based on George Lennox Barrow's measurements recorded in *The Round Towers of Ireland* (1979). All those which I have checked personally correspond closely to his measurements, give-or-take some centimetres, an acceptable discrepancy, allowing for the uneven nature of the stonework, and the probability that dimensions were not taken in precisely the same position. Identifying the type of stone in some towers is problematic due to discoloration of the surface of many towers. It has been assumed here, as a general principle, that all towers were originally complete, although there is no means of substantiating this. The fact that some towers display phasing in their construction can indicate that they were built over an extended period, which also leaves open the possibility that some were never finished.

Possession of a collapsible ladder will provide access to entrance-floor level, and thereby to the interiors of most towers, other than to eccentric and inaccessible examples like Kilmacduagh. Intrepid souls who ascend the outside of a Round Tower to entrance level, and descend into its interior, must become inured to the presence of the live pigeons, rooks, bats, other fauna and creepy-crawlies which inhabit virtually all towers, and to standing thigh-deep in a disagreeable mulch of collapsed nests, guano, feathers and dead birds, as well as all manner of bones, modern grave goods and soft-drink cans, flung in through the open door from the surrounding graveyards by present-day pilgrims.

SCATTERY, CO. CLARE

ANTRIM

Left: Despite the roughness of its masonry, Antrim has an excellent profile and is characteristic of the form and proportions of the finest Round Towers. The mature trees which now surround the tower, and the raised platform upon which it stands, are the result of 19th-century landscaping. The bullaun is visible in the bottom left of photo. (See photos pp. 63, 65.)

Below: The lintelled doorway has a low-relief, ringed cross with foot on the relieving stone above the lintel; Antrim is the only early tower to have a decorated doorway. The articulated four-quoin

INVENTORY

An alphabetical listing of Round Towers by county.

1 Antrim, Co. Antrim   Antrim town is at the north-east corner of Lough Neagh, just south of the A6. The Round Tower (one of only two complete towers in Northern Ireland) is in the grounds of Steeple Park, Steeple Road, now the offices of Antrim Borough Council, north-east of the town centre. The growth of the town has obscured the fact that the monastery was originally located not far from the shores of the lake. The foundation of the monastery of which little is known, is attributed to St Comgall of Bangor in the 6th century.

The Tower: Antrim is a complete tower, with cap. It is unusual among towers around which towns have developed, in that it is now neither located in a ruined ecclesiastical site nor surrounded by a later graveyard. The tower stands in a small area of parkland, enclosed by mature trees and with the exception of a fine metre-high double bullaun boulder located some distance from its base, is devoid of any evidence of its original ecclesiastical setting. It is probable that the tower acted as a folly within the conventions of 18th-century Romantic ideas of landscape, when the parkland was laid out during the Georgian era.

Antrim stands 28 metres high from the ground to the apex of the cap. The batter is quite visible but the wall line is in places uneven. The tower is constructed of random basalt rubble, unevenly coursed; the stones are roughly squared with many spalls. An earthen platform on which the tower stands has been created around it by lowering the surrounding surface by one metre. There are two offsets at the base of the tower, with the door-sill placed 2.3 metres above.

The granite doorcase which faces north-east is lintelled with inclined jambs; the jambs are each composed of four quoin-like ashlars – a commonplace treatment over a lengthy period. Above the lintel a relieving block carries a low relief carving of a ringed cross with an elongated stem, which ends in curved terminals. There is no reason to doubt that this feature, which is unique to Antrim, is contemporary with the construction of the tower, although there is no means of substantiating whether it is in fact contemporary or a later embellishment. At other towers which display decorated entrances (Donaghmore, Timahoe, Kells among others), it is clear that the embellishments are integral, rather than, as has been suggested, later additions. Both lintel and monolithic sill are split. If the tower was originally rendered in lime plaster, the doorcase and the lintel with a cross would not have been covered. The windows of the drum are rectangular and lintelled. The window on the second floor, the 'Treasury' window, which is to the left of the entrance is substantial, and the same width as the entrance and almost as high. The bell-floor windows are small, rectangular and face the cardinal points.

Antrim was struck by lightning in 1819, after which the cap was reset. A small plaque with a neo-classical frame is set on the external wall of the tower, to the left and below the entrance. This may have been placed to record the

ARMOY

Above: The tall and narrow doorway is Armoy's most interesting feature, and displays important elements in the evolution of the door-opening – a lintel with cut-away soffit arch, as well as a rudimentary architrave around the doorhead. (See photo p. 62.)

Left: Like many other Round Towers during the early 19th century, Armoy served as bell-tower to the nearby church. The masonry below the level of the lintel is composed of smaller courses than those above, a factor which generally implies some phasing in the tower's construction.

Left: Masonry found above the door lintel.

restoration, but no inscription is now visible. Antrim is distinguished by being among the first Round Towers of which a post-medieval visual record exists. It was drawn *c.* 1699, by the antiquarian and keeper of the Ashmolean Museum, Edward Lhuyd (1660-1709), while on a tour of Ireland.

Suggested date: 10th century.

Dimensions: height 28 metres; diameter at base 4.8 metres; height of door-sill 2.3 metres.

Unique features: cross above the entrance.

Access: open access to site from Steeple Road; no floors or windows in tower, some windows glazed.

2 Armoy, Co. Antrim   Armoy is on the B15, 2 km east of Armoy village on the A44, 10 km south of Ballycastle. The tower is in the churchyard of St Patrick's Church of Ireland parish church (1820-69), and was adapted for use as a belfry to the church during the 19th century. A later gabled building abuts the base of the tower. The location of the Round Tower, in a churchyard with a souterrain surrounded by a broad sweep of roadway, powerfully suggests the outline of a circular monastic enclosure. St Patrick appointed Olcan, founder of the monastery, as bishop in the 5th century. Olcan was a nephew of the Dalriada king, Fergus Mor Mac Erc, who granted the land to Patrick.

The Tower: Armoy, charmingly sited at the back of the churchyard on slightly rising ground, is a fragmentary Round Tower, standing to a height of 10.8 metres, and is built of roughly dressed sandstone blocks, evenly coursed. The external masonry joints have lost a lot of mortar, which gives Armoy a more ragged appearance than other towers of similar construction that have been conserved: four lifts of putlock holes are visible externally.

The most interesting feature of the tower is the south-facing entrance doorway, which is remarkably tall and narrow and, at 50cm, the narrowest. The doorhead, well worked to the curvature, is a monolithic lintel, four courses high, from the soffit of which a round-headed arch has been cut. Armoy, like many other proto-Romanesque towers, represents an attempt to accommodate the form of a round arch without actually going to the bother (or perhaps, more plausibly having the expertise) of constructing one. There is a shallow raised band, expressing the extrados of the door-arch in low relief on the lintel.

There are no windows in the surviving portion, which indicates that the first and second floors were unlit.

Internally, the floor supports of three levels are visible, corbelled at the entrance floor and with offsets above. The tower was used as the church belfry until 1869, when the current west bell-tower was built.

Suggested date: 11th century.

Dimensions: height 10.8 metres; diameter at base 4.6 metres; height of door-sill 1.6 metres.

Unique features: none.

Access: to site and interior of tower, no floors or ladders.

RAM'S ISLAND
Above: At the base of the tower the blocked-up 19th-century opening appears like a badly healed scar on its surface.

Left: Dense undergrowth and encroaching trees surround the tower which stands on an artificially created plateau on the ridge of the island. The original doorcase has been removed, and replaced by a crude blocking.

Left: Surrounded by the rough waters of Lough Neagh, Ram's Island looks dark and forbidding. Of the seven island sites with Round Towers, Ram's Island is the least visited.

3 Ram's Island, Co. Antrim

The bird sanctuary of Ram's Island – a long, thin strip of land, heavily wooded – is 2 km offshore from Sandy Bay on the east shore of Lough Neagh. Other than Cony Island, associated with St Patrick, it is the only island of any significance in the lake, which at 276 sq. km (23 km long by 12 km broad) is the largest stretch of inland water in Britain and Ireland. The tower is all that remains of a monastery of which nothing whatsoever is now known; there are no other ecclesiastical remains on the island. The legend, as related by Giraldus Cambrensis, that the Round Towers of submerged monasteries could be seen on calm days by local fishermen, may be a fanciful distortion of the sight of the Ram's Island tower (before the tree plantation had surrounded it), reflected in the waters of the lake.

Ram's Island was extensively landscaped during the 19th century, with a plateau being created down the spine of the island by abruptly cutting away the land between the summit and the foreshore. This plateau is now totally overgrown with saplings, in the midst of which stands a fine avenue of mature trees; grouse and pheasants scurry among the dense undergrowth. The tree cover is so thick around the tower that it is quite difficult to see. Directly below the level on which the Round Tower stands is the roofless ruin of a Georgian single-storey villa. The level of Lough Neagh has dropped during the 20th century, revealing more of the foreshore of the island.

The Tower: Ram's Island is an almost featureless and enigmatic tower – it does not reach above the tree-line and is invisible from the water. Three typical base-offsets are seen on the east side confirming, if there were any doubts about it, that this is a genuine tower.

The basement of the tower has a ragged breach which was made during the 19th century, thus elevating the tower to the dignity of a romantic 'grotto', as part of the landscape scheme. This breach has been unsympathetically blocked up by a wall which fails to correspond to the circumference of the original.

The door is missing, leaving another gaping breach in the wall. Only a single lintelled second-floor window survives. The thickness of the wall (less than that of any other tower), based on earlier accounts, is 82cm, a good 30cm less than the average (Antrim, 1.12 metres, Drumbo, 1.14 metres, are the two closest towers), which casts doubt on the probable height of the tower being even comparable to Antrim, itself far from the tallest at 28 metres. The masonry, which resembles Antrim more than Drumbo, is extremely rough-looking, constructed of poorly coursed hewn and unhewn boulders. Much of the external surface has reddish-coloured pointing which looks similar in appearance to the rendering of the villa, that is located below the tower. The batter is quite noticeable.

Suggested date: 10th century.

Dimensions: height 12.8 metres; diameter at base 4.16 metres; height of door-sill 4.38 metres.

Unique features: none.

Access: by boat from Kinnigo Marina at Oxford Island in the south-east corner of the lough.

ST MULLINS

Above: A cluster of roofless churches stands at the rear of this cluttered grave-yard, surrounding the base of the Round Tower. The proximity of the church buildings is unusual for a multi-church site.

Left: The tower viewed from above. The sandwich technique of the early medieval masons can be clearly seen in plan form in this view of St Mullins. External and internal skins of well-coursed ashlar stonework are separated by an infill of unhewn fieldstones, bound together by mortar.

4 St Mullins, Co. Carlow

St Mullins is off the R729 in the Barrow Valley, 12 km north of New Ross. This interesting and cluttered site was traditionally the burial place of the kings of south Leinster. The entire graveyard is congested with tombstones and an absolute plethora of ruins – all of the latter are crammed into the east end of the graveyard, in the typical 'parked cars' manner of early medieval church settlements. County Carlow boasts only a single tower, St Mullins, and not much of that survives.

Perched on top of the slope above the river valley, the churches and tower of the monastery were magnificently sited, although their presence is now obscured by trees. Remains include those of two nave-and-chancel churches, the later of which the tower adjoins, St James' Oratory, an unusual High Cross and the disused Church of Ireland parish church. A well-preserved Norman motte stands by the roadside outside the churchyard.

The monastery was founded by St Moling, Bishop of Ferns and Glendalough, who died in 696. The Book of Mulling (8th century), in Trinity College Dublin, has as a colophon, an idealised plan of the monastic enclosure, recording a total of twelve crosses of which only one now survives, but indicating neither oratory nor Round Tower.

The Tower: St Mullins is a stub of a Round Tower, discovered in 1880 by the Office of Public Works. No features survive except five courses of granite masonry of a good quality but uneven dimensions, with rather open joints. The tower abuts the remains of the later medieval church. Judging by the size of the base and the importance of the site, this must have been a fine tower in a beautiful location of the Barrow Valley. It is possible here to get a very good idea of the wall-structure of a Round Tower, with the inner and outer masonry and rubble infill visible. St Moling's day, 17 June, is a day of local pilgrimage.
Suggested date: 12th century.
Dimensions: height 1 metre; diameter at base 5.1 metres.
Unique features: none.
Access: free access to site and most of the ruins.

5 Drumlane, Co. Cavan

Drumlane is 1 km south of Milltown village on the R201, on the Killashandra to Belturbet road, 5 km south of Belturbet. The lonely churchyard site is on the reedy banks of Lough Oughter, with the substantial remains of a late medieval parish church, which continued roofed and in use up to the early 19th century. The 13th-century church was extended during the 15th century and has an excellent west doorway and some label-stop sculpted heads on the door and windows. The monastic foundation is associated with St Maedoc, who was the abbot in the late 6th century. Of the early monastery, only the tower survives.

The Tower: Drumlane tower stands 11.6 metres high and is divided clearly into two phases of construction, the original vastly superior to the later. The lower limestone masonry, with diagonal tooled finish, is among the finest

DRUMLANE

Above: The fine doorcase indicates the quality of construction found among the late towers. (See photo p. 79.)

Left: Two phases of construction are evident in the contrasting styles of masonry.

DRUMCLIFF

Above: Masonry found at the base of the tower.

Left: The Round Tower and medieval church dominate the steeply sloping graveyard site. As in so many sites, the tower perches on the perimeter wall of the graveyard, indicating an attempt in more recent times to include the towers within a used graveyard.

known among Round Towers, comparable to Clonmacnoise, Ardmore and Devenish. The masonry is remarkably well cut, with vertical diagonal and joggle-jointed ashlars, beautifully worked to curve and batter. However, some courses sag noticeably from the horizontal.

The well-proportioned doorway with four stone jambs is externally decorated by a distinct architrival band incorporating the door-sill. It has a tripartite arch for the doorhead, of which the one-metre-long voussoirs penetrate right through the wall. This is a true arch, rather than the adapted lintel of Armoy, or semi-corbelled examples found in Scattery. On the left-hand side of the door passage is a rectangular raised border of unknown purpose.

The upper portion of the tower, also of limestone, is constructed of roughly finished rubble stonework with a single round-headed window, with a monolithic arch, directly above the entrance. The carving of this window is superior to the surrounding stonework of phase II, and may suggest a date contemporary with the building of the medieval church for the upper section. The second phase stonework begins directly below the sill of the first-floor window. This implies the continued construction or re-construction of a Round Tower in the 13th century, a date later than is generally considered to include the construction span of the towers. The architectural emphasis of the window in the upper phase belongs stylistically to the manner of late medieval building. Tower doors are generally lintelled or arched, while the windows are lintelled or triangular-headed, making the Drumlane arched first-floor windows extremely unusual.

Two quite indistinct carvings, which have been identified as birds, are two metres up on the north face of the tower. Their position suggests that they could have been executed only when either the original or second phase was still scaffolded. If the interpretation of one of the birds as a cock is correct, this may suggest a Christian context of the Crucifixion. The identification of the other birds as a various menagerie of domestic and wildfowl does not help explain their significance. A medieval date is likely.

A late 18th-century engraving of Drumlane shows numerous small and regularly positioned holes in the north face. These may have been putlock holes which were subsequently filled.

Suggested date: 12th century.

Dimensions: height 11.6 metres; diameter at base 5.09 metres; height of door-sill 2.74 metres.

Unique features: exceptional masonry; carvings of birds on external wall.

Access: to site; no floors or ladders.

6 Drumcliff, Co. Clare   Drumcliff is on the N85, 4 km north-west of Ennis. There are two Round Towers of this name. The other, which is more well-known, is the burial place of W. B. Yeats in Drumcliff, Co. Sligo. There are no annalistic records for this Co. Clare monastery, the foundation of which is associated with St Conald. The site is a graveyard on the side of a hill, with a ruined 15th-century church which has an undecorated 12th-century Romanesque window in the west

DYSERT O'DEA
Left: Tripartite 13th-century lancet windows dominate the east gable of the reconstructed 12th-century church, while remains of the unusually placed Round Tower lie close to its north-west corner.

Above: The surface-area of the wall surrounding the large breach at the base of the tower displays considerable evidence of fire damage. The wall overhanging the breach is now supported by a square masonry pillar.

Left: The evolution of the Romanesque round arch passed through many contortions before achieving perfection: here the extrados, the exterior outline of the arch, has been clumsily treated on the left hand side, where it fails to reflect the curve on the inside.

gable which, although not likely to be contemporary with the tower, is a survival of a church which was replaced by the present one. The steeply-sloping and extensive graveyard has a fine planting of mature yews, and many interesting 18th- and 19th-century tombstones.

The Tower: Drumcliff is a ruined tower, standing to a height of 11 metres on one side and falling to within 3 metres of the ground. The unhewn or hewn hammer-dressed and roughly squared limestone masonry is coursed, but with large irregular boulders interspersed with smaller stones comprising the bottom one metre of wall, then regularly coursed above, with occasional larger stones. The batter, in so far as it can be judged, is not considerable.

The interest of Drumcliff is the insight which it presents into the construction of a Round Tower. The interior floor offsets for the first, second and third floors are clearly visible from outside, as is the sandwich wall-construction of the masonry outer and inner face, with a mortared rubble core binding them together. There are two pairs of non-structural corbels, one each at first-and second-floor level. No other features survive.

Suggested date: 10th – 11th century.

Dimensions: height 11 metres; diameter at base 4.88 metres.

Unique features: none.

Access: free access to the site.

7 Dysert O'Dea, Co. Clare　　Dysert O'Dea is west of the R476, Ennis to Corrofin road, 5 km south of Corrofin. The tower is part of an important early monastic site with Romanesque and late medieval church remains, as well as a fine 12th-century High Cross in an adjoining field to the east (possibly a collage of fragments from two crosses), which has been reconstructed at least twice by local landowners, in 1683 by the O'Deas and 1871 by the Synges. St Tola, who is probably the bishop represented on the east face of the cross, founded the monastery in the late 7th century or early 8th century. Dysert O'Dea Castle stands nearby.

The Tower: Dysert stands 14.6 metres high, of fine coursed and hammer-finished limestone masonry, with a reduction in its diameter above the first floor. There is a single offset at ground level and an ugly breach on the north-west side, blocked by a supporting pillar of masonry; this may represent the position of a late entrance, introduced when the medieval window was installed in the upper wall. The external wall in this area exhibits considerable fire-damage, a feature which might be expected more frequently, considering the number of towers known to have been torched.

The large breach in the wall on the north-west side, where the lower wall stands only to the height of the doorhead, is, as it now appears, totally misleading. Photographs (Dunraven *c.* 1870) demonstrate that this breach originally went within two metres of the ground and extended to the left-hand side of the doorcase. Such reconstructions can create curious anomalies in Round Towers

INIS CEALTRA

Above: The superb setting of Inis Cealtra, on an island in one of the Shannon's finest lakes, makes its location particularly attractive, and it is among the most important of the island monastic sites with Round Towers, being rivalled only by Scattery for the number of its churches and the preservation of the remains. (Photo 1981)

Left: Inis Cealtra Round Tower rises above the treeline of the island. To medieval pilgrims it eloquently announced the presence of the monastery.

and makes them extremely difficult to evaluate and date. Without clear documentary evidence that the repair is modern it could be seen as an earlier repair although the late masonry is clearly different in style. This difficulty emphasises the value of the modern practice of placing a barrier between original and reconstructed masonry.

The doorcase is round-headed and projects slightly proud of the face of the tower, with a six-voussoired true arch with projecting keystone; the extrados of the arch fails to replicate the internal curve. The voussoirs penetrate through the 1.16 metre depth of the wall. The four- and three-stone doorjambs are unusually, very nearly vertical. The significance of repairs and alterations arises again with the setback in the wall-face which occurs at 8.6 metres above the ground level. The diameter above the offset is 5.29 metres. It is unclear whether this upper level is a late medieval reconstruction or original masonry

A single window, close to the top of the wall, looking north-west, is ogee-headed and late medieval at its earliest; this section of the tower with its reduced diameter probably belongs to a second phase in the construction of the tower.

Suggested date: 12th century.

Dimensions: height 14.6 metres; diameter at base 5.89 metres; height of door-sill 4.46 metres.

Unique features: largest diameter at the base.

Access: to site, no floors or ladders in tower; sign-posted.

8 Inis Cealtra, Co. Clare Inis Cealtra or Holy Island is a beautiful and seemingly remote island site in the south-west of Lough Derg, 1 km offshore from Mountshannon on the R352, the Portumna to Scarriff road, 8 km north-east of Scarriff, and reached by boat from Mountshannon harbour. There is little evidence of disturbance or rebuilding, other than the curiously oriented modern boundary walls which enclose the church sites as graveyards, and as protection from roaming cattle.

Inis Cealtra, was from its foundation in the 7th century up until the 17th century, an important site of pilgrimage. It has significant early and late medieval church buildings, surrounded by the remains of the rampart of the earthen monastic enclosure, as well as other abundant and complex earthworks which are clearly visible from the ground. There are four churches, one of which, the Romanesque St Caimin's Church, dedicated to the 7th-century founder, stands adjacent to the Round Tower; it is a nave-and-chancel type, now re-roofed. There is also a possible hermit's cell or tomb-shrine, as well as two High Crosses. Many of the early inscribed cross-slabs from the graveyard are now displayed in St Caimin's. The aerial photo shows the site during the excavations carried out by de Paor (1970-80), with excavated squares directly behind the tower and to the right, cutting across the earthen embankment.

Unlike Scattery, with which Inis Cealtra may easily be compared (both are multi-church island sites, and among the most interesting in the country), the ecclesiastical landscape has hardly been interfered with by later agricultural practices or wall-building, and the ambience of an early Christian monastic

INIS CEALTRA

Above: The relationship of tower to church as shown here is typical. The Round Towers, as though pendants to the west door, swing from right to left in their position, and at varying distances from the west gable.

Left: Two of the island's churches can be seen; in the foreground is St Brigid's Church, which has a reconstructed Romanesque doorway, and in the distance the recently roofed and reconstructed 12th-century St Caimin's Church with antae and Romanesque doorway. The Round Tower stands facing it to the north-west.

KILLINABOY

Left: Although the remains are those of a well-built tower with ashlar masonry, much of the ruin is concealed by ivy and covered with long grass.

island is much easier to appreciate here than in other more altered sites. The prospect of the settlement from the lake, with the tower rising above the island's trees, cannot be so different from what the 12th-century monks and pilgrims might have seen as they approached by boat from the surrounding lakeshore. The beauty of the island location in its inland sea is as exceptional as any monastic site in Ireland.

The Tower: Inis Cealtra is a finely built almost complete tower, missing its bell-floor and cap. There is a single offset and the base is of excellent coursed cyclopean stonework, the proportions of which diminish as the courses rise to the door-sill level, a phenomenon common to many towers.

The round-headed doorway faces north-east in the direction of the west doorway of St Caimin's Church, which is 12th-century Romanesque with antae. This type of elaborate recessed church entrance was first developed in the early 11th century, at Speyer Cathedral in the Rhine valley, and in its decorated form reached Ireland most probably from Britain during the late 11th or early 12th century.

The tower door has a three-voussoir arch with a rudimentary keystone, the stones of which span the 1.05 metres depth of the wall; only the intrados is expressed. The jambs are very slightly inclined off the vertical.

There are four windows in the drum; that on the second floor, the north-facing Treasury window, is triangular-headed and of impressively large proportions. Those in the drum above it are quite small and rectangular, one of which is directly above the door, demonstrating, if any demonstration were needed, that the positioning of the tower windows has nothing whatsoever to do with defence, since only by reversing the positions of the first- and second-floor windows would they be of any value in providing protection for the tower's most vulnerable point, the entrance. Only in Roscrea is the differentiation between the second-floor window and the others as clearly demonstrated as in the example at Inis Cealtra.

Within the drum there are four floor offsets; the second floor is an exception here as the remains of the floor slabs are supported on corbels.

Suggested date: 11th – 12th century.

Dimensions: height 22.3 metres; diameter at base 4.58 metres; height of door-sill 3 metres.

Unique features: exceptionally large Treasury window; stone floor at second-floor level.

Access: by boat from Mountshannon; no floors or ladders in tower.

9 Killinaboy, Co. Clare   Killinaboy village is on the R476, 4 km north-west of Corrofin. The Round Tower stands in a churchyard at the centre of the village, with a late medieval rebuilding of an earlier church which has a Sheela-na-gig over the south door. The remarkably unusual double-barred 'Cross of Lorraine' (13th century) is an integral part of the masonry; it is displayed on the external doorless west gable of the church. The monastery was founded by the daughter of Baoithe.

SCATTERY

Left: Four churches and the Round Tower can be seen in this aerial view with, at the shore, the Church of the Dead. Facing the Round Tower are the cathedral and a 12th-century oratory with, further north, Temple Senan.
(Aerial photo 1971; see photo p. 99.)

Below left: The ground-level position of the entrance door, uneven profile and eccentric or incomplete cap suggest that Scattery may be the earliest of the towers to survive. The drum windows are tiny rectangular openings.

Below: Scattery's most unusual and intriguing feature is the ground-level corbel-headed doorway. Is this an archaic example of corbel construction, or a rudimentary attempt at creating an arch?

The Tower: What remains at Killinaboy is only the stub of a tower, of which no architectural features survive. The eleven or twelve courses of limestone masonry are of roughly squared construction, hammer-dressed and quite unevenly laid. During the 1990s rubbish and graveyard detritus has been allowed to accumulate in the interior, while the top is totally concealed by an overgrowth of ivy.

Round Towers that stand in currently used graveyard sites are generally being encroached upon by the increased use of modern tombstones and the expanded boundaries of burial plots; Killinaboy has suffered the added indignity of having a memorial slab attached to its wall.

Suggested date: 11th century.

Dimensions: height 3.6 metres; diameter at base 5.08 metres.

Unique features: none.

Access: free access to site.

10 Scattery, Co. Clare   Scattery Island is in the Shannon estuary 2.5 km off the Clare coast, reached by regular ferry from Kilrush Marina, Kilrush town, on the N68. St Senan, who was the teacher of Ciaran of Clonmacnoise, founded Scattery during the 6th century. It was here that, according to legend, the saint defeated the monster Cata, who is commemorated in the Island's name. The Scattery Island Centre at Merchant's Quay in Kilrush has a small display devoted to the history, flora and fauna of the island. It is a settlement rich in historic remains, a multi-church site with a number of standing churches and a unique Round Tower.

The 10th – 12th century church with antae, the Cathedral of S.S. Mary and Senan with later alterations, stands to the east of the tower, while a smaller 12th-century nave-and-chancel Romanesque church abuts the cathedral on its north face. Another well-preserved church, Temple Senan, further to the north, has an inscribed early gravestone 'OR DO MOENACH AITE MOGROIN; OR DO MOINACH' – 'A prayer for Moenach, tutor of Mogrón; a prayer for Moinach'. To the south-west is the ruinous Church of the Hill of the Angel, 10th century with later alterations. On the shore adjoining the village housing, which consists of a single row of cottages, is the substantial c. 15th-century Church of the Dead, surrounded by the island graveyard. There are also the remains of a ruined 17th-century tower house by the village pier. In contrast to Inis Cealtra, where the medieval landscape is undisturbed, 19th-century land enclosure has divided up the ecclesiastical lands.

Scattery Island was inhabited until the late 1970s, and although it is now deserted, its landscape is still used for grazing cattle. The aerial photograph is viewed from the south-east and was taken when the island was still inhabited. The landscape of the island is a combination of poor quality rough grazing land, now much overgrown, and small areas of tillage near the village.

The Tower: Scattery has a reasonable claim to being the oldest surviving Round Tower and might possibly be the prototype for all later developments.

The outline of the batter is far less accomplished than later towers, and the architectural features of entrance door and windows are indecisive in their proportions and detail. The roughly coursed sandstone masonry of unwrought fieldstones is skilfully fitted to curve and batter and generally composed of relatively small stones. Single courses of larger rectangular stones are interspersed among the cruder stonework.

The doorway of Scattery is on the external ground floor level, a situation which is paralleled only at Castledermot. Compared to Kilmacduagh with its door at 8 metres off the ground, there is a tremendous difference of emphasis. The jambs of Scattery are inclined, and the doorhead is created by corbelling from the line of both jambs with a lintel to close the gap; the result is clumsy looking and can be interpreted as a corbelling solution, predating the monolithic lintel, or alternatively, as a proto-arch, the most rudimentary move in the direction of the true arch. Obviously, these different interpretations have a bearing on where the tower occurs in the development sequence, corbelling implying an early period, while any attempt at creating an arch suggests a later date. From a distance the doorhead looks like an arched one. Despite this, the combination of other features, such as the position of the door and lack of articulation, the window design and masonry, all suggest an early date. The doorway of the cathedral is lintelled with a large monolithic slab. Because the tower must be later than the church, the peculiarities of its design may be no more than anomalies.

It is possible to walk straight into the tower and, depending on available light conditions, see right up through the empty drum of the tower to the underside of the cap. The floor-offsets are clearly visible.

In the drum, courses of large stones placed at irregular intervals, contrast with courses of much smaller ones. The light source in the drum is provided by the five quite small-lintelled windows. They are sufficiently insignificant and unarticulated to make little or no impression when viewed from the exterior of the tower. However, the bell-floor windows are taller and have large inclined jambs, and therefore can be seen more clearly from the outside of the building.

The cap of Scattery is truncated, as though unfinished, although this condition may have some other explanation, such as being struck off by lightning, according to the annals a not uncommon experience, or may even represent the original design: if the tower is a prototype, anything abberant is possible. The incline of the cap is exceptionally steep, even more acute than at Ardmore; this suggests that about approximately half the cone may be missing.

A lengthy and structurally dangerous-looking fissure on the west side is recorded in 19th-century photographs; it split the drum of the tower, virtually from cap to base, and was most probably caused by lightning. The damage was repaired at a later date. All towers are now protected by lightning conductors from further damage.

Suggested date: 10th – 11th century.

Dimensions: height 26 metres; diameter at base 5.08 metres.

Unique features: ground-floor entrance, smallest tower drum windows.

Access: direct access into base of tower; no floors or ladders.

11 Cloyne, Co. Cork   Cloyne village is on the R629, 8 km south-east of Midleton on the N25. The tower stands between Georgian houses halfway down Church Street, in a small gated enclosure like a little garden. The tower was originally part of the ecclesiastical site from which it is now orphaned by the public roadway. St Coleman's Church of Ireland Cathedral of the diocese of Cloyne, occupies the remains of a 13th-century foundation, much altered and rebuilt during the 18th century, its nave now occupied by a synod of marble bishops. An early oratory, known as the 'Fire House', is in the churchyard, north-east of the cathedral, and may be the remains of the original church. An early 12th-century metalwork equal-armed cross, thought to be from the cover of a book-shrine, was discovered in the chapter house in the 19th century. Its workmanship is sufficiently close to that on the Lismore crozier (NMI) to suggest that they are the work of the same hand. Each arm of the Cloyne cross has a single figure on it with Scandinavian *Urnes* style decoration at their feet. The monastery was founded in the 6th century by St Colman Mac Lénine, who was granted the land by Coirpre Cromm, King of Cashel.

The most famous incumbent was the philosopher George Berkeley (after whom the University of Berkeley in California is named), Bishop of Cloyne 1734-52. He wrote *The Querist*, an important contribution to Irish social and economic thought, while incumbent in Cloyne.

The Tower: Cloyne is an exceptionally fine and well-preserved Round Tower, lacking its cap, which has been replaced by a parapet with battlements to which there is access. The tower was damaged by lightning on 10 January 1749, but the cap was already missing at that date. It is still in use as the cathedral belfry with a bell of 1857. Berkeley wrote of the 1749 incident:

> *'Our round tower stands where it did but the little stone arched vault on the top was cracked. The bell also was thrown down and broke its way through three boarded stories but remains entire. The door was shivered into very many small pieces and dispersed and there was a stone forced out of the wall. The thunder clap was the loudest I ever heard in Ireland.'*

Cloyne is built of a dark purplish sandstone with a fairly uneven hammer-dressed finish: the stonework is of coursed and roughly squared quarry-stones. Its foundations on a rocky outcrop are visible from the west side.

The door is tall, with a lintelled head and visibly inclined jambs, the bases of which were cut away in the 19th century in order to admit the bell. There is no external articulation or differentiation of the doorcase.

There are five windows in the drum, all lintelled except those on the third and the fifth floors, which are triangular-headed. The fifth-floor window, directly above the entrance, is exceptionally large and would in later towers be expected to occur on the second floor. The bell-floor windows have inclined jambs and are lintelled. The combination at Cloyne of lintelled doorway with lintelled bell-floor windows (the two most distinctive featured in the fenestration of a tower) consign the tower to an early date. Conversely, the single large

CLOYNE
Above: The public roadway passes between the Cathedral (here seen from the parapet of the tower) and the Round Tower, severing the fundamental relationship between church and *cloicteach*.

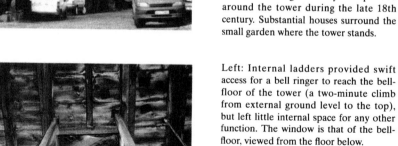

Left: The village of Cloyne expanded around the tower during the late 18th century. Substantial houses surround the small garden where the tower stands.

Left: Internal ladders provided swift access for a bell ringer to reach the bell-floor of the tower (a two-minute climb from external ground level to the top), but left little internal space for any other function. The window is that of the bell-floor, viewed from the floor below.

triangular-headed windows would be more commonly found in a tower with round-headed door. This argues for some transitional date, approaching the appearance of the round-arched doors of the 11th – 12th century.

Cloyne belongs to the half-a-dozen towers to which there is complete internal access. It is of exceptional interest for this reason, as the original internal arrangement of a Round Tower can be appreciated only from within a still-floored tower. The darkness, sense of claustrophobia and lack of contact with the outside world is here very evident. Cloyne's internal floor plan, with the access ladders on the side rather than in the centre, invites speculation as to whether this is a more probable arrangement than that at Devenish, with central ladders. Cloyne's floor arrangement gives a better floor use than any other alternative plan.

The bell-floor is occupied by pigeons, the denizens of all towers to which there is any form of upper access. From this floor a ladder leads to the parapet from which there are views over Cloyne village. Only from such a vantage point can the Round Tower's potential as a lookout post be truly appreciated; in this case a 360° view of the landscape is possible; in towers with a cap a more limited prospect would be possible through the four axial windows.

Suggested date: 10th – 11th century.

Dimensions: height 30.5 metres; diameter at base 5.17 metres; height of door-sill 3.4 metres.

Unique features: access to roof.

Access: an almost complete tower with floors and ladders: the keys are kept at the caretaker's cottage, located to the left inside the gates of the cathedral opposite.

12 Kinneigh, Co. Cork Kinneigh is on the R588, 5 km north-west of Enniskean village on the R586 Bandon to Bantry road set in the lush and hilly landscape of west Cork. The tower is on the edge of the extensive churchyard of St Bartholomew's Church of Ireland parish church. When I visited Kinneigh in the 1980s the shaky internal metal ladders were still accessible, although climbing them was a terrifying experience. The lowest of these has now been removed (1997) and an iron-barred gate placed in the interior of the entrance doorway prevents access. The monastery was founded by St Mo-Cholmog in the 6th century, but no other early buildings survive and little is known of its history. In Charles Smith's *Ancient and present state of the county and city of Cork* (1749), the author refers to an unidentified manuscript source which mentions the tower as nearing completion in 1015, but this seems improbably early.

The Tower: Kinneigh is unique among surviving Round Towers on account of its hexagonal plinth which supports a round superstructure. The hexagonal portion, based directly on bedrock with two offsets, contains the basement and entrance floor; the drum is round. Kinneigh, which is constructed of local slate, is built on a high scarp of rock, rising some 4 metres above the surrounding land, located to the east of the parish church. The masonry of exceptional

KINNEIGH

Left: Kinneigh stands to the rear of the 19th-century church and still carries the bell installed in 1856. Unusually for a Round Tower, this example stands on an outcrop of rock which rises above the surrounding land, so that it and the church which it served were not on the same plane. The windows are almost as small as those in Scattery, but the base indicates that this is a tower of late date. (See photo and drawing p. 50.)

Far left: Few towers exhibit such accomplished masonry as that in the base of Kinneigh, where the angles of the hexagonal base are aligned with a precision and sharpness unexpected in Irish early medieval architecture.

Left: Close up of one of the arrises of the base where the planes of two faces meet.

quality, is diagonally comb-finished, beautifully bedded, and the arrises of the hexagon are superbly cut. The transition from hexagon to circle is skilfully achieved by six corner squinches above the arrises, which graduate the change in plane.

The entrance is lintelled with inclined jambs and a well-defined doorcase, although there is no change in the type of stone used. Both lintel and sill are well-formed monoliths, running through the wall.

All the windows are small and rectangular, one each on the four floors of the drum. Those on the second and third floors (30cm x 40cm) are among the smallest Round Tower windows. The upper metre-and-a-half of the wall is probably a rebuilding, *c.* 1857, when the 19th-century church was built, and the current bell installed.

Directly inside the entrance on the first floor is what appears to be the original slate floor in situ, composed of large slate slabs, cantilevered from corbelled stonework which projects from the walls of the basement below. On inspection the floor surface was so covered in guano that this feature was difficult to evaluate, but it has every appearance of being original. In the centre of the entrance floor is a rectangular opening giving access to the basement. The floors above are poured rough concrete semi-circular platforms, from which the metal ladders rise.

Severe cracking has occurred in the base with a displacement of the arrises by up to 10cm. Movement gauges have been placed on the cracks, dated 17-11-1987: no movement is evident since that date. The absence of similar cracking in the bases of other towers suggests that the structural stability of the circular plan-form may have been better able to carry the load of the superstructure than this ambitious experiment.

Kinneigh is so eccentric that it presents dating difficulties. The lintelled doorway and rectangular rudimentary windows argue an early date, whereas the experimental plan-form, as well as the very high quality of the masonry, suggest a later dating. If Kinneigh is a prototype, which is probable, it is an experiment which was not followed. It can be seen as a transitional tower, related to Trinity Church (Glendalough III) and Kilmacnessan on Ireland's Eye, where Round Towers were based upon rectangular base structures. Polygonal building of any type are non-existent in Irish early medieval architecture – with the exception of this sole surviving example. One parallel structure which does exist is the two-storey octagonal lavabo at Mellifont which is dated to *c.* 1220. The sophistication of mind which produced the Mellifont lavabo is a product of Continental influence; the evidence of a skilled hand in the design.

Similarly at Kinneigh the concept is too fine to be the chance product of some isolated local mason, and implies the touch of a master mason's hand. Despite the archaic door and window features, it is unlikely that this is an early tower; rather the opposite. It most probably dates from the mid-12th century, and can possibly be identified as exhibiting influence from either Rhenish cathedral towers, such as St Pantaleon, Cologne (*c.* 966), where the west towers have a rectangular four-floor podium, an octagonal three-floor middle section, and round two-floor top section, which is finished with a steep cone.

KINNEIGH

Left: The manner in which the public roadway loops around the graveyard at Kinneigh is suggestive of the prior existence of a monastic enclosure. The 19th-century church probably represents the position of the early church. (Photo 1979)

DUNGIVEN

Left: Like Kinneigh, Dungiven was an eccentric tower, rectangular at the base, and circular higher up. The sole surviving example of this type at Ferns, gives an impression of what the Dungiven tower may have looked like. It is not an orthodox Round Tower in the sense of being freestanding, circular and tapering with a conical cap, yet it belongs within the function and time frame of orthodox examples.

Kinneigh resembles nothing so much as a stripped down version of the second section upwards, the octagon simplified to a hexagon, the string courses removed and the window size reduced to Irish norms (**fig. 12a-b**). Comparison of the plans of both towers provides plausible evidence of the intellectual debt Kinneigh owes to St Pantaleon or some similar building. The squinches at St Pantaleon which join the hexagon to its rectangular base, are quite similar to those at Kinneigh, joining the circular drum to the hexagon; this detail is also seen on the 12th-century tower at Ferns.

The hexagon of Kinneigh, unique in Irish terms, is also extremely rare in Continental ecclesiastical architecture. An example which relates to both Mellifont and Kinneigh is at the Cistercian monastery of Le Thoronet (1150 – 1200) in southern France, where, as at Mellifont, a polygonal lavabo projects into the cloister garth. Here, however, the lavabo is hexagonal rather than octagonal.

The origin of the axially oriented bell-floor windows is also to be found in westwork church towers, such as those of St Pantaleon, in the range directly below the bell-floor.

Suggested date: 12th century.

Dimensions: height 21.5 metres; maximum diameter at base 6 metres; height of door-sill 3.24 metres.

Unique features: hexagonal base; stone internal floor.

Access: free access to site; inaccessible floors and ladders; locked gate in door-opening.

13 Dungiven, Co. Derry

Dungiven Priory, 1 km south-east of Dungiven town centre on the A6, was founded *c.* 1100 by the O'Cahans as an Augustinian Priory. The church was modified during the 13th and 14th centuries and its chancel contains the recumbent table tomb of Cooey-na-nGall (d. 1385). A plantation manor-house with bawn was added during the 17th century. The graveyard has a fine collection of headstones.

The Tower: Dungiven is a significant inclusion in any inventory of Round Towers, although looking in isolation at the photograph, its inclusion seems to be stretching the bounds of credibility to claim the remains as those of a Round Tower. These walls are slight in the extreme, and consist of a rectangular structure projecting into the south-east corner of the nave, of well-built ashlar construction. An early 19th-century drawing records this church tower as having, like Ferns, a round superstructure on a rectangular base, the bottom metre of which still stands.

This is an engaged tower, although in form more closely related to late attached examples. Such structures are a distant remove from freestanding Round Towers, yet not only did this type of tower develop from the orthodox Round Tower, it presumably performed the same function as a bell-tower, although its small floor-plan would not have recommended it as a place of either storage or refuge.

TAMLAGHT
Beneath a canopy of briars and ivy, the base of a Ferns-type tower stands on the external corner of this small medieval chapel.

TORY
Left: Electricity poles form an honour-guard for Tory's Round Tower, swathing it in cables. Unlike Cloyne, where the tower seems an honoured and respected element in the streetscape, here no concessions have been made to the fact that an important early medieval building stands between the houses.
(See photo p. 74.)

Below: With its multi-voussoired true arch, the doorway of Tory indicates that this is a late tower, contemporary with the more finely constructed examples at Clonmacnoise and Devenish.

Like the base of the north tower of Cormac's Chapel, which formed a porch with two doors, Dungiven has three doorways, giving access to the interior of the building. Access to the superstructure of the tower would have been, like in Kilmacnessan, from the attic of the nave roof area.

Suggested date: 12th century.

Dimensions: height *c.* 1 metre; dimensions of base *c.* 2 x 2 metres.

Unique features: originally round above, rectangular below.

Access: free access to site; signposted.

14 Tamlaght, Co. Derry

Tamlaght is 1 km east of the B69, 4 km south-west of Ballykelly on the A2. The site is a small rural churchyard beside the road, with the ruins of a medieval church.

The Tower: The north-west corner of the single-cell church has a rectangular projection which is the base of an attached tower. The remains are overgrown but it is possible to observe the circular interior of the tower. Like Ferns, Tamlaght would have been rectangular to the line of the eaves and round above. The circular interior of the tower suggests the former presence of a spiral staircase. Since there is no evidence for a stone staircase, it may have been made of timber. The significance of towers such as Tamlaght is the fact that contemporaneously with orthodox and freestanding Round Towers, there was a wide range of variations on the theme, all of which derive from the freestanding originals.

Suggested date: 12th century.

Dimensions: height 1.5 metres; dimensions at base approximately 3.5 x 3.5 metres; internal diameter 1.62 metres.

Unique features: remains of attached tower.

Access: free access to site.

15 Tory, Co. Donegal

Tory Island is 12 km off the Donegal coast, and can be reached by boat from Bunbeg or Meenlaragh, both on the R257. This is by far the most remote of all the tower sites, although the sea journey can be an exhilarating experience if the weather is not too rough to permit passage, which it frequently is. The island landscape is desolate, treeless and barren-looking, with few concessions towards adapting the environment to human needs; the remaining community are mostly lobster fishermen.

The tower is in the centre of West Town, one of the two small *clachan* villages of dispersed houses on the island. The remnants of a minute, ruined oratory are east of the tower, now preserved as a platform for a collection of archaeological bric-à-brac: farther uphill to the west are the more substantial remains of another oratory.

A fine 'T' shaped Tau cross has been re-erected on the pier. The tower site, although in the centre of the village, has an unkempt and neglected appearance, with the area surrounding the tower festooned by a disarray of electricity poles and wiring. The foundation of the monastery is attributed to St Columba during the 6th century.

The Tower: The tower, the most northerly located in Ireland, is built of heavily weathered, sea-rounded granite blocks which have lost a lot of their external mortar. Like Dysert O'Dea, the remains of Tory are more substantial now than they were a hundred years earlier! The outside of the tower on the west side displays a number of rows of what look convincingly like putlock holes, but this area of the wall is a repair of a large breach, carried out in 1880. The stones of the repair are smaller than those in the authentic portions of the wall which also display putlock holes, irregularly placed.

Tory is one of the few towers to have a true arch, composed of more than three rudimentary voussoirs, for its entrance door. Here, there is an arch of thirteen voussoirs, with corresponding intrados and extrados, although it lacks a distinct keystone. The arch penetrates halfway through the wall, where there is a corresponding inner arch. The door opening is narrow with visibly inclined jambs, each composed of four, quoin-like worked boulders. Halfway up the right-hand internal door jamb is an integral projecting stone boss, into which a bolt housing has been sunk. Its position clearly indicates that the tower door was conventionally hung on the inner face of the opening, with the hinges on the left. This detail in Tory is the most convincing evidence in any tower of the original door position. In many other towers which were re-used as belfries during the 19th century, the internal jambs have been tampered with.

There is a single small lintelled window on the second floor, directly above the door, the arched interior detailing of which is unusual. Instead of the internal window jambs being flush with the curved wall-surface, they project farther inward, and are surrounded by a flat plane of masonry, at a tangent to the curve. On the floor above is evidence of three axially positioned windows, one of which is intact and lintelled. It seems probable that this is the bell-floor, because what appears to be an extended fragment of the cornice lies directly above the surviving window-head, acting as the lintel. If the top of the wall, three courses above the lintel, does represent the base of the springing of the cone, then Tory would never have stood taller than 17 metres, making it an authentic half-size tower. An alternative interpretation would be that what appears to be the cornice is in fact a string-course, as at Ardmore: the towers must be roughly contemporary for the reason that however radically their masonry differs, their arch construction is among the most sophisticated of surviving towers. Tory's arch suggests that it is a late tower; Ardmore is one of the few others, such as Clonmacnoise I, with a multi-voussoir door arch.

The cornice alternative seems the more likely and it opens up the possibility that there is a sub-species of towers, similar to Tory, which were never intended to rise more than half the usual 30 metres height. If the required height of a tower can be related to its perceived hinterland, then the size of Tory island may be a guide to the need for only a short tower.

Internally, at about 7.3 metres from the ground, that is above the window of the second floor, is what appears to be a stone corbelled dome projecting from the inner wall surface – this may represent the original floor structure. The rounded stonework of the tower masonry could hardly be less suitable for any kind of arch or dome construction, yet the remains do look convincingly like the springing of a corbelled floor support. The phenomenon of a corbelled dome floor level, directly below the roof-cone, is certainly unique to Tory.

Suggested date: 12th century.

Dimensions: height 12.8 metres; diameter at base approximately 4.8 metres; height of door-sill 2.64 metres.

Unique features: stone door furniture; least number of internal floors; almost complete half-size tower.

Access: free access to site, no floors or ladders.

16 Drumbo, Co. Down

Drumbo village is 1 km south of the B23, 5 km north-east of Lisburn. The tower is at the rear of the churchyard of Drumbo Presbyterian Church, at the centre of the village, and overlooks the Lagan valley. The monastery, of which little is known, was reputedly founded by St Patrick, or his follower, St Mo-Chumma (6th century). No evidence of the monastic foundation has survived, other than the ruin of a medieval church.

The Tower: Drumbo has lost most of its features and two-thirds of the tower is missing; the lower portion of the door has been much damaged and the upper portion of the wall on the north side is a late 19th-century repair. The remaining masonry, of roughly squared slate blocks with many spalls, is unevenly coursed but well trimmed to the curve, and strongly resembles the masonry to be found at Dun Aenghus on Inishmore, where the similarly squared masonry is of a drystone construction. The modern burials in the churchyard encroach directly on the tower, making viewing of it unsatisfactory. Like many towers on the perimeter of graveyards still in use, Drumbo has been subject to numerous indignities, being surrounded by tombstones and its interior filled with the detritus of the funerary trade.

The door, which faces east, is tall and narrow with a short lintel, and in need of urgent repair: the bottoms of both jambs are loose and the sill and supporting stones entirely missing. There is no articulation of the doorcase. The drum seems to display slight entasis, and to be concave in profile, which can hardly have been the intention of the builders.

There are no windows in the surviving portion of the tower, indicating that Drumbo was one of those towers which, at least in its second and third floors, was without internal illumination. Neither are there any offsets internally in the surviving portion, which suggests that the floors were supported by beams set into the internal wall during construction.

Suggested date: 10th century. (Annals reference for 1130 – 31.)

Dimensions: height 10.25 metres ; diameter at base 5 metres; height of door-sill 1.5 metres.

Unique features: absence of windows in surviving portion of drum.

Access: free access to tower, no floors or ladders.

DRUMBO, CO. DOWN
(See photo p. 79.)

MAGHERA

Left: The fact that the tower is constructed of Mourne granite fieldstones is not necessarily proof of its being an early example. The absence of any architectural features makes it quite difficult to date. Any immediate evidence of surrounding earthworks has disappeared beneath the present-day agricultural landscape. (See photo p. 79.)

NENDRUM

Left: The Round Tower of Nendrum, when complete, would have commanded a great sweep of landscape on the west shore of Strangford Lough. Base offsets, inner and outer masonry are visible here, although the surfaces have been reconstructed and are therefore not reliable. (See photo p. 26.)

17 Maghera, Co. Down   Maghera is on the Newry to Newcastle road, 5 km south of Dundrum village on the B180, 4 km north-west of Newcastle. The stump of the tower stands in the middle of a field to the north-west of the Church of Ireland parish church, in a beautiful part of County Down, overshadowed by the Mourne mountains. The ruins of a 12th-century church stand to the east of the modern church. The monastery is associated with the 6th-century St Donard.

The Tower: Maghera, a sad remnant of a Round Tower, stands alone and deserted by its context, more so than almost any other tower, with the furrows of a ploughed field around it. Excavations around the tower, conducted in 1965, indicated early medieval occupation. The distance between the medieval chapel and the tower give some sense of the extent of the early enclosure. It can be assumed that the tower and the site now occupied by the church were originally enclosed by a circular rampart. The remaining stump has a large breach where the door might have been located, if it was a low one. Through this it is possible to climb into the interior. The base of the opening is 1.5 metres, which would indicate a sill level of *c.* 1.8 metres. A relieving arch has been built into the upper portion of the breach; this is probably a 19th-century repair. The tower is built of rough, uncoursed granite field-stones, and demonstrates the fact that it is not quality of masonry which has preserved the towers, but the binding quality of the lime mortar constructional system, which has given them their stability and strength. The wall treatment is similar both externally and internally.

In Walter Harris' *Ancient and Present State of the County of Down* (1744), he relates how the tower of Maghera had collapsed in a storm earlier in the 18th century, and '*lay at length and entire on the ground like a huge gun without breaking to pieces, so wonderfully hard and binding was the cement of this work*'. This anecdote, hearsay to Harris, who had unfortunately not witnessed it, is not as improbable as it may seem. Large portions of the walling of the Bishop's Tower on the Rock of Cashel, and the castle at Clonmacnoise, have collapsed intact, the masonry bound together by the mortar. That a Round Tower, whose *modus operandi* is its iron-like mortared construction, should have fallen over intact, is an equally plausible, if unsubstantiated, possibility.

Maghera is probably an early tower, although the absence of any visible architectural features makes its date difficult to comment upon.

Date: not known.

Dimensions: height 5.4 metres; diameter at base 4.85 metres; height of door-sill *c.* 1.8 metres.

Unique features: none.

Access: from the churchyard by a stile, signposted on local roads.

18 Nendrum, Co. Down   Nendrum is 10 km south-east of Comber on the A22. The road meanders along the shore of Strangford lough, before crossing a causeway to reach the monastic site on Mahee Island, off the north-east coast of the lough. The monastery was unknown until 1844, when William Reeves, later Bishop of

Down, Connor and Dromore, recognised it as an early ecclesiastical site. This is one of the most beautiful and least spoiled monastic sites to survive, and more than any other which retains a Round Tower, it is possible here to easily appreciate the form of the original concentric ramparts, which have not been seriously encroached upon. The foundation of the monastery in the 6th century is attributed to St Mochaoi, whose name may survive in the title of Mahee Island; its site covers 2.4 hectares within the boundaries of an enormous trivallate cashel, the outer ring of which runs along the shoreline of the lough, 20 metres below. The middle circle is occupied by the remains of buildings, both round and rectangular, one of which was identified as a monastic school by its excavator. These buildings were constructed against the outer rampart of the middle enclosure. Within the inner circle is a church (c. 1000), with a later medieval extension, which most probably occupies the position of the original timber church. Located to the north-west is the stub of the Round Tower.

Nendrum (figs. 4 & 5) was excavated extensively by H.C. Lawlor, 1922-24, with fascinating results, although the archaeological methodology of the time has made it difficult for his conclusion to be ratified by modern scholars. Since that date there has not been published a similarly extensive excavation of a comparably important monastic site. The range of finds (Ulster Museum, Belfast) emphasise the variety of crafts and domestic tasks carried out within the self-sufficient settlement. Among the most important is an early bell, similar to St Patrick's Bell (National Museum, Dublin), found concealed in the outer cashel wall. It is typical of the 7th – 9th centuries, made of beaten iron sheet, dipped in tin. This indeed is 'a bell, the best of bells' which might be directly associated with a particular Round Tower. Some of the carved stones found during the excavations are now in the Display Centre on the site. The reconstructed sundial (c. 1000) was used to indicate terce, sext and none (9am, 12 noon, 3pm), the three main times of daily prayer.

The Tower:

> 'Oendruim, that is, one hill, is the entire island, and in Lough Cuan it is.'
> Martyrology of Oengus

The tower stands on the summit of the rising land, within the innermost ring of the cashel; its wall is breached down virtually to the double offset on the south side. This may represent the position of the entrance, in which case it must have been very low, a possible indication of an early date, but there is no means of establishing this with certainty. The present appearance of the tower is totally unreliable, for when it was originally identified as a Round Tower in 1844, most of its external facing had fallen off, leaving only the mortared core (it had previously been thought to be a lime kiln). The outer face was restored using stones found around the tower. The masonry cannot therefore be evaluated for stylistic evidence. Despite the unreliability of Nendrum's appearance, its internal diameter of 2.06 metres indicates a tower of unusually small diameter which suggests a fairly slim and, therefore, shorter than average tower. Located as it is on the summit of the island it would, nonetheless, have been a prominent feature of the Strangford Lough landscape.

Date: not known.

Dimensions: height 4.4 metres; diameter at base 4.2 metres.

Unique features: none; significant site.

Access: free access to the site.

THE DUBLIN TOWERS

During the later centuries of the early medieval period the linguistic and religious uniformity of the island became fragmented by the appearance of settlements of Norse seafarers, who over the passage of little more than a century graduated from raiding to trading. Viking presence in Dublin, which began as an overwintering settlement on the Liffey in 841, was re-established more permanently at a different site in 917. The tower of Slane, some 45 km north-west of Dublin, was burned by the Norse in 950. This is the first mention in the annals of a Round Tower, and an indication of the state of Norse – Irish relations at that time.

The Round Towers in the immediate Dublin area, as well as in the greater area of Dublinshire, *Dyfinnarskiri*, known to have been controlled by the Dublin Norse, deserve some consideration as a group. The area under Norse control, the extent of which varied during the 9th – 12th centuries, extended as far as Arklow to the south, Skerries in the north and inland to the west as far as Leixlip.

By the end of the 10th century the inhabitants of Dublin had become Christianised, intermarried with the Irish and developed into Hiberno-Norse settlers. Dúnán, the first bishop of Dublin, was appointed in 1030 and the church of Holy Trinity (which later became Christ Church Cathedral) was built. Church sites proliferated both within the walls and in the countryside around Dublin, with one, St Michael le Pole, due south of the town, having a Round Tower within sight of the settlement. The other Round Tower sites within the area of Hiberno-Norse influence are Clondalkin, Lusk, Kilmacnessan, Rathmichael and Swords.

Significantly, four of these towers, three of which are substantially intact, are early examples, probably early 11th century. From an analysis of the door and window forms of Clondalkin, Lusk and Swords, and from 19th-century drawings of the demolished St. Michael le Pole, it can be seen that they all belong to the early phase of lintelled opening, which preceded the arched doorways and towers with Romanesque decoration. Rathmichael is a mere stub, but since it is associated with a small single-cell church, it also probably belongs to the same period. The influence of Canterbury in the consecration of Dublin's bishops may not have encouraged the continuance of tower building in the surrounding areas.

Kilmacnessan, which is an engaged example, is an anomaly among the Dublin towers. The vaulted chancel which supported the Round Tower dates it to the 12th century, and separates it from the other towers of the region probably by a hundred years or more.

CLONDALKIN The unusual features of this exceptionally slender and complete building are its apparent concave profile and the circular enveloping buttress which surrounds the base. (See photo p. 62.)

19 Clondalkin, Co. Dublin

Clondalkin village is immediately north of the N7, Dublin to Naas road, 10 km south-east of central Dublin. The tower, on the northern edge of the village, is separated by the public road from the core of the original monastic site, now the churchyard of the 19th-century Church of Ireland parish church, some remnants of which are medieval. There are two early crosses and a baptismal font in the churchyard. The monastery was founded by St Mo-Chúa or Crónán, in the late 6th century or early 7th century. The street surface around the tower has recently been treated as a paved area, with concentric setts radiating from the base of the tower, in a misguided municipal attempt to turn the tower into a piece of street furniture.

The Tower: Clondalkin is the finest and only complete tower in the Dublin area, and is doubly important for the fact that it is the only complete tower which has not had its cap reconstructed or re-set during the intensive conservation work carried out by public and private bodies on Round Towers during the late 19th century. The angle of the cap is shallower than that of other partially surviving caps. In the late 18th century, a neighbouring powder-mill, containing 250 barrels of gunpowder, exploded, demolishing the existing parish church. The tower, remarkably, survived the force of the explosion.

Clondalkin is built of roughly coursed hammer-dressed Dublin calp limestone, with many smaller insertions and spalls. It is one of the slenderest of all the towers and exhibits a tendency towards concave entasis in the drum, where there seems to be a narrowing which widens again just below the cornice. This phenomenon is most probably an error on the part of the builders.

The base is surrounded by a one metre-wide circular masonry buttress, which encloses the tower to a height of 3 metres, where it is curved inward to meet the wall surface. A flight of steps, cut into the buttress to give access to the entrance door, are cantilevered out over the inclined surface of the buttress below the doorway. The date of the buttress is unknown, but it is certainly not original, and may date from as late as the 18th century. The base and steps are possibly not contemporary.

The door, which faces east towards the present parish church, is lintelled and with inclined jambs. The well-articulated slender doorcase of four jambstones on either side, with sill and lintel, is of granite.

The two windows in the drum, which lit the original second and third floors, are also lintelled and with inclined jambs. The windows of the bell-floor are rectangular and facing the cardinal points. These windows have had modern glazing installed.

The internal organisation of the timber floors has been altered, and the present arrangement of four floors (which date from 1827 or earlier) differs from the original five. A curiosity of the internal profile is the almost total absence of floor offsets (a feature paralleled at Glendalough), giving the interior a tube-like profile, rather than the series of inverted buckets which is more normal. There is a single offset to support the entrance floor.

Clondalkin's cap, probably the most perfect to survive, is at a less acute angle than others, and sits on a conventional cornice.

CLONDALKIN
Of the three substantially intact Dublin towers, Clondalkin, Lusk and Swords, this is the only one to retain its original cap.

KILMACNESSAN

Above: The chancel vault, viewed from the nave. No example of an engaged or attached tower supported on a vault has survived. At Kilmacnessan the inclined and chamfered wall below the tower indicate that it resembled what is seen in the surviving 18th-century drawings of Glendalough III, Trinity Church, which has a Round Tower standing on the projecting rectangular base.

Left: Kilmacnessan stands in a great sea of bracken, between the uplands of Ireland's Eye and the shoreline. The chancel arch which stands at the west end of the oratory can be seen rising above the nave walls.

Suggested date: 10th – 11th century.

Dimensions: height 27.5 metres; diameter at base 4.04 metres; height of door-sill 3.9 metres.

Unique features: narrowest tower; eccentric base and internal profile.

Access: there are floors and ladders; key available from the caretaker.

20 Kilmacnessan, Co. Dublin

Kilmacnessan is on Ireland's Eye, an uninhabited island, with an important bird sanctuary, which lies off the north coast of Howth promontory. Motor boats from the east pier of the harbour regularly take passengers to the island during the summer season. Howth, 12 km north-east of Dublin, is reached from the R106. The monastery is said to have been founded in the 6th century by three brothers, Diuchaill, Mo-Nissu and Neslug, sons of Nessan.

The Tower: Kilmacnessan, like Trinity Church at Glendalough, is the site of a missing yet intriguing engaged Round Tower (**fig. 15c**). The small nave-and-chancel church which survives is located on a bleak slope of the island, without any other monastic remnants. It has an arched chancel which acted as the sub-structure to the tower. During extensive reconstruction in the 19th century the west door was removed and the present remains of the tower may have been interfered with, although, at 3.6 metres diameter, it is close to the engaged tower of Glendalough III, which was 4 metres in diameter.

The existing tower remains consist of a single course of stones, sitting on the extrados of the chancel vault. The surface area between the external walls of the chancel and the tower base is paved on the north, south and east by an inclined coping, chamfered at the corners. This certainly looks original and unaltered; a similar feature can be seen in the surviving 18th-century drawings of Glendalough III. Since there is no indication of access to the tower through the chancel arch, there must have been an opening on the west side of its base, from within the apex of the east gable of the nave roof.

In each of the surviving engaged towers the position of the tower is different, emphasising the experimental nature of these buildings, and the fact that they represent a break with tradition. Kilmacnessan is the sole example to have its chancel treated in this manner. From the invention of the Round Tower to its demise as an architectural form, the engaged tower represents the only radical development of the idea to occur between the 10th and 12th centuries.

Suggested date: 12th century.

Dimensions: height of tower from supporting vault 50cm; diameter at base of tower 3.6 metres.

Unique features: engaged tower on the chancel arch.

Access: free access to site.

21 Lusk, Co. Dublin

Lusk village is on the R127, 3 km east of the N1, Dublin to Drogheda road, 20 km north-east of Dublin. The tower is in the churchyard of the former Church of Ireland parish church (1847) and attached to a late medieval belfry, in the

LUSK

Left: Lusk is a dream in geometry, one of the most extraordinary buildings in Ireland, where the late medieval master masons have been inspired to emulate the genius of their forebears. The 15th – 16th-century church belfry was built to incorporate the Round Tower (left) into its design, and has seamlessly merged buildings, constructed five hundred years apart. A 19th-century parish church (disused) adjoins the fortified belfry.
(See photos pp. 37, 70, 81.)

Below: Although the Round Tower (left) has lost its cap, it is otherwise intact, well preserved and provided with floors.

ground floor of which are some medieval and later tombs. The finest of these is the Renaissance-style table-tomb of the Barnewalls, with double recumbent effigies dressed in fashionable clothing and the continental armour of Sir Christopher Barnewall (d. 1575) and his wife, Marion Sharl. The original church would have been located somewhere in the area where the west end of the parish church now stands. Nothing, other than the Round Tower, survives from the original monastery, founded by St MacCuilinn during the late 5th century. The street layout, which surrounds the churchyard of Lusk, retains the concentric rampart-lines of the original ecclesiastical enclosure.

The Tower: Lusk Round Tower is an integral unit of one of the most distinctive and dramatic medieval ecclesiastical complexes. During the 15th and 16th centuries, a church belfry with circular corner turrets was built adjacent to the Round Tower which occupies the position of the fourth turret, on its north-eastern corner. Lusk gives the clue as to what should be expected at the destroyed tower at Duleek which, similarly, has a medieval belfry attached to it, and its influence can be seen in the round corner turrets of the belfry of nearby Balrothery. Lusk is a complete tower, missing its conical cap, which has been replaced by a flat timber roof to which there is no access.

The masonry is of roughly hammer-dressed limestone blocks in relatively horizontal courses, with a fine profile to curve and batter. The unarticulated granite doorcase faces east and is lintelled with inclined jambs. The sill height above the external ground level is misleading, as the ground level within the graveyard has risen in the last few centuries. There is an indistinct architrival band around the door-opening. With eight internal floors, as well as a basement, Lusk differs from all other towers, where the general number is less. Each floor is lit by single-lintelled windows which vary in size, the largest being on the seventh floor, almost directly above the entrance. Two windows, one on the second floor and another on the sixth, have been blocked up where they face onto the wall of the later belfry. This has left the second floor unlit. The bell-floor windows that face off the cardinal points are significantly smaller and unusually narrow.

There are internal non-structural corbels on the fourth and fifth floors, the most interesting of which is the fine hooked corbel on the fifth floor, clearly designed to support suspended objects.

Suggested date: 10th – 11th century.

Dimensions: height 26.56 metres; diameter at base 5.06 metres; original height of door-sill 2.6 metres (now 90cm).

Unique features: eight floors internally.

Access: the tower has floors and ladders and is open to the public during the summer months.

22 Rathmichael, Co. Dublin Rathmichael is west of the M11 on Carrickgollan Hill, 3 km south-west of Cabinteely village, 15 km south-east of Dublin. The site is approached by a long and narrow track from the south side of Rathmichael Road. The location

RATHMICHAEL
The remains of a well-built tower now stand totally submerged in the church-yard planting of a quiet country grave-yard. The tower closely adjoins the late medieval extension to an earlier church.

SWORDS
Although Swords retains a cap, this is not original, but an ill-proportioned and unsuccessful late attempt at restoration. Possibly the earliest of the Dublin towers, nothing of the early monastery survives as the site was subsequently much built upon and retains late medieval and 19th-century buildings. (See photo p. 62.)

is particularly beautiful and secluded, with a strong sense of other-worldliness about it. The tower stands in a churchyard overshadowed by yews, with a medieval nave-and-chancel church, surrounded by a cashel which most probably represents the original ecclesiastical enclosure. The fabric of the eastern end of the nave is the same as that of the tower, and this is possibly the single cell church for which the tower was built.

A small collection of early Christian grave slabs from the site are displayed on the south wall of the church. The monastery, dedicated to St Michael, may possibly have been founded by St Comgall of Bangor.

The Tower: Despite being only the stub of a tower, Rathmichael is an impressive ruin, standing close to the south wall of the later portion of the church. The masonry is coursed granite and limestone rubble, roughly dressed to the curve, and evidently a tidied-up version of its condition a hundred years previously. No architectural features survive.

The interior of the Round Tower has been for many years the recipient of graveyard rubbish, and like many other towers to which there is open access, anything from tin-cans to discarded bones have been thrown over the wall, making the interior look like a rubbish tip, particularly inappropriate in so beautiful a location.

Suggested date: 10th – 11th century.

Dimensions: height 1.9 metres; diameter at base 4.96 metres.

Unique features: none.

Access: free access to site.

23 Swords, Co. Dublin   Swords village is on the MI/NI Dublin to Drogheda road, 12 km north of Dublin. The Round Tower is in the graveyard of the Church of Ireland parish church. A medieval tower with interesting sculpted decoration and inscriptions stands nearby with, on its south wall, the gable-end imprint of the vanished medieval church. The Round Tower acted as belfry to the present parish church. The establishment of the monastery, of which nothing survives but the tower, is attributed to St Columba in the 6th century.

The Tower: Swords is a crudely built tower, of rough-looking random rubble limestone field and quarry stones which are laid unworked to the curve and batter, with much exposed loose lime mortar.

The door, which faces east, is on ground floor level and is lintelled and has inclined jambs. The two stone steps which lead to the door are modern.

There are four rectangular windows in the drum, with a larger one directly over the door which can be construed as an early example of a Treasury window. The original second floor, of which elements remain in situ, was constructed of slabs of stone corbelled out from the tower wall; the significance of a stone floor at this level can be associated with the presence of the large window, emphasising its importance. Decayed fragments of a 19th-century timber floor into which the floor remains were incorporated survive, here and above.

DEVENISH I

Left: Seen in the background of the late medieval stone cross, the complete Round Tower stands on the slope before a ruined Romanesque church. The cornice, between the bell-floor windows and the cap, is decorated with sculpted human heads and running motif decoration, the only tower to be treated in this manner. (See photos pp. 42, 78, 82, 85.)

Left: Among the lakelands of Upper and Lower Lough Erne it is often difficult to distinguish between islands and mainland, so variegated is the shoreline. Here, a few miles north of Enniskillen in the lower lake, the reedy waters surround Devenish and the perfection of its Round Tower.

The bell-floor appears to have been totally reconstructed, but not very skil-fully, during the late 17th century or early 18th century. It has four large arched windows which clearly belong to a later period than the tower; they face the cardinal points. The upper reconstructed portion of the tower appears like a classical garden folly which suggests an 18th-century date. The cap likewise is crude and misshapen.

Suggested date: 10th century.

Dimensions: height 26 metres; diameter at base 5 metres; height of door-sill 70cm.

Unique features: fragment of original stone floor.

Access: to interior of tower; there are later timber floors but no ladders.

24 Devenish I, Co. Fermanagh   Devenish Island is situated in Lower Lough Erne, reached from the A32 by the west lakeshore, 3 km north of Enniskillen, and is one of the most glorious early Christian monastic sites in Ireland. Its location, on an island off the reed-fringed shores of Lower Lough Erne, makes it a place apart. Devenish is the best preserved and internally most easily accessible of all the Round Towers. The remains include 'St Molaise's House', a 12th-century oratory or tomb-shrine; the Teampull Mór, a 13th-century church with domestic buildings, and the 15th-century priory which crowns the hill to the west of the tower. There is also an unusual and rather beautiful late medieval pierced stone High Cross which shows the inspiration of contemporary metalwork. The monastery was founded in the 6th century by St Molaise; one of its great treasures, the 11th-century *Soiscél Molaise* book shrine, is in the National Museum of Ireland in Dublin. A 1609 plantation map of the Barony of Magheraboy has a schematic drawing of the tower. The small site museum has a display of finds from the site.

The Tower: Devenish I is a superbly built example of what was aspired to by many monastic communities but seldom achieved. This statement requires qualification. In fact we do not know if among the ruins of other towers there was one as fine or finer than this. Mostly, the remains of towers which do not rise to door height tell little more than the masonry style of what quality of tower has vanished. Devenish, like Ardmore, which it hardly resembles, must be among the last group of towers to be built, and represents a point close to the apogee in their development. The masonry, some of the lower courses of which are extremely large, is of fine, well cut and dressed sandstone blocks which exhibit diagonal comb-dressing; the courses are occasionally joggle-jointed. Triangular putlock holes are visible on the external surface.

The doorcase is round-headed with inclined jambs and its tripartite head is a true arch composed of a keystone and two voussoirs. A broad band architrave surrounds the external arch and jambs. Internally, the right-hand doorjamb has a pair of bolt holes sunk in its masonry, but it is difficult to confirm that they represent the original fittings. Their position, which is similar to Tory, at least suggests that they may be original.

Almost directly above the entrance and a little to the right is a fine large tri-angular-headed window opening to the second floor, possibly the Treasury level of the tower. In the drum, which in this instance has only two further floors, are two rectangular lintelled windows. The bell-floor windows are unfortunately glazed. They are tall, with inclined jambs and lintelled, and are oriented slightly off the cardinal points, preventing much of the surrounding landscape being seen from above.

The interior of Devenish I is reached by a ladder which gives access to the doorway. The entrance floor is provided with a timber trapdoor to the basement area. Centrally placed openings in the timber floors have ladders between them, which allow the visitor to ascend to the bell-floor and to clearly see the interior construction of the cap. The climb of eighty-two steps to the top floor can be achieved from external ground level in two minutes. Depending on the agility of the climber and familiarity with the tower interior the climb might probably be achieved within a minute.

Devenish I is dark inside, except on a very bright day when the sun can illuminate the interior. The central positioning of the access ladders means that very little use could be made of the surrounding floor-space. This suggests that the floor-plan in Cloyne provides for a more economical use of the internal spaces. Between the first, second and third floors, there are eight projecting wall corbels, of which three are hook-shaped. Presumably some of these corbels were placed to provide hanging places for leather satchels for manuscripts or other precious objects; others are on the same level as the floor-offsets and seem to provide 'belt and braces' stability for the floor.

Above the bell-floor windows is Devenish I's claim to absolute uniqueness, a feature which is without parallel on any other tower. The four sculpted heads and decorated cornice are, unfortunately, so far above ground that it is difficult to examine them with any clarity, except with the help of binoculars. All known external decoration on Round Towers is associated with the entrance doors, or in the case of Timahoe, the door and second-floor window. There is no parallel for the placing of such decoration, and like the string-courses at Ardmore, it indicates a late interest in experimentation and enhancement of the basic and, by the late 12th century, well-established form of these towers. The heads represent either three males and one female, or perhaps three older bearded and one younger clean-shaven man. The identities of the first interpretation could be St Patrick, St Columba, St Molaise and St Brigid or, alternatively, the four evangelists, Matthew, Mark, Luke and John. The cornice, which is three courses above the bell-floor windows, is divided by the heads which project not quite directly above the windows, and between them is the decorative band which connects them. This band is composed of different running motifs, large lozenges between borders, s-shaped bands between borders, and small lozenges between borders. The best preserved of the heads is that facing east; from the vigour of this carving which has withstood 700 years of weathering, it must have been exceptionally beautiful when freshly carved. The east head represents a male with a moustache and beard carved in an interlace pattern. The head is either bald or wearing a close-fitting cap. The other two bearded

DEVENISH II
The ring of stones represents the position of a previously unknown tower base discovered during excavations.

heads (west and south), are more weathered and damaged. The fourth head, that facing north, is clean-shaven, with a heavy lock of hair falling over the forehead. While it could represent either a woman or a young man, the latter seems more likely. Unless they are purely decorative, identification of the four heads with the evangelists seems the most probable, considering the widespread use of their symbols (surrounding Christ in majesty) on the west portals of countless Continental churches and in Irish manuscripts.

The corbelled internal structure of the roof-cone which springs from the internal wall surface has, unusually, an internal cornice (corresponding to the conventional external one). The internal shape is not a dome but a cone with a flat capstone closing its apex. This beautifully pointed and proportioned cap was damaged in 1835 but repaired the following year.

Suggested date: 12th century. (Annals reference for 1176.)

Dimensions: height 25 metres; diameter at base 4.82 metres; height of door-sill 2.59 metres.

Unique features: sculpted and decorated cornice.

Access: by boat from the east shore of lake or from Enniskillen; complete floors and ladders to the top.

25 Devenish II, Co. Fermanagh

The Tower: Devenish II stands directly to the north of Devenish I. Here, one must imagine the vanished tower, like a hollow tube of air penetrating the sky, for nothing survives beyond the fairly minimal foundations and their reconstruction above ground level. Clearly this was not a case of two Round Towers standing within metres of each other, like the westwork towers of a Continental cathedral. It is more than likely that Devenish II is the earlier building, which was either not proceeded with, or collapsed at some point, and was replaced by Devenish I. If the standing tower does replace the earlier collapsed one, it is an important example of the fact that this spot was the desired location for the tower, close by the position of the earlier one. Many more Round Towers can be expected to be identified on the basis of this discovery and that at Liathmore, and in time the small number of previously unknown towers may become much larger.

Date: not known.

Dimensions: height 50cm; diameter at base 5 metres.

Unique features: none.

Access: directly adjacent to Devenish I.

26 Ardrahan, Co. Galway

Ardrahan village is on the N18, Gort to Galway road, 12 km north of Gort. The tower, or what remains of it, is in the churchyard of the Church of Ireland parish church (1809), on the edge of the village. Ruins of a late medieval church stand in the churchyard.

The Tower: Ardrahan is an almost-vanished tower; what remains is a stub; five courses of masonry partly outside the graveyard, south-west of the church. All that can be seen is a portion of the outer wall of the tower, where it projects

ARDRAHAN
The large stones beneath the outcrop of bushes are all that survive of the tower, the remainder of which is within the graveyard and below ground. Even such slight survivals as this are important for the evidence which they provide of a vanished church complex.

KILBENNAN
Kilbennan stands on the edge of the churchyard, in the half in, half out situation, commonplace to many tower sites. The large breach at the top of the tower reveals, as at Drumcliff, the constructional system adopted by the tower builders, with a mortar and rubble core sandwiched between outer and inner skins of masonry.

through the perimeter wall of the churchyard into the adjoining field, the level of which is considerably lower. The churchyard wall abuts that of the tower and is clearly a later structure. The remainder of the circumference, the top of which is obscured by gorse and ivy, is within the churchyard. An ivy-covered 19th-century grave-slab stands within the overgrown interior of the tower, presumably indicating a burial actually in the tower. The tower is best viewed from the lower ground.

Four courses stand above a single offset composed of crude boulders, one stone of which has a stepped profile, as in Faughart. The visible tower remains are of impressively large unwrought and irregular limestone blocks. Below the offset are a few courses of small stones, which may represent exposed foundations or a later underpinning.

Suggested date: 10th – 11th century.

Dimensions: height 2.9 metres; diameter at base 4.7 metres.

Unique features: none.

Access: free access to site.

27 Kilbennan, Co. Galway

Kilbennan village is west of the R332, Tuam to Claremorris road, 4 km north-west of Tuam. The tower stands in a graveyard at the centre of the village, in which there is a late medieval parish church, and the fragmentary remains of an earlier Romanesque church. The foundation of the monastery is attributed to St Benen or Benignus, a 5th-century saint, and successor to St Patrick in Armagh.

The Tower: The tower of Kilbennan stands, as is found in numerous other Round Tower sites (Ardrahan, Clones, Kilree), half-in and half-out of a later graveyard boundary wall, an indication of a shrinking ecclesiastical territory. With the build-up of land from burials within the walls there is usually, as here, a considerable change of level between the inside and the outside of the site which is lower by one metre, revealing a single base offset. The tower is built of inconsistently coursed, dressed and relatively uniform limestone blocks, occasionally joggle-jointed. There is an extensive breach on the west side, where there is a drop of some 7 metres in the wall height, which exposes the wall section to view.

The round-headed doorcase, facing north-east towards the side of the medieval church, is articulated in sandstone, with a well-cut true arch of five voussoirs with keystone; its jambs are quite steeply inclined.

Despite the fact that parts of the tower stand 16.5 metres high, there are no surviving windows. There is a possible window-reveal in the exposed section of the breach, which also shows one of the two sets of floor-corbels.

Suggested date: 11th century.

Dimensions: height 16.5 metres; diameter at base 4.8 metres; height of door-sill 4.56 metres.

Unique features: none.

Access: free access to site.

KILCOONA
What survives of Kilcoona suggests that it was originally a fine tower. In the Dunraven photograph (1870) of Kilcoona it stands no higher than it does today.

KILLEANY
Left: In the foreground stands a cross shaft while on the summit of the hill is seen the outline of Temple Benen. Between them on the slope, the tower stands on a plateau of rock.

Below: Temple Benen is one of the most beautifully proportioned of the steep-roofed churches which, with the Round Towers, are the great architectural achievement of the Irish early medieval period.

28 Kilcoona, Co. Galway

Kilcoona is off the N84, Galway to Headford road, on the east side of Lough Corrib, 6 km south-east of Headford. The tower stands in a well-maintained graveyard in which there are the ruins of a medieval church. St Cuanna (7th century) is recorded as being the founder.

The Tower: Kilcoona is another tower stub, built of well-coursed ashlars with some joggled interruptions to the lines of the masonry. Above the surviving five courses no architectural features survive. Kilcoona has been partially rebuilt, but the repair has been archaeologically indicated by a barrier. The core is visible through a large breach in the base of the wall, situated directly above a pair of finely cut offsets at the base; the interior is filled with rubble and rubbish to the top of the wall.
Suggested date: 11th – 12th century.
Dimensions: height 3 metres; diameter at base *c.* 5 metres.
Unique features: none.
Access: free access to site.

29 Killeany, Inishmore, Aran Islands, Co. Galway

The tower is outside Killeany hamlet, on the north-east coast of Inishmore, the largest of the Aran Islands, which is 15 km offshore. Killeany or St Eany's monastery was founded by St Enda in the 7th century. The tower is among the more minor antiquities of the exceptionally rich landscape of the Aran Islands which includes eight early churches – Temple Benen, Tighlagh Eany, Temple MacDuagh, Templenaneev, St Kieran's Church, the slightly later Temple an Cheathair Aluinn, Temple Soorney and Temple Brecan – as well as the extraordinary barbaric splendour of the Iron Age Dun Aenghus and other monuments. The Round Tower is reported to have stood relatively complete until the 17th century, when its stone was allegedly re-used in the construction of the nearby Cromwellian fort.

The Tower: Killeany is situated on the lower slopes of a rugged hillside near St Eany's Well and the shaft of a High Cross which has non-figurative decoration. On the summit of the slope is Temple Benen (unusually oriented north-south), one of the most beautiful, well-preserved and dramatically sited of all the early steep-roofed oratories. Of the church, for which the tower was built, and which must have stood further east, nothing survives. On the plateau surrounding Temple Benen are remains of structures occupied during the 17th century. Tighlagh Eany (and St Eany's Grave), which stands further to the east, is a fine early church with antae, although some of its features are late or post-medieval.

Like Kilcoona, Killeany is yet another tower stub: eight courses over a single offset are all that still stands of a tower which, if it stood to a height of approximately 30 metres, would have provided a remarkable landmark for the island monastery and been visible from the mainland. The masonry is of well-squared, but irregularly coursed, limestone ashlars. A single internal corbel probably indicates the level of the entrance floor, although possibly not the

149

KILMACDUAGH

Above: Despite extensive restoration and a tendency to look as though it might topple over, the sleek outline of Kilmacduagh identifies it as among the finest of the surviving towers. It has the greatest number of windows of any tower. (See photos pp. 65, 71.)

Far left: It is probable that the door, at 8 metres above ground level, was reached from a freestanding timber stair structure rather than by ladder.

Left: The small lintelled upper-basement window has few parallels and was possibly intended more as an air vent than as a source of light.

orientation of the door. No other features have been preserved.

Suggested date: 11th – 12th century.

Dimensions: height 3.02 metres; diameter at base 4.82 metres; height of door-sill 3.3 metres.

Unique features: none.

Access: free access to site; the shortest journey is by ferry from Rossaveel in Connemara.

30 Kilmacduagh, Co. Galway

Kilmacduagh is north of the R460, 8 km south-west of Gort, and shares with Clonmacnoise, Glendalough and Inis Cealtra, the distinction of being a multi-church site. In the large graveyard and the fields which surround it are an outstanding collection of medieval churches, the most important of which is the 11th-century to 15th-century cathedral with late transepts, which stands adjacent to the Round Tower. In a field to the north is the 12th-century nave-and-chancel St John's Church, with the 13th-century domestic building of 'Glebe House' further north of it. To the north-west is sited the 13th-century O'Heyne's Church, as well as a further 15th-century church, and on the east, the 12th-century St Mary's Church. The monastery was founded by St Colman MacDuagh in the 7th century.

The Tower: Kilmacduagh is the Irish equivalent of the Leaning Tower of Pisa, which it probably pre-dates: Pisa was begun in 1174, has the same number of storeys (eight), but is both twice the height and, at 5 metres off the perpendicular, leans considerably more than Kilmacduagh at a mere 1.02 metres. The tower is both the tallest standing and has the highest doorway. Kilmacduagh should be a late tower if the doorways, rising like a lift, can be considered an indicator for dating, although this is at best an unreliable principle. The excellently preserved appearance of Kilmacduagh today belies the condition of the tower slightly more than a hundred years ago. A large breach existed on the south-west side (possibly dating from a collapse of *c.* 1859), from the sixth floor to halfway up the cap, the apex of which was totally missing. The 19th-century photographs show Kilmacduagh in a very battered condition; the breach was repaired in 1878, preserving the tower from further deterioration.

The tower's stonework is of limestone throughout, with no articulation of doorcase or windows, and the profile in silhouette is a superb example of the medieval master-mason's artistry. The bottom eight courses, above a single offset, are of almost cyclopean dimensions, indicating the height to which available lifting equipment was capable of manoeuvring large boulders; the phenomenon of cyclopean masonry below the sill-level is common to many towers. Above, the stonework appears uniform and well-coursed (deviating off the horizontal) with occasional joggle-joints, hammer dressed with a pocked finish, spalls and many smaller stones.

The basement of Kilmacduagh (the tallest and among the narrowest known) shares with Glendalough an unusual and unexplained feature, a thin wall-shaft in the masonry which could function as a minimal light source, air-vent or drain; none of these suggestions particularly recommend themselves. An unstopped putlock hole seems possible, yet hardly more plausible. The shaft, about 50cm high and 15cm wide, penetrates right through the wall at a radius to the circumference. Unlike at Glendalough, where the shaft is positioned just above the base offset, here it is 6.5 metres above the external ground level.

If the door, at 8 metres from the ground, were slightly higher, it would be a quarter way up the tower which is 34.89 metres from the external ground level to the apex of the cone. The doorway has a round-headed arch, made in the primitive mode by being cut from a pair of butted corbels; the jambs are visibly inclined. Considerations of security and display appear paramount here; convenience clearly ranks much lower. As well as the sheer inconvenience of gaining access to the tower, the practical question of stowing the access ladder within the tower is a conundrum to which there is no simple answer. A timber ladder of the height necessary to reach the door could not be drawn inside – except by passing it up through the floor openings of the second, third and fourth floors, and this could be achieved only if it were constructed of pliable timber. Only a rope ladder would be capable of being pulled in with ease, a consideration which casts doubt on the image of some Lector-like Caineachair of Slane scrambling for safety with an armful of manuscripts, even if he were young and agile. This problem of withdrawing the access ladder is common to all towers because of the wall depth. At Kilmacduagh the problem is merely accentuated. In most cases the wall thickness, at an average 1.1 metres alone, would prevent a ladder being pulled inside a tower.

The five floors of the drum each have a single triangular-headed window. The bell-floor has six triangular-headed windows, evenly spaced: three of these were reconstructed and installed during the 19th-century repairs. Kilmacduagh, with eleven windows (and thirteen apertures overall), has the largest number of any intact tower.

Increasing the number of bell-floor windows appears to be a modification which was not followed in such later towers as Ardmore or Timahoe, lending support to the understanding that observation was not a primary function in tower design, although here its possibilities were greatly enhanced by the insertion of two additional bell-floor windows.

Kilmacduagh is significant as a window case-study for examining the general question of fenestration. Rattoo, in terms of the door-typology, is slightly later than Kilmacduagh, yet has a single drum window and an orthodox four windows on the bell-floor. Kilmacduagh is also significant for the light which it casts on the clockwise and anticlockwise ordering of the window-openings. It can be argued that the rising windows are arranged in either manner; the only convincing reason for choosing one over the other is the proximity of the second floor window to the entrance, suggesting that this is the orientation to be followed. It is hard to avoid the conclusion that, in either clockwise or anticlockwise order, the arrangement is a residual survival of windows thus arranged in some unidentified, probably Continental, prototype which was provided with a spiral staircase. There is no other satisfactory explanation for a window arrangement which is quite arbitrary. The obvious proposition that the ascending spiral of windows distributes viewing positions and overlooks a greater span of landscape is undoubtedly the case, yet in Kilmacduagh (with the exception of the bell-floor) the north-western quadrant of the drum is entirely without windows. Within the drum, north, east and west cardinal points have a window each, as have the two southern quadrants; the door is in the remaining north-eastern quadrant.

The cap is eccentric as it has no cornice but sits overhanging the wall like an eaves detail. Visually, this treatment is less strong than, for instance, Clondalkin or Devenish I, where the cornice more definitely articulates the transition from one plane to another.

Suggested date: 11th – 12th century.

Dimensions: height 34.89 metres; diameter at base 5.68 metres; height of door-sill 8.22 metres.

Unique features: extreme height of the door above the ground; the tallest standing Round Tower; the greatest number of windows; a leaning tower (2 degrees off the vertical, to the south-west).

Access: to site; there are no floors or ladders; keys to the locked churches are available from the caretaker.

31 Roscam, Co. Galway   The site is on the north shore of Galway Bay, 1 km south of the N6 Galway to Oranmore road, 10 km east of Galway, and approached from Roscam hamlet. Roscam stands in a splendid location among open fields, surrounded by the remains of a vast ecclesiastical cashel. This circumvallation (2 metres high, 1 metre wide) which has been absorbed into the topography of field walls, is of enormous interest and in itself an impressive antiquity. The settlement's orientation was seaward rather than from the land. Nearby is a ruined *c.* 1400 medieval church which has been used as a repository for field-stones gathered from the adjoining fields. A beautiful early graveyard, still in use (in which are two mammoth bullaun slabs, one with three cups), stretches down the slope from the church. Little is known about the foundation of the monastery, which is associated with St Patrick.

The continuing heavy development of sites for domestic housing is in serious danger of encroaching on the beauty and importance of this site.

The Tower: Roscam is well constructed of a silvery limestone, unevenly coursed, roughly squared and hammer-dressed. The wall has widely dispersed and regularly arranged putlock holes. Although they are seen on other towers, this is the sole example of a tower as it might have appeared at the time of construction, the holes still unplugged. The putlock holes give valuable insight into the actual building of this and, no doubt, many other Round Towers. The putlock holes are in seven levels or lifts, slightly more than a metre above each other. Those of the top four lifts penetrate through the wall and can be seen on the surface of the inside wall.

The doorway, facing south-east, is rectangular and lintelled with a single stone which spans the depth of the wall. The jambs are slightly inclined and

ROSCAM

Galway Bay forms the backdrop to the site of Roscam, with the tower standing above the late medieval church. The entire site is surrounded by an impressive stone cashel.
(See photo p. 76.)

AGHADOE

Poised above the roadway, and on the edge of the graveyard, the remnants of Aghadoe have been so frequently restored that little of the original outer surface remains.

stand on a sill, almost as massive as the lintel. The door height above ground is less than the average, and presumably points to an early date, as do all the other features of the building. Both internal jambs have a rebate to receive a door, with housing for a timber door-pivot on the top left-hand side. The combed tooling of the rebate is later than the treatment of the tower masonry.

There is a single rectangular window on the third floor, almost directly above the door, and only slightly smaller than the entrance. The uppermost courses of the wall, a mere 40cm thick, are clearly later, as possibly is the single rectangular window which is most uncharacteristic of a Round Tower.

Internal floors were supported by string-courses of corbels rather than the conventional offsets, with the exception of the second floor which was supported on joists inserted in the wall during construction.

Suggested date: 10th – 11th century.

Dimensions: height 10.98 metres; diameter at base 4.77 metres; height of door-sill 1.85 metres.

Unique features: complete system of putlock holes.

Access: to site and interior of tower, no floors or ladders.

32 Aghadoe, Co. Kerry

Aghadoe lies north of the R562 and 3 km north-west of Killarney. This is a truly stunning site, perched on the hills to the north-west of Killarney town, with an unrivalled view south over the lakes of Killarney and their mountain backdrop. Unfortunately, what remains of the monastic settlement is slight: the stub of a Round Tower, on the edge of a graveyard, which contains a ruined medieval church, 12th century and later. In its south wall lies an ogham stone, inscribed BRRUANANN. The monastery was founded by St Finian the Leper during the 7th century.

The Tower: Aghadoe has been so 'restored' and repaired that it looks more like the parapet of a garden centre wishing-well, missing only its milkmaid and collection of garden gnomes, than the vigorous remains of an early medieval Round Tower. Without the valuable record of Lord Dunraven's photograph (*c.* 1875), it would be difficult to form any impression of the true appearance of the tower. Originally, it was constructed of irregularly coursed and joggled red sandstone blocks, well worked and trimmed to the curve. All other facing stonework (the majority of which is now visible), must be considered modern intrusions.

The surviving masonry here exhibits a characteristic manner common to many towers, where the horizontality of the courses is not maintained and they tend to sag noticeably. Around the eleventh course of the squared ashlars from the ground the horizontal plane has been lost by the masons, but recovered in the courses above. The graveyard wall undercuts the north face of the tower.

Suggested date: 11th century.

Dimensions: height 5.5 metres; diameter of base 4.6 metres.

Unique features: none.

Access: free access to site; signposted.

RATTOO

Above: The keystone of the arch has paired volutes which extend down the shoulders of the arch into a terminal pair of similar form. (See photo p. 65.)

Left: Few surviving Round Towers display such elegant proportions as Rattoo, with its superb profile and sharply pointed conical cap. The single drum window is the only light source between the doorway and the bell-floor. A medieval church is concealed behind the demesne wall on the left.

33 Rattoo, Co. Kerry Rattoo is approached down a side road, 3 km south-west of Ballyduff village on the R551, 16 km west of Listowel. Rattoo, among the most beautiful and well-preserved of all the towers, stands in the midst of open farmland on the edge of Ballyduff village. The tower is directly outside the perimeter wall of a churchyard, in which is a ruined medieval church with, to the east, the slight remains of an Augustinian priory. The churchyard and some of the surrounding large fields are enclosed by high demesne walls which completely separate the tower from the position of the chapel. Aerial photographs show the traces of the now-removed monastic enclosure. The original foundation is attributed to St Lughach.

The Tower: Rattoo is superficially an exemplary, orthodox Round Tower, with good proportions, elegant batter and a tall, well-formed cap which was repaired during the 19th century. The tower stands 27.37 metres from ground level to the cone's apex. There is an offset at the base and the sandstone masonry is of well-coursed, regularly sized ashlars, well-dressed to the curve and batter, with erratic red-sandstone intrusions. In fact, Rattoo is in a number of respects an extremely eccentric tower.

The round-headed doorcase faces south-east away from the late-medieval church. It has the conventional inclined jambs but the three-stone round arched doorhead is unusual in having a keystone, with the other two stones of the arch forming the upper quoins of the doorcase. Is this formulation a transition between the butted corbels of Kilmacduagh and the tripartite treatment of Devenish I? There is a low-relief broad band which acts as the architrave surrounding the doorhead and jambs; the sill carries the line of the band while slightly projecting from the wall-face. Above the architrave, and integral with its carving, is a decorative feature of no evident religious associations. This bas-relief detail is in the form of paired scrolls or volutes resting on the shoulders of the arch, with a symmetrical double scroll centrally positioned over the keystone which may have terminated at its apex, with some detail (a cross perhaps), now missing. This feature has no parallel on surviving towers as a door decoration; however, one of the internal decorated corbels at Ardmore has on its sides a scroll form decoration, which looks quite similar in conception to the one at Rattoo.

Rattoo is clearly out of order by the standard of most towers in having only a single window in its drum, a small triangle-headed one with inclined jambs, lighting the fourth floor, and placed directly above the entrance – the window-head is like an inverted V, cut from a single stone, rather than being composed of two inclined slabs. The Stygian gloom of the intermediate floors of Rattoo must have been almost total. No tower is less defensible, habitable or usable, except to provide access to the bell-floor and for storage purposes. In the claustrophobic confines of Rattoo, Margaret Stokes' proposal of up to eighty monks sheltering in a tower assumes nightmare proportions.

The four tall bell-floor windows are triangle-headed and face the cardinal points. Where a tower is lacking a window in the drum, it is plausible to speculate that the masons may have accidentally missed a single floor. At Rattoo the

CASTLEDERMOT
Left: A reconstructed Romanesque doorway stands in front of the 19th-century church, which repeats the formula with a Romanesque revival doorway. A High Cross base stands in the foreground to the left of the early doorway.
(See photo p. 73.)

Left: The tower's position, on the north side of the church, makes it a very eccentric example of a Round Tower. The tower is original only to the level of the bell-floor window sills.

absence of windows can hardly be attributed to error.

The unexpected presence of a small Sheela-na-gig (30cm high), on the internal side of the left jamb of the north-facing window is another feature unique among Round Towers, and the source of speculation as to whether it is integral or a later insertion. The function of the Sheela carvings, normally displayed on the exterior of medieval churches or tower-houses as warnings against the blandishments of the flesh, suggests the lonely figure of a monk, who isolated in his tower from the world below, is sternly admonished to keep his mind on ringing his hand-bell for the hours of the daily office, rather than on the distant sight of a woman from a neighbouring ringfort.

Suggested date: 11th century.

Dimensions: height 27.23 metres; diameter at base 4.6 metres; height of door-sill 2.83 metres.

Unique features: decorated doorcase; single window in drum, Sheela-na-gig on bell-floor.

Access: free access to site, no floors or ladders in the tower; signposted.

34 Castledermot, Co. Kildare

Castledermot is on the N9, Dublin to Carlow road, 12 km north of Carlow, with the important remains of a monastery established by St Dermot *c*. 600. It is significant as an ascetic foundation associated with the 9th-century *Céli Dé* religious reform movement.

The tower is in the churchyard of St James' Church of Ireland parish church, at the centre of the village. The site is of equal interest to the Round Tower, which is both early and eccentric. The decorated Romanesque doorway which stands in front of the west door of the 19th-century church, is shown in early drawings of the site from the west, with the roofless walls of the church still standing, and a small portion of the chancel still roofed and in use. Then, the tower would have had a conical cap, rising from inside the striking medieval battlements.

In the churchyard are two extremely interesting sculpted 9th-century High Crosses, the base of a third, and numerous early grave markers, including a 'hogback' grave-slab, which may be a Christian Viking memorial. The north and south crosses are richly ornamented with scripture panels. The principal scenes on the north cross are the Crucifixion and Adam and Eve. The south cross also has a Crucifixion and a hunting scene on the base. There is a pedestrian approach to the church from the main street, through a tree-lined avenue with monumental granite benches and neo-classical ironwork, laid out on axis with the Romanesque arch.

The Tower: The Round Tower is attached to the 19th-century church by an interconnecting passageway, which has an external entrance doorway facing west, and another which provides access to the north side of the nave. Towers are normally located to the north-west or south-west of the church, with the entrance facing diagonally towards the west door of the church. Castledermot's position on the north side of the church, with its door facing south, could indicate that it is among the earliest of the towers to be built. The arrangement of this plan can be found at S. Apollinare in Classe (7th century), where the freestanding medieval campanile occupies the identical position, slightly to the north of the sanctuary of the church.

Castledermot is built of undressed random rubble granite field-stones, well laid to the curve and batter, and in style resembles Maghera, Co. Down. The upper portion of the tower, which begins from about the base of the bell-floor windows, is evidently a reconstruction dating from the early 18th century, and may have been contemporary with the installation of the bell. The bell, dated 1735, still hangs in the bell-floor.

The entrance door, now enclosed in the connecting passage, is almost on the ground level, and for want of evidence to the contrary, must be considered the original. This also suggests that the tower is of an early date, roughly contemporary with Scattery, as does the narrowness of its diameter and general architectural features. The doorcase is lintelled and of large granite blocks; there is no basement.

A single ground-floor window, obviously a later insertion, probably dates from the 18th century, when the tower was adapted as a belfry to the church. It lacks an external lintel and is unlike the authentic windows of the drum. The two drum windows are small and lintelled. The sill-level of the bell-floor windows sit almost directly on top of the fourth-floor window, above which everything must be a late re-building because a change of character in the stonework is apparent.

Internally there are now five floors, but the walls are without setbacks or corbels. A damaged stone vault positioned half way up the first floor may represent an original floor level; it is similar to that at Tory.

On the bell-floor, above the four tall and round-headed bell-floor windows, the wall surface is projected proud of the plane below, supported on a course of corbels. The battlemented parapet also projects beyond the surface of the intermediate section of wall below. Unfortunately, there is no access to the roof parapet.

Castledermot is either a prototype Round Tower or, alternatively, an early and eccentric one. The absence of a basement and the eccentric door orientation distinguish it from other late towers.

The location of the original church for which the tower was built is not known. It is possible that it may have been situated further east, and the tower's orientation may be less unorthodox than its relationship to the present church suggests. No tower which is known to be of a late date has a ground-floor entrance.

Suggested date: 10th century.

Dimensions: height 20.12 metres; diameter at base 4.74 metres; height of door-sill 53cm.

Unique features: tallest door-opening; internal stone floor; extremely narrow tower.

Access: free access to site, tower closed, although internally it has floors and ladders.

35 Kilcullen, Co. Kildare

Old Kilcullen is 2 km south of Kilcullen village on the N9, Naas to Carlow road, 15 km south-west of Naas. The tower is in a graveyard on an elevated site overlooking the surrounding countryside, east of the main road. There are the remnants of three High Crosses and the remains of a 12th-century church with later alterations. The foundation of the ecclesiastical site is attributed to Patrick in the 5th century.

The Tower: Kilcullen is built of random, roughly squared slate, unevenly coursed; the courses of stones below sill-level are considerably larger than those higher up.

The round-headed doorcase is articulated in contrasting granite with inclined doorjambs: its low sill-height may be misleading as the external ground level has probably risen. Like Kilmacduagh, the doorhead is constructed of twin pairs of corbels, cut back on the soffit in order to create the appearance of an arch, with both corbels butting over the centre of the opening. This arrangement, a development of that at Scattery, is a very primitive, even if structurally sound, approach to arch construction. Only two towers have doorheads with this peculiar arrangement.

There is one small lintelled window in the drum and the straight-sided projection of the wall, facing west at the top, may represent the embrasure of another, although the masonry of the jamb looks late. Records from the 18th century show that Kilcullen, at that time, retained four top windows over which a cornice ran, indicating that it was a capless yet complete tower of reduced height. Assuming this to be a correct interpretation, Kilcullen (11 metres high to underside of the bell-floor lintels), with Tory (12.8 metres to three courses above the cornice), together with numerous towers which stand to similar heights, possibly represent a sub-species of half-size towers, similar in appearance to the present-day condition of Dromiskin which stands 15.24 metres to its apex. While this understanding may be a severe jolt to the conventional image of the tall and willowy Round Tower, it merely represents a further variation on the theme, as do engaged towers.

Suggested date: 11th century.

Dimensions: height 11 metres; diameter at base 4.62 metres; height of door-sill 1.8 metres.

Unique features: none.

Access: free access to site, no access to tower interior; signposted.

KILCULLEN

Recently (1998) the doorway of Kilcullen has been sealed by a metal grill. This move is indicative of the gradually decreasing number of towers to which access is possible.

36 Kildare, Co. Kildare

Kildare town is on the N7, Dublin to Portlaoise road. The tower is in the churchyard of St Brigid's Church of Ireland Cathedral off the market square. The 13th – 15th-century cathedral was a roofless ruin by the 19th century when it was extensively reconstructed by the architect George E. Street, who also restored Christ Church Cathedral in Dublin; much of the north side had disappeared, and only the south wall of the crossing tower remained standing.

There are some medieval tombs in the cathedral and in the churchyard is St Brigid's 'Fire House', possibly the ruins of an early oratory. An undecorated

KILDARE
Left: The tower, in the churchyard of Kildare Cathedral, dominates the town and can be see from a great distance across the plain of the Curragh. Variants on the battlemented top are to be seen at Castledermot and Kilkenny.
(See photo p. 32.)

Below: Remains of a tangential gable surmount the much damaged Romanesque doorway.

High Cross stands in the churchyard to the south-west of the cathedral. The ground plan of the churchyard boundary wall and that of the adjacent streets still reflect the circular plan of the early medieval bivallate ecclesiastical enclosure (**fig. 8a**). The monastery was founded by the 6th-century St Brigid, Ireland's principal female saint, after whom countless holy wells are named.

The Tower:

> *'From the time of Brigid a noble falcon was accustomed to frequent the place, and to perch on top of the tower of the church.'*
> Giraldus Cambrensis, *Topographia Hibernica*, 1188

This and another (see Ram's Island) oblique reference to the tower of Kildare, by the credulous Giraldus, are the only written sources, other than annalists' notations, to mention a Round Tower before the antiquarian interest of the 17th century. Kildare is one of the finest surviving towers, the second tallest, and has the good fortune to be fitted with floors and ladders. It stands 32.6 metres high, and is built of a variety of stones, owing either to the availability of individual quarries or possibly to economic considerations.

The bottom 3 metres of the tower (11 courses) are built of well-worked large granite ashlars, with a visible 19th-century repair of the courses below the doorway. Above the ashlars the masonry is much less finely finished, built of uncoursed random rubble limestone with occasional sandstone insertions. A further variation occurs at 10 metres above the granite, where there is a colour change to a lighter limestone. Some courses of sandstone occur in the drum, as well as individual stones.

The sandstone doorcase, which faces south-east in the direction of the cathedral and, therefore, towards the site of an earlier church, must have been among the finest of its day since it is not only a four-ordered Romanesque doorway, it is surmounted by an acutely angled tangential sandstone gable, similar to that on the church of Roscrea. Unfortunately, the doorcase has been badly mutilated and is now a sad remnant of its original form.

The four floors of the drum each have a single window which are, respectively, triangular-headed, two lintelled and a further triangular-headed. The bell-floor has five windows, above which a string course is surmounted by the high parapet, which has stepped Irish battlements surrounding a flat roof. The round-headed windows of the bell-floor resemble those in Swords, and are, with the uppermost section of the wall, a late medieval or possibly even later alteration to the tower.

Internally, there are six floors over basement, with all floors, other than the first-floor entrance level, supported on offsets.

Suggested date: 12th century.
Dimensions: height 32.6 metres; diameter at base 5.35 metres; height of door-sill 4.67 metres.
Unique features: decorated entrance door.
Access: open during the summer season.

OUGHTERARD
Left: Visibility was a significant, although not a primary, consideration in the placing of a Round Tower. Here at Oughterard the elevated site provided maximum visibility for the presence of the monastery.

TAGHADOE
Left: Other than the 19th-century parish church and the Round Tower, no other ecclesiastical remains stand on the site. (See photo p. 62.)

37 Oughterard, Co. Kildare

Oughterard is located north of the N7, Dublin to Kildare road, 4 km south-east of Sallins village and 5 km north-east of Naas. The topographical name of the site could hardly be more apt since, from its elevated site, it overlooks a vast sweep of countryside (*Uachtar Árd* – high upper place). Oughterard stands in a beautifully well-maintained graveyard, with a ruined late medieval barrel-vaulted chapel (*c.* 1400), with remains of domestic buildings and an accessible stairs turret, which leans precariously off the vertical. The foundation of the monastery, of which the tower is the only remnant, is usually attributed to a 6th-century St Brigid, who is contemporary with but distinct from the saint associated with Kildare.

The Tower: This tower is quite unusual in the randomness of its rubble stonework (possibly shale). The surface is well-dressed, yet the wall has a crazy-paving look about it. Above the doorway the wall surface is scarred by many stones missing from the surface, while at the top there appears to be a change of masonry with many small stones or spalls.

The articulated granite doorcase which faces east has significantly inclined jambs and is round-headed. The doorhead is tripartite, with the keystone and two voussoirs supported on three-stone jambs. The overall appearance of the doorcase is much more contained than those where the quoins of the doorjambs extend further into the body of the external wall.

The single surviving second-floor window is round-headed, with an internal monolithic arch. Three floor-offsets are visible in the interior.

Suggested date: 11th century.

Dimensions: height 9.5 metres; diameter at base 4.58 metres; height of door-sill 2.65 metres.

Unique features: none.

Access: to site, no internal floors or ladders; a solid steel door blocks the entrance.

38 Taghadoe, Co. Kildare

Taghadoe lies east of the R407, 8 km south-west of Maynooth. The tower stands elevated above the bend in the road, in the churchyard of an abandoned, roofless Church of Ireland parish church (1821). The gaunt Tudor-Gothic church ruin creates a somewhat surreal presence, of which the tower forms part of the ensemble. The manner in which the public road circles the churchyard is strongly suggestive of the former location of a circular monastic enclosure. The origins of the monastery, attributed to St Tua, are obscure.

The Tower: Taghadoe is the only surviving remnant of another lost ecclesiastical settlement. The masonry is of limestone, evenly coursed, and this must have been a very fine tower when complete. There is a sharpness and clarity about the stonework, which is in marked contrast to towers where the coursing is less prominent and regular, or the masonry of uncoursed random work.

The entrance, facing south-east, has a finely cut granite doorcase, round-headed and with a clearly defined external architrave which runs around the

AGHAVILLER

Left: Below the conventional base offset can be seen the highly unusual rectangular foundation pad. The upper door is the original one. (See photo p. 75.)

Below: The voussoirs of the door arch span the wall thickness. This internal view shows the quality of masonry and attention to detail of which the master masons who built the towers were capa-

Left: The remains of a 12th-century church and a late medieval residential building stand in the foreground of the Round Tower.

arched, slightly inclined left-hand jamb and sill; the right-hand jamb is of limestone and does not carry the moulding. The arch is tripartite with a prominent keystone. On the stone directly above the keystone there is a protruding boss which may be a much-weathered head, similar to those which flank the entrance at Monasterboice.

There are three windows in the drum; all are small and narrow, lintelled with inclined jambs of dressed granite. That on the third floor is directly above the entrance. Slightly below the top of the tower is a row of what appear to be putlock holes which penetrate through the wall. This may be a surviving example of an attached scaffolding system, which rose with each level of stonework as the tower was completed.

Suggested date: 11th – 12th century.

Dimensions: height 19.8 metres; diameter at base 4.96 metres; height of doorsill 3.56 metres.

Unique features: rudimentary head on keystone.

Access: free access to site, no floors or ladders in tower.

THE KILREE GROUP (39 & 42)

The Round Towers at Aghaviller and Kilree are distinguished by the use of a rectangular stone pad-foundation which are visible at both sites. They are presumably the work of the same master-mason or local building tradition and importantly represent in microcosm the stylistic advance from square-shouldered to round-shouldered treatment of the upper contours of the doorhead, an important step toward acceptance of the true arch.

39 Aghaviller, Co. Kilkenny   Aghaviller is 2 km east of Killmaganny village on the R697, 20 km south of Kilkenny. This site, an old graveyard with a medieval church and tower-house, has been encroached upon by modern afforestation and the tower backs on to the trees of the plantation. There are foundations of a 12th-century church, with a complete chancel arch and *c.* 15th-century residential accommodation above it. A mural staircase leads to the upper chamber which overlooks the tower. The identity of the founder of Aghaviller, or anything else about the monastery, is unknown.

The Tower: Aghaviller is the squat remains of a good quality Round Tower. At the base of the wall there is a single offset, founded on a broad rectangular pad-foundation of large stones, a detail also found at the nearby Kilree. The fine sandstone ashlar masonry is unusual in the manner in which the height of the courses and the size of the stones varies, with large courses both at the base and above the door, and smaller courses in between.

The door-opening is round-headed, beautifully proportioned and cut with steeply inclined jambs. It is composed of four-stone acutely inclined jambs, monolithic sill and tripartite true arch with a defined keystone which rises above the extrados; the stones of the doorhead span the depth of the wall. An architrave-like band is visible on the jambs and partially on the arch. A late doorway has been introduced at ground level. This has a horizontal lintel and

FERTAGH

Above: Even without its conical cap Fertagh presides over the surrounding landscape with a dominant presence. The extraordinary verticality and visibility of the Round Towers has in many cases been negated by collapsed upper portions and encroachment. Where an almost intact tower stands unencumbered by buildings or vegetation, some suggestion of their original power can still be felt.

Left: A typical drum window. The windows were generally placed just above the internal floor level.

Far left: It has been the fate of a number of towers to have their original doors removed.

leads directly into the interior of the tower. The nearby church, which retains an altar, was used as a parish church to which the tower acted as belfry; the lower doorway must date from this period. There is a single small triangular-headed window in the topmost surviving courses of the tower.

Suggested date: 11th century.

Dimensions: height 9.6 metres; diameter at base 4.92 metres; height of door-sill 3.98 metres.

Unique features: rectangular foundations.

Access: free access to site and tower interior.

40 Fertagh, Co. Kilkenny

Fertagh is 4 km north of Johnstown and west of the N1, Cashel to Portlaoise road. It is signposted as Grangefertagh. The tower stands in open farmland and can be seen from a considerable distance, demonstrating the high visibility of the complete towers in their original context. It is one of the tallest and slimmest towers, lacking only its cap. With the cap complete it would have been the tallest Round Tower known. The tower stands in a churchyard with the remains of a late medieval church (in use until the late 18th century), which has been barbarically converted into a handball-alley, its features cemented over! An adjoining roofless late medieval chapel has a damaged 16th-century table-tomb of the Mac Gillapatricks, with a recumbent double effigy. It was carved by one of the well-known O'Tunney family of master masons, whose work can also be seen at Kilcooley Abbey, near Urlingford, and in St Canice's Cathedral, Kilkenny.

During the 19th century, remnants of the vanished medieval buildings turned up elsewhere in the locality; the west door and east window of the Mac Gillapatricks' Chapel were installed in Johnstown village in the Church of Ireland parish church, while in the Catholic church are the baptismal font and a crucifixion bas-relief panel. The monastery was founded in the 6th century by St Ciarán of Seir.

The Tower: This is an exceptionally fine tower and it is regrettable that there is no access to its interior because the view from the top would be of a vast sweep of unrestricted countryside. It is built of evenly coursed squared limestone blocks and stands 31 metres high without its cap; with the cap complete it could have stood 35 metres high, dominating the small church buildings. The tower profile is excellent.

In the position of the doorway, a large jagged opening faces north-east and is now supported by a modern replacement, recessed from the tower face. It has a shallow arch of small voussoirs which are clearly a late intrusion; they resemble the similar 19th-century repair at Maghera. This opening is blocked with a stone wall, preventing any inspection of the interior. The round-headed door-case was removed, allegedly by a local farmer before 1800, because he believed that the stones had magical fire resistant properties! The five windows in the drum are, in ascending order, triangular-headed, two lintelled, and two triangular-headed. The bell-floor windows which face the cardinal points are tall

KILKENNY

Above: Velvet Lane leads up a steep flight of steps beneath the arch, from Irishtown to the cathedral. The house directly in front of the tower, like many in the area, is late medieval.

Left: The doorway of Kilkenny faces away from the Cathedral, suggesting that the church for which the tower was built lay in the immediate foreground. No evidence survives of the earlier building.

Left: No original tower furnishings have survived, either floors or ladders. Restorations have been based on an understanding of what probably existed – timber floors supported on the offsets of the internal walls, with connecting ladders.

and triangular-headed. A portion of the cornice survives, above which are a number of courses of the cone. High up on the east side of the tower are what appear to be putlock holes.

Suggested date: 11th century. (Annals reference for 1156.)

Dimensions: height 31 metres; diameter of base 4.77 metres; height of door-sill 3.3 metres.

Unique features: extreme height; putlock holes.

Access: free access to site; interior sealed.

41 Kilkenny, Co. Kilkenny   Kilkenny is 22 km south-east of the N8, Portlaoise to Cashel road, at the junction of the N10 and N77. The Round Tower, one of the finest in the country, stands close to the south transept of St Canice's Church of Ireland Cathedral, in Irishtown, on the north-west side of a settlement of considerable historic and architectural importance. Medieval remains in the town include Kilkenny Castle, the Black Abbey, St Mary's Church and the cathedral to which the tower acts as a belfry. St Canice's is the second largest medieval church in Ireland, after St Patrick's in Dublin, and contains a unique collection of early and late medieval monumental tombs, including a number of exceptionally fine recumbent table-tombs. The monastery was founded by St Canice in the 6th century.

The Tower: Kilkenny is one of the best-known Round Towers in the country, and its siting on high ground above the Nore valley, with its backdrop of the medieval cathedral, rivals Cashel, which this site must have resembled before the encroachment of the modern town. There is a noticeable inclination off the vertical which is best not considered when climbing the tower or venturing out onto its small parapet. Kilkenny stands 30.2 metres high without its conical cap, and must have been among the tallest of the towers when complete. The masonry, which shows little evidence of tooling, is mainly limestone with erratic intrusions, beautifully cut to curve and batter, and the quality of the profile is excellent. There are two offsets at the base.

The doorcase faces south-east, away from the location of the cathedral, and has inclined, four-stone jambs and an indeterminate doorhead, composed of a round tripartite arch with poorly defined extrados. It has no external decoration. The treatment of the arch displays a feature seen also in other towers (Dysert Oenghusa, Kells, Meelick), where the inner and outer circumference of the arch do not correspond, and the horizontal courses above the arch appear to impinge upon it. This load-bearing lintel, which sits directly above the arch spreads the downward pressure of the superstructure.

The tower's small internal floor areas leave little room for anything more than the access ladders. Numerous corbels project from the internal wall but their purpose is unclear. Rectangular and triangular putlock holes are visible on a number of internal levels.

There are four windows in the drum, all lintelled and rotating clockwise. The bell-floor has six tall, well-formed lintelled windows, their jambs dressed

KILREE

Above: In the foreground of the Round Tower stands an early example of the great High Crosses which at the peak of their development led to the growth of an important school of medieval figure sculpture. The Kilree example is a stone version of a timber prototype, the round bosses representing the rivets necessary to hold together a timber structure. The tower doorway faces towards a slightly earlier church with antae, and a later medieval chancel.

Left: The mists of the Suir Valley sweep around the tower of Kilree and the ivy-covered trees of the churchyard.

in a contrasting stone. The roof-parapet, now enclosed by an unsightly cage, conceals a flat roof surrounded by a precarious low wall from which there are magnificent views over the town and Nore valley. The bell-floor windows may have been reconstructed during the late medieval period, although they appear integral, as does the external masonry, although the parapet is later. It is certainly possible that towers like Kilkenny and Kildare were adapted within the period of their construction to a more effective use as lookouts, without a conical cap and with a more generous supply of windows.

Suggested date: 11th century.

Dimensions: height 30.2 metres; diameter at base 4.5 metres; height of door-sill 2.78 metres.

Unique features: none.

Access: the tower has floors and ladders and is open to the public daily.

42 Kilree, Co. Kilkenny Kilree is west of the N10, Kilkenny to Waterford road, 15 km south of Kilkenny, and 4 km from Kells village on the R697. This is a beautifully sited Round Tower, perched on the circular boundary wall of an old churchyard which probably represents the position of the inner rampart of the monastic enclosure. A 9th-century sandstone High Cross with geometric and figurative ornament in an adjoining field, west of the tower, may indicate that this was a bivallate complex. Inside the churchyard, which is shrouded by mature trees, is a 10th- to 11th-century church with antae, with a later medieval extension of the chancel, reached through a broad chancel-arch. The churchyard is still in use for burials and therefore in danger of abuse by present-day insensitive burial practices. The site is reached through a field gate and across a field.

The Tower: Kilree is a fine, well-preserved tower, lacking its cap, and with evidence of rebuilding of the bell-floor level. From the base of the wall there are two offsets, which are clearly visible on the portion of the wall which stands in the field outside the churchyard. These offsets stand on a monolithic rectangular pad-foundation which, so far, has only been confirmed elsewhere at Aghaviller, a few kilometres to the south-east. This is a significant technical detail, distinct from other towers and identifies Aghaviller and Kilree as belonging to the 'Kilree Group'.

The tower is built of irregularly coursed limestone with sandstone dressings on the well articulated doorcase, which faces south towards the door of the church with antae. The opening is round-headed, the arch being cut from the soffit of a monolithic lintel which is now cracked. An architrave-like band runs around the outside of the entrance. The treatment of the doorhead is more rudimentary than that at Aghaviller, and assuming they are the work of the same hand, this is probably the earlier building.

The three drum windows are articulated in sandstone; the first floor is triangular-headed, the remainder lintelled. The four rectangular bell-floor windows face the cardinal points. Above them are what appear to be stone waterspouts to drain the now-vanished roof, and un-stepped battlements, which may

TULLAHERIN

Above: Urgent conservation is required here, in order to stabilise the condition of the damaged entrance, and the cracking which has developed from it.

Left: The architectural phasing of Tullaherin can be observed in the change in window style between the rectangular lintelled version in the drum and the arrow-slit mullioned type in the bell floor. There is also a visible change in masonry style and an increase on the conventional four axially placed windows.

belong to the same period of alterations, possibly when the nearby church was used for worship during recent centuries.

Suggested date: 11th century.

Dimensions: height 26.75 metres; diameter at base 4.86 metres; height of door-sill 1.64 metres.

Unique features: pad-foundation.

Access: free access to site and tower; no floors or ladders; signposted on the public road.

43 Tullaherin, Co. Kilkenny   Tullaherin is east of Dungarvan on the N9, 12 km south-east of Kilkenny. The tower stands on the edge of a graveyard, close to the south-west corner of a ruined medieval nave-and-chancel parish church. The eastern portion of the nave with antae is probably late 10th century, and is the church for which the tower was built. The remainder of the enlarged church is in a number of phases dating from the 12th century to the 17th century. A damaged ogham stone has recently been placed by the south wall, close to the base of the tower. This is another monastery of obscure origin, but its foundation is attributed to St Ciarán of Seir. In the surrounding fields are extensive late medieval earthworks. The statue of the Virgin which dominates the graveyard is a French 19th-century cast iron figure, painted to resemble a plaster image.

The Tower: The tower, which lacks its cap, stands 22.5 metres high, the top 3 metres of which are a second phase of masonry. The sandstone masonry of the tower is well coursed and dressed. The doorcase is entirely missing, leaving a jagged hole in the wall, now blocked by an unsightly rectangular pillar which impedes investigation of the interior. Above the opening there is an extensive and ominous fissure running up the tower wall, where the structure has been destabilised by the removal of the doorcase, while below the doorway there is a poorly repaired breach in the wall. The opening faces north-east and is 3.7 metres above ground.

The four windows in the drum, rotating clockwise, are small and lintelled. The bell-floor windows are likewise rectangular but taller, with finely dressed and chamfered jambs and lintels in cut stone, which resemble the possibly 13th-century windows in the east end of the chancel; above the bell-floor windows are the remains of a cornice. The annals record damage to the tower by lightning in 1121, when a falling stone killed a student in the church. Most probably it was after this date that the bell-floor was rebuilt on the same principle as Clonmacnoise I, with eight windows, of which here only four remain. All towers which exhibit late medieval alterations have a greater number of windows in the later work.

Suggested date: 11th century. (Annals reference for 1121.)

Dimensions: height 22.5 metres; diameter at base 4.92 metres; height of door-sill 3.7 metres.

Unique features: none.

Access: free access to site, no floors or ladders in tower; signposted.

TIMAHOE

Left: All the significant features of Timahoe can be seen here; triple base offsets, Romanesque decorated entrance door and Treasury window standing proud of the wall surface, tall and triangular-headed bell-floor windows with steeply inclined jambs. Timahoe is the most architecturally conscious of the late towers. (See photos pp. 40, 75, and drawings pp. 52, 69.)

Below left: Seen from below, the entrance door has a wrap-around look, rather than one of penetration.

Below: As in the 12th-century Romanesque churches with decorated west doorways, the same details have been grafted on to a Round Tower without the result achieving the same degree of appropriateness. The thickness of the wall encloses two separate doorcases, one behind the other, in a rather half-hearted attempt to accommodate the doortype to an exceptional wall thickness.

44 Timahoe, Co. Laois   Timahoe village is east of the N8 on the R462, 12 km south of Portlaoise. The unique tower stands in a beautiful location on the banks of a small stream, shaded by fine trees and on the edge of the village green. All that remains of the monastery is enclosed in the churchyard of the former Church of Ireland parish church, which now houses the local library. The 15th-century church, which obliterated all evidence of an earlier Romanesque one, was fortified as a castle during the 17th century, but little of either remain beyond a cannibalised east arch and tower wall. The 12th-century Round Tower is all that survives of a monastery originally founded by St Mochua in the 7th century.

The Tower: Timahoe is another leaning tower, constructed of large sandstone ashlars for the first 3 metres, with smaller, different coloured limestone above this line, to a point halfway up the drum where there is a further change of stone to limestone of a darker colour. What looks like polychrome banding is created by the introduction of courses of limestone into the base courses of sandstone below the doorway. These discrepancies would not be visible if the tower was externally rendered.

It is both a complete Round Tower, and one of great importance, on account of the Romanesque orders of the doorcase. This is the most elaborately decorated of all the towers and, although the blending of a door-form intended for rectangular structures and flat wall surfaces to an elevated situation on the curve of a Round Tower is quite unsuccessful, if not actually ridiculous – there is really no attempt at achieving an integrated solution, the combination is nonetheless fascinating. However unsatisfactory it may be to position an architectural feature, designed to embellish a flat surface at ground level, up in the air and inserted in a curved structure, the idea finds a precedent (although not on a curved surface) at the Rhine Valley Benedictine Abbey church of Maria-Laach (*c.* 1156), where the transepts have similarly designed 'floating doorways'.

Timahoe is a point of particular significance in the development of the Irish Round Tower, and like all the structures which were built in the 12th century, a source of speculation as to the direction which indigenous style might have taken had the arrival of the Continental monastic orders (Mellifont, consecrated in 1147) and the Norman invasion of 1169 not imported a more coherent and vigorous architectural aesthetic, one which brought an end to the building of these towers.

Three concentric offsets are clearly visible at the base and their graduation contributes to the elegance of the tower. The masonry, which is coursed, has larger stones in the courses below the door-sill. The diameter at base (5.58 metres) is among the widest of the towers, narrower only than Kilmacduagh (5.68 metres).

The east-facing doorcase, which stands proud of the wall surface of the tower, displays a noticeable batter, and is divided into two separate doorcases. The outside one is composed of flanked double columns with bases and capitals and a well constructed arch. Inside this the second order has a strong chevron moulding, and a second pair of columns and caps. The decoration of the inner doorcase is less elaborate. The detailing of the carving of the right-hand outer jamb of the doorcase is inconsistent, but it is hard to explain the anomaly. Whereas the paired heads of the capitals are matching, and the base on the front left has a corresponding head and spool, the spool matching those on the bases of the inner two orders, the front right hand base has the spool and head reversed. It looks as though the doorcase, which can hardly have been carved in situ, but was doubtless prepared at ground level, was incorrectly assembled. Within the doorcase a flight of five steps ascends to the interior. The entrance floor was supported by a ring of corbels, unlike the more conventional offset for the other floors.

The three windows of the drum are triangular-headed, round-headed and lintelled respectively. The badly weathered triangular-headed window on the second floor, like the doorcase, has a window frame which projects beyond the surface of the wall, an innovation not repeated on the higher levels, or seen on any other tower. The projecting gable moulding is supported on pilasters with human-head capitals and spool bases, within which is a round-headed window. In H. S. Crawford's reconstruction drawing (1923), its original form was so close in general appearance to the window design of the 9th-century Torhalle from the destroyed Carolingian monastery of Lorsch (125 km south of Maria-Laach), that they might as well have been from the same pattern-book. The Lorsch window details are skeuomorphic (stonework derived from carpentry designs), like similar features from Anglo-Saxon Britain, and show a common ancestry in timber construction for building details across Europe. The principal difference between the Timahoe window and those at Lorsch is that the Timahoe capitals are in the Irish manner of human heads, whereas the Lorsch capitals are classical in concept.

The bell-floor level has four tall triangular-headed windows. The cornice and cap, which were restored in the late 19th century, are well-proportioned. A photograph of Timahoe in Dunraven, *c.* 1870, interestingly shows the top of the tower in a dilapidated state, with a considerable portion of the cap missing. It can be assumed that the cap was restored after this date.

The projecting doorcase and window highlight the issue of profile, and its importance to the success of Round Towers as an architectural type. At Timahoe the unobstructed line of the profile has been broken; this clearly is not a successful innovation, and suggests a growing confusion concerning the manner in which towers might develop. In point of fact, the Round Tower as an architectural form expired rather than taking an imaginative leap into the future, although it can be claimed that liturgically the crossing towers of late medieval abbeys and friaries are their ecclesiastical equivalents, despite Cistercian proscriptions against the ostentation of towers.

Suggested date: 12th century.

Dimensions: height 29.26 metres; diameter at base 5.58 metres; height of door-sill 4.3 metres.

Unique features: decorated Romanesque doorcase and window; exceptionally wide base.

Access: to the churchyard, no floors or ladders.

45 Ardpatrick, Co. Limerick

The site is on a hill east of Ardpatrick village, on the R512, Kilmallock to Fermoy road, 8 km south of Kilmallock, and reached by a track which rises steeply from the village to reach the magnificently sited remains. The Ballyhoura Mountains provide a backdrop to the south, and the tower would have been visible from the Limerick plains to the north. All that now remains of the original monastery, beyond the dedication of the graveyard, is an undecorated church with antae, some subsidiary buildings, and the base of a destroyed Round Tower, standing outside the graveyard wall to the north-west, and surrounded by extensive rectangular earthworks.

The paucity of the tower remains are more than compensated for by the interest and drama of the site. On the sides of the hill are earthworks, with the remains of an exceptionally large ditch and bank enclosure surrounding the monastic site at the top. A fine stone wall, some of the stones of which look suspiciously as if they might have been cannibalised from the early buildings, encloses the older portion of the graveyard. The establishment of the monastery is attributed to St Patrick.

ARDPATRICK
Ardpatrick is one of many towers on the verge of disappearing altogether. It crowns a significant archaeological site.

The Tower: Ardpatrick is among the slightest of tower remains. Nine courses stand on the north, dropping away to ground level on the southern side; the entire circumference is visible. Much masonry debris has accumulated around the base of the tower. The masonry, of well-cut horizontal courses with vertical joints, suggests a late tower of fine quality, of which both external and internal surfaces are extant. Lime mortar is visible in the exposed joints. When fully standing, the tower would have dominated the landscape, even from a great distance and is among the finest sited of all towers.

No architectural features survive, nor is a base offset visible, although this may be concealed by the accumulated debris around the base.
Suggested date: 11th – 12th century.
Dimensions: height 3 metres; diameter at base 5.3 metres.
Unique features: none.
Access: free access to site.

46 Dysert Oenghusa, Co. Limerick

Dysert Oenghusa lies west of the N20, Limerick to Ráth Luirc/Charleville road, 3 km west of Croom village. Dysert stands in open farmland at the north-east corner of a medieval church which is 15th century, with evidence of an earlier building on the same site. The foundation is attributed to the mid-8th century Oenghus the Culdee (d. 815), founder of the *Céli Dé* ecclesiastical reform movement, which sought to return the monastic church-members to anchorite values of poverty and self-denial, and which was instrumental in promoting the abundant religious and secular manuscript literature of the 9th century. The monasteries of Finglas and Tallaght in Co. Dublin were its principal centres. The site is approached by a long farm-track from the main road, and its surroundings, despite being in the grounds of a substantial farm, are rather bleak. If the tower was conventionally oriented towards the west door of an earlier church, this was probably located further east.

DYSERT OENGHUSA

Above: The central voussoirs of this handsome decorated doorway are a repair and lack the original pellet and double moulding.

Left: The doorway of Dysert faces away from the nearby late medieval church towards the position of a now-vanished early church. Stonework of sharply contrasting colours distinguishes this tower as one which was probably of exceptional beauty when newly built.

Left: The tower stands in a treeless landscape on the edge of an extensive modern farm complex. The angle of batter is more extreme than is usual.

The Tower: Dysert is a well-built tower, four stories high over the basement, with its bell-floor and cap missing. It is constructed of coursed but uneven masonry of irregular stones, with considerably larger stones in the lower courses. The masonry is of limestone, with brightly contrasting red sandstone dressing for the doorcase and windows, an arrangement which must have been extremely impressive when the stonework was freshly cut. Heavy pointing conceals most of the joints, except at the top of the tower.

There is a single offset, founded on bedrock visible below the thin soil cover of the site. For what must be a late tower, as well as an architecturally conscious one – the decorated doorcase and articulated door and windows – Dysert has a surprisingly uneven profile. There is a large rectangular breach in the base of the tower to the west but this does not penetrate through the wall.

The round arch of the east-facing doorcase has seven voussoirs, the central four of which represent an inaccurate repair. This doorcase belongs to the category of those having true arches but with diminished extrados. The original arch-stones and vertical jambs are decorated externally by traces of a double-band architrival moulding with a repeating pattern of pellets.

The three windows are in concentric ascending order, triangular-headed, round-headed and lintelled, and have clearly articulated jambs.

Suggested date: 12th century.

Dimensions: height 20.65 metres; diameter at base 5.28 metres; height of door-sill 4.6 metres.

Unique features: decorated doorcase.

Access: to site but not to tower; inaccessible floors and ladders; signposted.

47 Kilmallock, Co. Limerick   Kilmallock town, which has considerable remains of its civil and religious medieval architecture, is on the R515, Tipperary to Ráth Luirc/Charleville road, 10 km east of Ráth Luirc/Charleville. Gabriel Beranger's late 18th-century watercolour of the town, with its walls and abundance of still-standing medieval towers, suggests the complexity of the Tuscan hill-town of San Gimignano. Less stands today, yet enough to give a clear picture of the importance and wealth of the town. Of the buildings visible in Beranger's picture, the 13th-century collegiate church of SS Peter and Paul is substantially intact and has incorporated into its outer walls the remnant of a Round Tower. This indicates the early presence of a monastery on the site, presumably founded by the 7th-century St Mo-cheallóg, who is commemorated in the naming of the town.

The Tower: As a Round Tower, Kilmallock is only significant for what its presence records, rather than for what remains. Its identity is so completely subsumed into the fabric of the later buildings that, without examples from elsewhere, it would probably be passed without comment. Only the bottom dozen courses can be said to represent the masonry of the tower; what stands above it is late medieval, although it is possible that some of the upper masonry conceals the core of the earlier wall. Damaged towers of which as little survive, but which have not been encroached upon, such as Killinaboy, St Mullins and

KILMALLOCK

Above: The collegiate church of SS Peter and Paul is in the bottom left of the picture, with the Dominican Priory on its right. The tower of the Collegiate church is built on the remains of a Round Tower. (Photo 1980)

Left: The Round Tower projects from the surrounding wall of the 13th-century church, and is original to below the level of the rectangular putlock holes.

Rathmichael, are far more credible as towers than this genuine example.

The masonry of the tower's superstructure, like the adjacent walls of the church, has putlock holes (absent in the original portion of the Round Tower), and the general aspect of the rebuilding, in a number of periods, is extremely dramatic in its profile and roofline.

Date: not known.

Dimensions: height 3 metres; diameter at base 5.2 metres.

Unique features: none.

Access: free access to the inside and outside of the site.

48 Dromiskin, Co. Louth

Dromiskin village is east of the N1 Castlebellingham to Dundalk road, 10 km south-west of Dundalk. The Round Tower is in the Church of Ireland church-yard at the centre of the village. The roofless Gothic Revival parish church dates from 1821; the tower was restored as its belfry in 1879. In the church-yard is a reconstructed High Cross and a 13th-century roofless medieval church, with a fine 15th-century, two-light east window in the only surviving gable. The foundation of the monastery is attributed to St Patrick.

The Tower: Dromiskin is the shortest Round Tower to have a cap, even if this is a late restoration. What remains of the original structure is the lower two-thirds of the drum. The masonry of Dromiskin is composed of unusually small random rubble, which resembles more closely an Anglo-Saxon poured-flint lime mortar and rubble wall than the stonework of an Irish tower.

The doorcase is the most interesting and, in fact, a unique feature of the tower. The door opening is recessed and arched with a true arch of five unequal voussoirs, without a keystone. This arch rests on imposts which are carried through the depth of the wall. Outside the inner arch, and flush with the surface of the tower wall, is a Romanesque doorcase with positions for two flanking freestanding colonettes, with capitals and bases integrated into the wall. Both colonettes are missing, as is the integrated base of the right-hand column which is, instead, composed of a number of stones; the decoration on the right-hand cap is the better preserved. Flanking the doorcase at impost level are a pair of projecting bosses which appear to be much-weathered heads. Dromiskin's doorcase, while not as elaborate as Timahoe, is architecturally both more simple and more sophisticated, and displays none of the manner-isms of the indigenous Romanesque style. Its integration into the form of the tower suggests masons with a better sense of harmony in those parts of the building. The details of this doorcase are very similar to the single surviving first-floor blind arcade arch on the external south face of Cormac's Chapel (1127-34), which the tower presumably post-dates. Dromiskin displays very slight evidence of batter, although its broad base would have allowed for a tower of considerable height. It has been suggested that the doorcase is a later insertion, but this seems without basis.

A single second-floor window in the drum dates from the original structure; this opening is quite small and triangular-headed. Directly above it are four

DROMISKIN

Above: The distinctive doorcase is missing a pair of columns which flanked the opening.

Left: The appearance of Dromiskin is misleading as a half-sized complete tower. Its ugly cap is a late restoration, as are the bell-floor windows. An original small triangular-headed window can be seen below the sill level of the rectangular window.

FAUGHART

Left: This disturbed ring of stones appears to represent original Round Tower curved ashlars, prepared for the base offset of the building.

large rectangular windows, facing the cardinal points. The bell-floor windows, cornice with putlock holes and cap are stylistically quite different, with cruder detailing than those on an authentic tower and must, considering the awkward window relationship, date from some period later than the body of the tower.
Suggested date: 12th century.
Dimensions: height 15.24 metres; diameter at base 5.22 metres; height of door-sill 3.7 m metres.
Unique features: Romanesque doorcase; shortest tower with cap.
Access: no access to tower; no stairs or floors.

49 Faughart, Co. Louth

The site is 2 km north of Dundalk, off the N11. Faughart is traditionally regarded as St Brigid's birthplace. The remains of a monastery, the foundation of which is attributed to the 6th-century St Monenna, consist of a small medieval church in a graveyard in an elevated position overlooking Dundalk bay. Edward Bruce was killed in a battle here in 1318, and his burial-place in the churchyard is marked by a large slab.

The Tower: Faughart is among the slightest of remains, and its identity as a Round Tower is possible rather than proven. The evidence consists of a single course of large stones forming a circle, consistent with the base course of a substantial tower, and located to the north-west of the church. The large dimensions of the individual stones and the fact that they are worked to the curve make them plausible as representing those of a Round Tower, although they are probably disturbed rather than in situ. One of the stones, to the west of the circle, appears to be a fragment of a stepped offset stone (similar to that at Balla) while other sections of the circumference seem to be inverted fragments of the offset course. It can be assumed that a tower was at least begun on this site, as there is no reason to suppose that they were brought to Faughart from another site.

The interior of the circle of stones is covered by an earthen mound on which is positioned the base of a high cross.
Date: not known.
Dimensions: diameter at base 5.75 metres; height 50cm.
Unique features: none.
Access: free access to site.

50 Monasterboice, Co. Louth

Monasterboice is an ecclesiastical complex of great interest, found west of the N1/M1, 8 km north of Drogheda. The site is surrounded by the rich and open farmland of County Louth, where the tower stands on the perimeter of a large walled graveyard enclosed by mature trees. Also in the graveyard are medieval church ruins and an early sundial.

Monasterboice and Kells, both with well-preserved Round Towers, have between them the most important collections of High Crosses. In Monasterboice are two of the finest surviving sculptured 9th-century crosses,

MONASTERBOICE

Above: The relationship of tower to landscape is seen here at harvest time, with the tower asserting its presence over the treeline. The site is significant for its sculpted High Crosses.

Far left: Between roofless churches a High Cross with bas-relief scripture panels stands at the base of the topless tower. Architectural treatment is of a high order on this tower, with distinctive door and window details. (See photo p. 63.)

Left: Monasterboice's doorway represents a transitional phase between earlier lintelled openings and later true round arches. The articulated doorcase is capped by a lintel into which a rudimentary soffit arch has been cut. The opening is surrounded by a broad architraval band.

as well as the remains of a third, the North Cross. The complete crosses are the Tall Cross and Muiredach's Cross. The latter carries the inscription, 'OR DO MUIREDACH LASNDERNAD ... RO' – 'A prayer for Muiredach who had [the cross] erected'. Unfortunately, in the annals for this period, there is more than one Muiredach mentioned, so his identity has not been established. St Buite, of whom little is known, founded the monastery in the 6th century.

The Tower: Monasterboice is a tall and exceptionally elegant Round Tower, missing its bell-floor windows and cap. The line of its wall, constructed of small slate slabs and spalls, is perfect, although the batter is not particularly pronounced.

The articulated sandstone doorway faces east towards the position of the medieval churches. Externally it is decorated by an indistinct double band which runs around the jambs and lintel, with what appear to be gaps, one directly above the door and another on the left-hand jamb, two courses below the lintel; the moulding is without breaks on the right-hand side. This door-head is essentially a lintelled opening, cut in the soffit to appear as an arch, while the jambs are clearly defined in quoins.

There are four windows in the drum, that of the second floor is triangular-headed and positioned directly above the entrance. For its small size, this is one of the stylistically most distinguished tower windows, beautifully constructed of cut stones which contrast with the rougher texture of the wall. Curiously for such a well-designed window, it lacks a sill. The next three floors have lintelled openings.

The top of the tower is uneven, with the jamb of one of the bell-floor windows still standing.

Suggested date: 10th – 11th century. (Annals reference for 1097.)

Dimensions: height 28.5 metres; diameter at base 4.98 metres; height of door-sill 1.84 metres.

Unique features: none.

Access: Monasterboice is provided with floors and ladders; there is no public access.

51 Aghagower, Co. Mayo   Aghagower village is on the N59, Westport to Clifden road, 5 km south-east of Westport. The tower is in a graveyard at the centre of the village which also has a ruined 12th – 15th century church with a fine east window, set against a distant backdrop of Croagh Patrick. The 7th-century St Senach is the reputed founder of the monastery.

The Tower: This is a much damaged and repaired tower, of coursed masonry with spalls. It has undergone a major and unskilful restoration in the late 1960s, when a large breach in the northern side, which exposed the interior almost halfway down the entire height of the tower, was built up. The line of the repair is quite visible on the exterior wall. Internally, there are no floor offsets, their place being taken by projecting corbels for the floor-support. There

AGHAGOWER

Above: Detailing of tower interiors is as varied as that of their exteriors. Here the floor support is provided by rows of projecting corbels. (See photo p. 86.)

Left: The extensive repair can be seen to the left above the late doorway, where the darker stonework represents original work.

are four floor-levels in the surviving portion of the drum.

The original doorway (with evidence of masonry sagging above the door-way), has a tripartite round-headed arch and slightly inclined three-stone jambs. The entire doorcase displays extensive evidence of fire-damage, as though the opening had been filled with inflammable material such as wood or straw. This is conclusive evidence of the vulnerable nature of Round Towers as places of security and refuge; they were not very effective as either.

A later lintelled doorway, facing north-west, was inserted at the base of the tower which gives access to the interior. There are three lintelled windows in the drum.

Suggested date: 11th century.

Dimensions: height 15.85 metres; diameter at base 5 metres; height of door-sill 2.18 metres.

Unique features: none.

Access: free access to interior of tower through late door; no floors or ladders.

52 Balla, Co. Mayo   Balla village is on the N50, Claremorris to Castlebar road, 12 km south-east of Castlebar. The tower is in the graveyard at the centre of the village, overlooking the square and backing onto the main street. This is a truncated tower, stand-ing only 10 metres high, with two doorways, one on the ground level and another higher up. The buildings of the town are encroaching upon the tower; the graveyard is totally neglected.

The Tower: Balla is a rogue tower: the prominent lintelled doorway, which suggests that it is an early example, was altered during construction to give an appearance different from the original builder's intention. The remains are those of a formerly fine Round Tower, well constructed in sandstone of coursed masonry, with larger stones towards the top of the surviving portion of the tower; there is little evidence of batter. The masonry indicates that, like Drumlane, Kildare and other towers, it was built in several phases.

Until the 1800s, Balla stood to around 15 metres and it continued in use, at least intermittently, into modern times; a bell was installed during the 1830s. Local folklore has ascribed fanciful explanations to the present-day condition of many incomplete Round Towers. There is no reason to suppose that this tower did not originally stand to its full height of approximately 30 metres.

There is a single offset visible which, unusually, has a moulding on its upper surface. In the courses immediately above the offset, what may be the remains of two bullaun stones are in secondary use. Above the offset, a round-arched entrance door leads directly into the interior of the tower, which has a paved floor. The lower door is certainly a late insertion, possibly 16th century, the inner lintel of which is a fairly indistinct, early medieval cross slab, also in sec-ondary use.

A small window with a monolithic arch and sill stones lights the upper level of the basement which is divided by an offset into two levels; this window form is also found in the north tower of Cormac's Chapel and helps to date the

BALLA

Above: At the base of the right-hand door jamb can be seen the decorated moulding which was the original builder's intention. Plain jambs and a lintelled doorhead are the result of a change in design, presumably following a gap in time. (See photo p. 63.)

Above left: Balla stands in a graveyard at the centre of the town, with the round-arched late doorway facing the viewer.

Left: The principal feature of the tower, two distinct phases of construction, is indicated by different masonry styles which change one course above the sill line of the upper doorway. The circular bullauns can be seen in the bottom course of masonary, left of the lower doorway.

tower as a late example. The convention adopted in this inventory is to regard the original entrance level as the first floor in all cases. It is unclear whether the basement did actually have two floor levels. Intermediate offsets, which also occur elsewhere, do not necessarily indicate a floor level (Timahoe), although the height of the basement is sufficient to allow for two levels, the upper one of which would have been lit by the small window, the lower without light. The Balla basement window is the strongest confirmation available in any tower that some of the tower basements were intended for use.

Externally, the basement window is far less prominent, appearing as a mere hole between two stones, and now lacking the clear architectural form of its interior detail. The second door, the original, is higher up than the basement entrance, and differently oriented. This straight-sided, small lintelled opening is remarkably narrow and taller than usual. The lower jambs have an external moulding which fails to continue on the upper jamb, above which the tower masonry also differs, being mostly composed of stones larger than those in the courses below. This roll moulding is similar to that on the door of Ardmore, as is the design of the Balla basement window to that resting on the second string course of Ardmore. It is evident that this masonry change indicates a break in construction; the original intention, no doubt, was to complete the door with a moulding and arched head, stylistically in keeping with the arched window of the basement.

Suggested date: 12th century.

Dimensions: height 10 metres; diameter at base 5.26 metres; height of door-sill 6.66 metres.

Unique features: bullauns in the wall; unusual window in the basement.

Access: free access to the site; locked iron gate in the lower doorway; no floors or ladders.

53 Killala, Co. Mayo   Killala town is on the R314, 12 km north-west of Ballina, on the west side of Killala Bay. This is a beautiful and complete Round Tower at the centre of the town, but so encroached-upon by buildings that it is difficult to view. The tower occupies a small yard, approached by a flight of steps from a side street. The distance between it and the Church of Ireland Cathedral of St Patrick gives some idea of the extent of the early monastic settlement which must have enclosed both sites; there is a souterrain in the cathedral grounds. St Muiredach was the first bishop, but the foundation is attributed to St Patrick. This is a classic example of a Round Tower, although not without some anomaly, a characteristic of all the towers. The miniature carving of a Round Tower at Rosserk Friary may be an attempt to represent Killala.

The Tower: At the bottom of the tower, where one or more conventional offsets might be expected, there is a plinth-like base which is similar to that at Kells; possibly this is just the cast drum-foundation which has been exposed and subsequently clad in stone. The tower masonry is of a fine hammer-dressed, well-coursed, dark limestone, with considerably larger stones used in

KILLALA
Left: The distinctive profile of Killala rises above housing at the centre of the town.

Below left: The drum is disfigured by an ugly discrepancy in the smoothness of the profile left of the window directly above the door.

Below: An unconventional foundation detail extends the form of the base offset into a plinth, possibly the underpinning of the offset necessitated by the exposure of the foundations.

the courses below the door-sill, some have a cyclopean character.

The door, which faces south-east, has visibly inclined jambs and a round-arched tripartite doorhead, composed of a keystone and two voussoirs. Quite unusually, the arch alone (rather than, as is more common, the entire doorcase) is articulated in pale beige sandstone; the jambs are in the well-tried formula of four quoin-like blocks. This detail, allied with three voussoirs for the arch, is frequently encountered, and is sufficiently characteristic to suggest the work of a travelling team of specialist masons; it is almost as individual a mannerism as a signature. At about the middle of the drum of the tower on the south-west side there is a peculiar bulge in the wall, the result of an unsuccessful masonary repair during the nineteenth century.

The windows of the drum are all lintelled and with inclined jambs. The second-floor window, which faces north-east, is larger and may represent the 'Treasury' floor. The four bell-floor windows are triangular-headed and face slightly off the cardinal points. The cornice and cap are well formed, although the cap was apparently incomplete during the 18th century.

Suggested date: 11th – 12th century.

Dimensions: height 25.6 metres; diameter at base 5.02 metres; height of door-sill 2.98 – 3.8 metres.

Unique features: plinth at base.

Access: free access to site; no floors or ladders.

54 Meelick, Co. Mayo

Meelick is 1 km north of the N5, Castlebar to Swinford road, 5 km south-west of Swinford. It stands, minus its cap and bell-floor windows, in a hillside graveyard. Of the origins of this monastic foundation nothing is known, nor are there any other early buildings still standing. A single early cross-slab survives, now displayed on the wall of the tower below the door. It carries the inscription 'OR DO GRICOUR' – a prayer for Gricour.

The Tower: Like the nearby tower at Turlough, Meelick is built of coursed sandstone. It has a number of courses of exceptionally large stones at the base. From below the door-sill level the stones are uniform and regularly coursed. There is evidence of fire-damage on the lower courses of the wall.

The doorway which faces south-east is round-headed with inclined jambs. Its doorhead is composed of six voussoirs with undefined extrados. The sill is of a monolithic slab; to the left it projects well beyond the line of the doorcase.

There are six windows in the drum, in ascending order, two triangular-headed and four lintelled. Internally, there is provision for five floors, supported on offsets for the first two floors with corbels for those above. The second floor-level is vaulted, springing from the offset, through which there is an access-hole. This phenomenon, together with similarly positioned features at Castledermot and Tory, confirm the identity of the second floor. In many other towers these are distinguished by the presence of a large window, as of more than average importance in the internal arrangements and function of Round

MEELICK

Far left: Was Meelick ever finished? This question might be legitimately asked of any site for which there is no documentary evidence of its completion. Fewer tower caps survive than any other architectural feature, no doubt as a result of their susceptibility to damage by lightning. After the caps, the bell-floor is the next most frequently missing feature.

Left: The fine masonry at Meelick is reflected in the quality of the doorcase.

ROSSERK

Far left: A characteristic feature of 15th-century ecclesiastical buildings is the use of finely executed low-relief realistic carving to decorate walls and furniture. The piscina of Rosserk Abbey has a unique representation of a miniature Round Tower carved on the left hand column (the lower of the two light-coloured octagonal pillar stones bears the carving).
(See photo p. 95.)

Left: Owing to the exceptionally subtle modelling of the carving, the tower miniature merges with the form of the

Towers. An unlocked metal barred gate has been installed in the doorway.

Suggested date: 11th – 12th century.

Dimensions: height 21.5 metres; diameter at base 5.44 metres; height of door-sill 3.42 metres.

Unique features: vaulted second floor.

Access: to site; tower inaccessible.

(A) Rosserk, Co. Mayo   The well-preserved Rosserk Franciscan Friary is magnificently sited, 10 km north of Ballina, on the shores of Killala Bay, to the east of the R314. This delicate bas-relief of a Round Tower, only 31cm high, decorates a column of the piscina in the chancel of the friary and can be dated to sometime after 1440, when the Third Order of St Francis (married men and women) established themselves here under the patronage of the Joyce family. The beautifully designed double piscina (used for washing altar vessels) has a pair of Gothic arches with, in the spandrels, angels holding symbols of the passion. A lion sits on the right-hand capital. The interior of the piscina is lit by a pair of oculus windows. The tower carving was executed over 200 years after the last Round Tower was built, and provides convincing evidence of the enduring power of the image. It relieves any doubt which may exist as to the general accuracy of the many 19th-century restorations of the caps of damaged towers – Glendalough, which was entirely reconstructed from fallen masonry, or others which have been heavily restored (Kilmacduagh, Timahoe).

Whether or not Rosserk is intended as a representation of nearby Killala is debatable: the window arrangement on the carving bears no particular resemblance to Killala, but neither does it relate to the specifics of any other nearby tower. Doubtless, it was carved by the mason from a mind's-eye image of Killala and it is a very spirited rendering. This little carving is the single known representation of a Round Tower, prior to the schematic representation of towers at Clonmacnoise and Devenish found in 17th-century manuscripts.

The Tower: All the essential elements of the Round Tower are recorded in this delightful miniature carving: battered sides, the entrance doorway above ground level and a conical cap. The dimensions of the representations correspond to those of the pillar block on which it is carved. The representation of a pair of windows on the second floor has no parallel in any surviving tower. The typically shallow foundations have been enhanced in a purely decorative manner, with a pointed feature replicating the cap as a base terminal, which bears no relationship to their actual construction. An interesting detail of the foundations here is that they are neither circular, as is conventional, nor square as in the Kilree Group, but octagonal; three faces of the octagon being visible. This detail replicates the form of the column which bears the carving.

Suggested date: 15th century.

Dimensions: height 31cm; diameter at base 4cm; height of door-sill 4cm.

Unique features: the carving is unique.

Access: free access to the friary buildings; signposted.

TURLOUGH

Above: The Round Tower with its complete cap seen through the chancel window of the 18th-century church.

Left: The juxtaposing of a Georgian parish church with a Round Tower occurs only at Turlough. Here the church architect might have improved the unhappy relationship which has been created by moving the new church away from the rather short tower, to the undoubted benefit of both.

Left: The corner of the southern transept encroaches upon the entrance doorway.

55 Turlough, Co. Mayo

Turlough is on the north side of the N5, 8 km north-east of Castlebar, and is a complete, although shorter-than-average, Round Tower. It stands at the north-east corner of a roofless cruciform 18th-century Church of Ireland parish church, which also incorporates some medieval 17th-century elements. There is a fine carved Crucifixion plaque inset into the east wall of the southern apse, next to the tower. Turlough is a further example of a monastery which has escaped from the annalistic records; nothing is known of its founder. The church and tower stand on the summit of an extensive hillside graveyard.

The Tower: There is a single offset visible at the base of the tower which is constructed of unevenly coursed and joggled sandstone ashlars, well dressed to the curve and batter. A late doorway, directly below the original one, was introduced into the basement of the tower, probably when the 18th-century church which abuts the tower was constructed. This doorway is now blocked and a modern gravestone has been placed directly in front of it.

The slightly tapered original door-opening has a round arch with eight voussoirs, without concentric extrados. A stone wall has been built into the back of the opening, completely sealing it.

The four windows in the drum are small with inclined jambs; all are lintelled. The four windows of the bell-floor are triangular-headed. Above the windows is a conventional cornice and cap which was repaired in the 19th-century by the Office of Public Works. The cap lacks the sheer outline and apex point of better examples, and the repair seems not to have been well executed.

The close proximity of the tower to the east transept of the 18th-century church weakens the impact of the Round Tower in the landscape. The manner in which the church abuts on the doorway is one of the most unsatisfactory adaptations of a Round Tower to a later ecclesiastical building context.

The varying heights of Round Towers (which can stand up to 12 metres higher than Turlough) is more likely to be explained by the economics of the individual church communities or their patrons, rather than by any reasons of topography.

Suggested date: 11th century.

Dimensions: height 22.86 metres; diameter at base 5.55 metres; height of door-sill 3.96 metres.

Unique features: none.

Access: access to site; tower interior sealed.

56 Donaghmore, Co. Meath

Donaghmore is on the N51, Navan to Slane road, 3 km north-east of Navan. This is a fine site overlooking the north-side of the main road, consisting of a well-maintained churchyard with the remains of a medieval church and Round Tower. The 15th-century medieval parish church, of which only one gable stands, has a double bell cote (probably 17th century), like Howth or Malahide. It replaces an earlier church of which only a sculptural fragment (a head), has been built into the south wall of the late church. The foundation of the monastery is attributed to St Patrick.

DONAGHMORE This tower still has a cap, but is lacking bell-floor windows. It is one of the curiosities of early medieval architecture. The gable end of a late medieval church with double gable bell cote is on the right.

The Tower: Donaghmore is an intriguing tower for a number of reasons. It stands to the top of its incomplete cone, with two base-offsets, and is built of fine-coursed masonry of limestone, with occasional darker chert insertions. The courses are fairly uniform in height.

The sandstone doorcase is of great importance, as it is the finest among the very small number of tower entrances with religious or sculptural decoration, rather than Romanesque orders or ornamentation. The opening has very slightly inclined jambs with a tripartite round-headed arch. A crucifixion figure, legs sharply canted towards the left, is carved in relief across the keystone and the relieving stone directly above it. The style of this crucifixion is uncommon to the Irish iconographic repertoire of crucifixion sculptures in stone, and more resembles an ivory or metalwork figure, such as that on the Domhnach Airgid (*c.* 1350), a book shrine in the National Museum, Dublin. This style of Romanesque crucifixion figure derives from Carolingian and Italian examples from *c.* 1050, although here it is most probably a century or more later. On either side of the doorjambs are bosses representing heads in relief, badly weathered. Inside the heads and running around the opening is a low-relief architrave band, which also incorporates the sill stone.

The only tower doorway which closely resembles Donaghmore is the single undoubted example of a 12th-century Irish Round Tower outside Ireland, that at Brechin in Angus, Scotland. There, the decoration is superior but the disposition of its elements identical, with a Crucifixion over the doorhead and a pair of figures on the jambs. At Brechin there are also supplementary decorations at the terminals of the sill, as well as projecting bosses outside the shoulders of the arch, also intended to bear decoration but uncarved. Although the four isolated examples of Irish-style Round Towers outside Ireland must be considered in general as examples of Irish ecclesiastical influence, it is difficult to avoid the possibility that in this instance the decorative influence worked in the opposite direction, with Donaghmore being influenced by Brechin.

The four drum windows vary, being in ascending order, lintelled, triangular-headed, round-headed and lintelled. The triangular-headed window on the third floor is prominent enough to have been the Treasury floor.

The major curiosity of Donaghmore is at the top where there is an absence of bell-floor windows and an unorthodox and incomplete cap. Unfortunately, accounts of the tower in the past differ, as do the 18th- and 19th-century drawings. As well as inconsistent accounts, there were a number of attempts at restoration and repair during the 19th century, both by the local landlord and by the Office of Public Works. These factors make it difficult to establish whether the present condition of the tower relates to its unrepaired state, or whether the top is a bungled restoration. Other than Temple Finghin at Clonmacnoise, which is in itself unorthodox and has two bell-floor windows, Donaghmore is the only tower which retains its cap but totally lacks bell-floor windows. If, as is possible, the cap and blank bell-floor are original, this has implications for a conscious change in the understanding of the purpose for which towers were built. Towers seen purely as monuments of ecclesiastical prestige would not require the windows, which are a standard feature of the

DONAGHMORE

Left: No other Irish Round Tower (excluding the extra-territorial one in Brechin, Scotland) has a sculpted cross as part of its door decoration. This 12th-century example considerably post-dates the ringed cross found in a similar situation at Antrim.

DULEEK

Left: The tapering scar which disfigures the side of the 15th-century church belfry was caused by the collapse or removal of a Round Tower against which, as at Lusk, the belfry had been built. The street-planning of the surrounding area also testifies to the prior existence of a circular monastic enclosure.

form, but then the bell-ringing function could not operate.

The cap, which rises above a conventional cornice, is of a much more slight angle than normal and lacks a pointed apex to its cone. If complete it would have been steeper even than Ardmore.

Suggested date: 11th century.

Dimensions: height 26.6 metres; diameter at base 4.98 metres; height of door-sill 3.4 metres.

Unique features: sculpted doorcase; absence of bell-floor windows.

Access: free access to site; no floors or ladders in tower.

57 Duleek, Co. Meath

Duleek is at the junction of the R150 and R152, 8 km south-west of Drogheda. This is only the ghost of a Round Tower, a wraith in stone, and if nothing were otherwise known of Round Towers the evidence here would hardly be sufficient to envisage one. However, in the light of knowledge from other sites, Duleek clearly had a tower to which a medieval belfry was attached during the 15th century, rather in the manner of Lusk. According to the annals, the cap of Duleek was struck by lightning in 1147, but the tower survived much longer and was integrated into the medieval works, only to collapse or be demolished like the rest of the buildings of the late medieval church. What survives are the foundations and the imprint of the tower on the north wall of the 15th-century belfry. Also standing are the walls of the south aisle, which contains a collection of late medieval funerary monuments. Aerial photographs of the site clearly show the outline of the circular ecclesiastical enclosure, preserved in the concentric arrangement of the surrounding streets. The churchyard also contains the ruins of the former Church of Ireland parish church of St Cianán (1816), which has an impressive tower with a needle spire. The massing of the two church towers and associated ruins form a dramatic complex when seen at dusk from the approach roads to the village.

The body of Brian Boru was brought here after the Battle of Clontarf in 1014. It is believed that the first stone church in Ireland was built at Duleek, and this is preserved in its corrupted name. A small but complete High Cross stands to the south-west of the 19th-century parish church.

The Tower: The imprint of the tower on the standing belfry rises to 14 metres, at which point its battered wall would have diverged from the vertical line of the late medieval belfry wall. No architectural features survive.

Date: not known. (Annals reference for 1147.)

Dimensions: height 14 metres; diameter at base 5.18 metres.

Unique features: tallest standing tower of the least substance.

Access: free access to the belfry and site.

58 Kells, Co. Meath

Kells town is on the N3, Navan to Virginia road, 15 km north-east of Navan. This is a particularly rich site, right in the middle of a busy market town, concentrated on the churchyard of the Church of Ireland parish church. On the

KELLS

Above: Rudimentary projecting bosses on the external door jambs represent human heads. The projecting keystone may have been intended to carry a Crucifixion figure, as at Donaghmore.

Left: The tower survives to the top of the bell-floor windows and has, like Killala, a plinth-shaped exposed foundation.

edge of the churchyard is the Round Tower, with nearby, three High Crosses and the base of a fourth, while a short distance away, outside the east gate, is a well-preserved, possibly 12th-century steep-roofed oratory, St Columb's House, which is open to the public and provided with an internal ladder to the attic. A rare opportunity exists to inspect at close quarters the roof construction of this type of early medieval building. A further cross, the Market Cross, stands at the junction of two streets in the town centre (probably not its original location), and has for some years been threatened by traffic. Having had its base, not for the first time, hit by a bus in 1996, it was removed for conservation. The Kells' High Crosses are the most important grouping of these ecclesiastical monuments, one of which carries the inscription 'PATRICII ET COLUMBAE CRUX' – 'The cross of Patrick and Columba'. The monastery was founded from Columba's settlement at Iona in the 9th century by monks threatened there by repeated Viking attack.

The Tower: Kells is a finely preserved tower lacking its cap; it displays a well-worked batter. There is a difference of 2 metres between the external street level, immediately below the tower, and that of the churchyard, which is considerably higher, making the entrance door appear closer to the ground than was originally the case.

The door, with distinctly inclined jambs, is round-headed, with the tripartite arch cut by the relieving stone of the course above, on to which the form of the keystone has been cut. The inclined jambs consist of, respectively, four stones on the right, five on the left. The unattractive detail in which the relieving stone appears to cut the extrados or natural outer circumference of the arch is a mason's mannerism found elsewhere (Inis Cealtra; Kilkenny). Two bosses protrude from the jambs: that on the left is a weathered carving of a head, the other is more severely eroded and too indistinct for identification. They closely resemble the bosses on nearby Donaghmore.

The windows of the drum are small with inclined jambs and lintelled. The triangular-headed bell floor windows are unusual in being five rather than the normal four.

Suggested date: 11th century. (Annals reference for 1076.)
Dimensions: height 26 metres; diameter at base 4.75 metres; original height of door-sill 3.6 metres.
Unique features: sculpted heads on door jamb; five bell-floor windows.
Access: free access to site; no access to interior of the tower.

59 Clones, Co. Monaghan

Clones town is on the N54, Cavan to Monaghan road, close to the border with Northern Ireland. Clones is a fine if incomplete tower standing in a beautifully undisturbed graveyard. This has an interesting collection of 17th- and 18th-century tombstones decorated in high relief, with symbols of the Passion and trade insignia, and an important 12th-century monolithic stone gabled house-tomb of St Tighernach, Bishop of Clogher, who was the 6th-century founder of the monastery. The tower stands, as many do such as Monasterboice and

CLONES

Above: This early example of a Round Tower door displays none of the features of developed later types. The lintel and sill remain rudimentary, while the door jambs are unarticulated.

Left: The roughly hewn, hammer-dressed and unwrought masonry of Clones give it an uneven profile, unlike later and more sophisticated examples.

INISHKEEN

The riverside meadow in which Inishkeen stands is an attractive site, as its topographical name, *Inis Caoin* – pleasant island, suggests.

Kells, on the very edge of the graveyard, indicating the fact that this represents a diminishing of the original ecclesiastical enclosure. A High Cross, reconstructed from an unrelated shaft and head fragments, stands nearby in the Diamond and was probably moved from the monastic enclosure. No evidence of a church exists in the present graveyard, although the remains of a 12th-century church stands in an adjoining street, at a fair distance from the tower.

The Tower: Clones stands up to bell-floor level but is without its cap. The low churchyard wall bisects the tower at the base, and an offset can be seen on the portion of the tower outside this wall. The masonry is composed of roughly coursed and dressed sandstone quarrystones with many spalls, and the batter is not very pronounced.

The door, which faces east, is narrow and lintelled with roughly squared jambs. Since the doorway is not an independently articulated doorcase, it tends to make the entrance look less distinct and less of a feature than in later towers, where different stone colour and texture were frequently exploited to give architectural emphasis.

The three small windows in the drum of the tower are lintelled, one of which is above the door, while the surviving two of the customary four on the bell-floor are straight-jambed and lintelled; two are missing their lintels. There is no evidence of a cornice visible.

Suggested date: 10th century.

Dimensions: height 23 metres; diameter at base 4.5 metres; original height of door-sill 2.12 metres.

Unique features: none.

Access: no access to the tower, which is sealed by a barred grill; the site is signposted, but the graveyard entrance is permanently locked: a path leads under an arch from the rear of the graveyard to a stile in the wall beside the tower.

60 Inishkeen, Co. Monaghan   Inishkeen village is 5 km north of the R178 Carrickmacross to Dundalk road. Short of being struck by an annalist's thunderbolt, Innishkeen has not been lucky in its treatment by the years. There are many sad towers, reduced to mere shadows of their original glory by 'improvements' or by vandalism; Inishkeen is of the latter category, a once-fine tower stripped of all its defining features. It is redeemed by the beauty of its location in the churchyard of the former Church of Ireland parish church (now a folk museum), on the banks of the Fane river. This is Patrick Kavanagh territory, the heart of what is now called 'Kavanagh Country', where the poet was born and is buried. The foundation of the monastery is attributed to the 6th-century St Daig.

The Tower: Inishkeen Round Tower stands about a third of the normal height, with a slight evidence of batter.

The door faces east-south-east in the general direction of the 19th-century church, suggesting that this was built on the site of an earlier church. The door-sill which is monolithic, looks original, the remainder of the door-opening

CLONMACNOISE I

Above: Unlike at Timahoe, where the emphasis is on embellishment, restraint prevails in Clonmacnoise.

Left: Clonmacnoise stands on high ground, with the broad reaches of the River Shannon directly below the monastery. On the extreme right of the picture is the corner of the cathedral, and in the foreground, between it and the Round Tower, is a replica of the early 10th-century Cross of the Scriptures, one of the most celebrated of the sculpted 'scripture crosses'.

Left: No other Round Towers display more accomplished masonry than those at Clonmacnoise. This quality is certainly the result of technical influence from Continental master masons.

however, appears to have been drastically altered. The shallow lintel is rather unconvincing and must certainly be a replacement. None of the windows has survived.

Photographs exist of a large hole in the wall at the base of the tower, into which a flat wall had been built with a door-opening, as though the tower were in use as a bicycle-shed. This gave access to the interior when the tower acted as belfry to the 19th-century church. The breach was repaired by the Office of Public Works *c.* 1909.

Suggested date: 10th – 11th century.

Dimensions: height 12.6 metres; diameter at base 4.5 metres; height of door-sill 4.1 metres.

Unique features: none.

Access: to site and outside of tower.

61 Clonmacnoise I, Co. Offaly

Clonmacnoise lies on the east bank of the River Shannon, 11.5 km south of Athlone on the R444, off the N62. This is one of the most beautiful and important of the Irish monastic sites. Its location at a bend on a broad stretch of the River Shannon, and the wealth of building remains and earthworks, identifies it as a place that, in its day, must have been of great significance and considerable ecclesiastical importance, and probably remained so for most of a thousand years after its foundation.

Clonmacnoise is at the cross-roads of Ireland where the waterway of the Shannon, flowing north-south, meets the *Slíge Mór*, one of the great east-west trackways of ancient Ireland. Evidence of a 9th-century timber bridge was recently identified offshore in the Shannon, and it is at present the subject of an underwater excavation. Here, on the east bank of the Shannon, the monastic city of Clonmacnoise was established. It became one of the wealthiest and most extensive medieval monasteries and proto-urban settlements, as well an important place of pilgrimage throughout the medieval period. The late medieval ecclesiastical 'city' of Clonmacnoise occupied the extensive stretch of land, between the castle on the west, and the Nuns' Church on the east of the inner enclosure, where the churches stand. The abundant remains, including two Round Towers, nine churches and a number of High Crosses, make it among the most interesting survivors of the great age of the early medieval Irish Church.

The churches, eight of which are within the enclosure, are dominated by the Cathedral, which dates from the early 10th century to the mid-15th century. To the east, and reached by an 11th-century stone-built causeway, is the Nuns' Church (1166), founded as an act of penitence by Dervorgilla, the abducted wife of Tiernan O'Rourke, King of Breffny. The Cross of the Scriptures (early 10th century) is among the greatest of all the sculpted High Crosses; it carries a damaged memorial inscription on its base which has been interpreted as 'OR DO RIG FLAIND MAC MAELSECHINAILL OROIT DO RIG HERREN OR DO COLMAN DORRO'– 'A prayer for King Flann, son of Maelsechnaill, a prayer for the king of Ireland. A prayer for Coleman who made this cross for King Flann'. The king referred to is probably Flann Sinna, High King (879-916): Coleman may be the abbot of the period or even the sculptor of the cross. The three High Crosses are arranged in a cruciform manner around the cathedral, with the Cross of the Scriptures on its axis.

Another fascinating feature of Clonmacnoise is the large collection of inscribed memorial stones, either to mark burials or donated by pilgrims who visited the settlement. Many carry the personal names of the donor and a request for a prayer in their honour: 'OR DO FINNACHTU' – 'A prayer for Finnachtu', and, 'OR DO MUIRETACH' – 'A prayer for Muiretach'. Some of the large collection of slabs are on display in the Visitor Centre at the entrance to the site.

The principal church, the cathedral, is substantially the stone church mentioned in the annals as having being erected in 909 – the *'daimhliag mor'*, or great stone church. This is the earliest dated stone church in Ireland, as well as its largest church building. Excavations have shown that the original south wall was further south than its present location, making Clonmacnoise Cathedral originally larger than that of Glendalough. The cathedral stood for over 200 years before the Round Tower was added to the complex. It begs the intriguing question: was there a timber predecessor to the tower ?

The Tower: Clonmacnoise I, known as O'Rourke's Tower, is among the most finely built of all the Round Towers, and if it stood to its intended height, would rank with Devenish I or Ardmore for sheer perfection. Its construction was completed in 1124, and according to the *Annals of the Four Masters*, it was built by King Toirdealbach Ua Conchobair, during the abbacy of Gillachrist Ua Maoileoin.

The tower, however, is both topless and altered, diminishing the stature of what must have been its original achievement. It may be considered to be missing slightly more than a third of its true height: the top 3 metres are of later medieval construction (probably post-1135 when it was struck by lightning). The superb limestone ashlar masonry is laid in courses of slightly alternating height, with strictly maintained vertical joints and with diagonally axed tooling, more reminiscent of the building technique of the European monastic orders than of the native tradition. A single offset is visible at the base. The lower courses of masonry have been cleaned, giving the tower the distorted appearance of being built of different types of stone. The masonry facing the cathedral is of finer quality than that on the other side of the tower, where repairs have been made.

The door faces south-east towards the cathedral. The opening is finely cut and has visibly inclined jambs with a round arch of eight voussoirs with a distinct keystone, a feature not generally so clearly defined as here. The arch-springing is from impost-blocks with chamfered soffits, a sophisticated constructional detail not found in other tower doorways, except those with Romanesque decoration, such as Timahoe or Dromiskin. Significantly, this detail is also found in the design of the string-courses on the towers of Cormac's Chapel on St Patrick's Rock in Cashel – significant because both are closely contemporary, dated buildings (Clonmacnoise 1124; Cormac's Chapel, begun 1129 and consecrated in 1134), of remarkably similar fine ashlar masonry, both built for or funded by kings. These two core buildings should be able to occupy a *terminus ante* and *post quem* position in the dating of other towers. The appearance of the impost block at Clonmacnoise I (its first appearance in a tower doorway) could indicate that both structures were supervised by the same master mason.

The lintelled windows on the first and second floor are narrow and reflect the proportion of the windows in the south tower of Cormac's Chapel. Above them, in what is now the bell-floor, are an unusual row of eight windows in the later portion of the wall (with inferior masonry), spaced regularly around the circumference of the tower. These windows represent a second phase of construction (post-1135). For the purpose of either bell-ringing or observation, eight windows must be more functional than four; this modification is found in a number of 12th-century towers, only one of which, unfortunately, retains its cap (Kilmacduagh).

Date: 12th century. (Annals references for 1124 and 1135.)
Dimensions: height 19.3 metres; diameter at base 5.62 metres; height of door-sill 3.5 metres.
Unique features: date of building and patrons known.
Access: access to site; no access to interior of tower.

62 Clonmacnoise II, Co. Offaly

The Tower: Clonmacnoise II, known as Temple Finghin, is one of only two surviving examples of an intact engaged Round Tower (**fig. 15d**). The idea that the Irish Round Tower is, by conventional definition, a freestanding structure, seems to be placing unnecessarily restrictive boundaries on an architectural form, the essence of which is its height, rotundity and conical cap, rather than whether it is independent or part of another building. Standing at 16.76 metres high, and complete to the apex of its cap, it is quite short for a Round Tower. The deciding factor in its height was evidently that it bears a proportional relationship to the church of which it is an integral element. This could not have been the case if it had stood in the region of 25 metres high. The masonry is of limestone ashlars, comparable to that of Clonmacnoise I; the tower probably dates from the late 12th century, *c*.1160.

Being an engaged tower, it exhibits different features within the basic formula of a battered drum and cone-shaped roof. The manner in which the masonry of the tower is cut back to accommodate the corner of the nave is structurally among the most accomplished details exhibited by any Irish building of the period, and has to be the work of a mason with experience outside Ireland. A feature of the tower is the absence of an elevated entrance door; this is found at ground-floor level within the chancel. Perhaps more significant is the lack of the customary four bell-floor windows beneath the cap.

Although the tower of Temple Finghin evidently served the same purpose as those towers with windows oriented to the cardinal points, here the window treatment is entirely different. The five small windows in the drum are all oriented to the south, towards the other churches, and correspond to those on the floor

CLONMACNOISE II

Above: Clonmacnoise II viewed through the two-light Gothic window of the cathedral. (See photo p. 31.)

Left: What appears to be the west entrance door of Temple Finghin is in fact the chancel arch; the walls of the nave have been reduced to almost ground level, giving the church a misleading appearance.

Below: The lowest window of the tower. There is no tower parallel for this window arrangement, where all but one of the windows of a tower appear on the same side.

levels of other towers. The bell-floor has a pair of windows facing north and south; these are unusually situated – well below the cornice – and are not distinguished by size or form from those in the drum. The drum windows are either lintelled or round-headed and have external architraval mouldings, slightly recessed from the wall surface. In ascending order, the five drum windows on the south, and sixth window of the bell-floor are, respectively, round-headed; two rectangular; rectangular in an arched surround, and again two round-headed.

Another singular feature of this tower is the treatment of the cap. Here, the normally horizontal external courses are laid in a herringbone manner, the only function of which is decorative. This must have been a very beautiful feature when the masonry was fresh, and the design more apparent than it is today. It is debatable whether such fine masonry as the Clonmacnoise towers exhibit was originally concealed by a lime-plaster rendering. The herringbone treatment of the cap argues against its being covered.

An illustration of Temple Finghin appears on an isometric perspective of Clonmacnoise reproduced by the antiquarian, Sir James Ware (1594 – 1666), in his *De Hibernia et antiquitatibus eius disquisitiones* (1658). Although the view was engraved in London by Prague-born Wenceslaus Hollar (1607 – 1677), the greatest topographical draughtsman and engraver of his day, it is obvious that the engraver had no personal knowledge of the site, and many of the details are incorrect (Clonmacnoise I is so distorted on Hollar's plan that, without prior knowledge, it is quite unrecognisable). This is, nonetheless, among the earliest visual records of any Round Tower (see Devenish I), and it is itself based on an earlier plan of *c.* 1620.

Suggested date: mid-to-late 12th century.
Dimensions: height 16.76 metres; diameter at base 3.97 metres.
Unique features: engaged tower with ground floor entrance; herringbone cap.
Access: to church but not to tower; no floors or ladders.

63 Seir Kieran, Co. Offaly

The site is at Clareen crossroads on the R421, Roscrea to Kinnity road, 8 km south-east of Birr. Seir Kieran is a complex of considerable interest and great natural beauty, surrounded by extensive and undisturbed earthworks on the side of an open valley which slopes down to the Fuarán River. This ecclesiastical site was traditionally the burial place of the kings of Ossory, and a modern grave-slab commemorates Cearbhall, King of Ossory in the 10th century. An Augustinian house was established here during the 12th century.

The earthworks consist of a large, circular, double bank-and-ditch which surrounds the Round Tower site, numerous sub-rectangular enclosures, a motte-like rectangular mound, souterrains; there are two 9th-century Cross fragments. The monastic site is now largely enclosed by the rectangular churchyard wall of the Church of Ireland parish church of St Kieran (1844). A circular turret with pistol-loops, within the graveyard, which marks the south-east corner of a destroyed late medieval building, might superficially be mistaken for the tower, which is located on the outside of the north-west corner of

SEIR KIERAN

Left: Until it had been excavated, some doubt remained as to the identity of this feature on the outside of the graveyard wall. Clearly it is the stub of a Round Tower, in a site where one might have been expected.

Below: Bullaun stones are frequently found at ecclesiastical sites. Here, a damaged double-cupped one is embedded in the basement wall of the tower.

ORAN

Concealed inside this most successful camouflage is a Round Tower. Oran's exceptionally wide base diameter suggests a tower of up to 35 metres high.

the churchyard wall. Judging by its relationship to the tower, the 19th-century church most probably occupies the position of the original older church. In the church is preserved one of a number of early medieval grave or memorial slabs, which have been be found elsewhere at the site. A 15th-century window has been installed in its east wall. The monastery was founded by St Ciarán of Seir during the 6th century.

The Tower: Little remains of Seir Kieran, yet it is an intriguing ruin. The wall stands some six courses high, with a recently constructed entrance at ground level, and a drop of about one metre to the internal floor. At the sill-level of the present-day entrance is a large damaged double bullaun, in secondary use as an integral part of the wall construction. The re-use of this particular bullaun in such a manner implies that by, at the latest the 11th century, but possibly earlier, it was no longer regarded as a necessary feature of the monastery, and might be re-employed in building work. The presence of the bullaun is the only remaining distinguishing feature of the tower.
Date: not known.
Dimensions: height 2.9 metres; diameter at base 5.14 metres.
Unique features: bullaun in the wall.
Access: interior easily accessible, fine view of the tower from the churchyard wall.

64 Oran, Co. Roscommon

Oran lies on the north side of the N60, Roscommon to Castlerea road, 12 km north-west of Roscommon town. Across the road from the graveyard, in the centre of which stands the remains of a once-fine Round Tower, is the Uaran Gared holy well which is still venerated. The well, marked by a large and garishly painted statue of St Patrick, has a succession of stone-walled pools. The monastery was allegedly founded by St Patrick.

The Tower: Oran belongs to that group of towers which have, by the sturdiness of their construction, defied time and the ever-pressing demand for reusable stone and despite inhospitable circumstances, have managed to maintain a presence into a more conservation-minded era. Enough survives to indicate that it was a structure of some quality. There is a single visible offset, above which the wall stands to a height of some sixteen quite uneven courses. No evidence of a door can be seen, nor are there any features of interest surviving other than the quality of the masonry. This is of finely cut limestone with some of the lower courses in a clearly contrasting coarser-grained stone from a different quarry, although the style of masonry does not differ. A breach in the base of the wall allows access to the interior; this aperture does not represent the position of the original door. The walls are so overgrown with ivy that the tower from a distance resembles a clump of bushes.
Suggested date: 11th century.
Dimensions: height 3.9 metres; diameter at base 6 metres.
Unique features: largest base diameter.
Access: to site and interior of tower.

DRUMCLIFF

Above: The sharp outline of Ben Bulben rises starkly behind the Round Tower.

Left: The Round Tower can be seen behind the High Cross. From the bottom of the High Cross, the panels represent Adam and Eve, a lion, David and Goliath, Daniel in the lion's den and, at the centre of the head, possibly the Last Judgement.

65 Drumcliff, Co. Sligo

The site of Drumcliff straddles the N16, 6.5 km north-west of Sligo town. The tower stands west of the road, while the churchyard and 19th-century St Columb's parish church are at the east. The site is associated with St Columb. The only other vestige of the monastery are two sandstone High Crosses, one merely an undecorated shaft, while the complete cross may be composed of an unrelated shaft and head. W. B. Yeats (1865-1939) is buried in the graveyard, of which he wrote in *Under Ben Bulben*:

'Under bare Ben Bulben's head
In Drumcliff churchyard Yeats is laid,
An ancestor was rector there
Long years ago; a church stands near,
By the road an ancient Cross.
No marble, no conventional phrase,
On limestone quarried near the spot
By his command these words are cut:
Cast a cold eye
On life, on death.
Horseman, pass by!'

The Tower: Had Drumcliff been a more aesthetic ruin, it might have received a mention in Yeats' poem. A century ago the little paddock, which now surrounds the tower on the edge of the main road, had a coppice of Scots Pines bristling around the tower, which then looked less desolate than it does today. It stands to a height which probably represents a third of the original. According to a 17th-century source, Drumcliff was struck by lightning in 1396, although there is no way of ascertaining whether the upper portion fell then or subsequently. The roughly level top of the tower suggests demolition rather than collapse, and there is unsubstantiated 19th-century testimony that some, at least, of the damage was done then. A single offset is visible at the base and the masonry is composed of roughly squared limestone boulders and unhewn field stones, unevenly coursed and fitted to the curve.

The narrow lintelled door-opening faces east-south-east. Only a single window survives and this is small and lintelled.

An early date is suggested by a combination of the remaining features, rough masonry, a low and lintelled doorway and a similar rectangular window.

Suggested date: 10th – 11th century.

Dimensions: height 9 metres; diameter at base 4.98 metres; height of door-sill 1.98 metres.

Unique features: none.

Access: to exterior only.

66 Cashel, Co. Tipperary

This site, which has been called 'The Acropolis of Munster', is on the north-east perimeter of Cashel town on the N8, Dublin to Cork road. The Rock of Cashel is one of the primary monuments of Irish architectural history, and is

CASHEL
Above: Cashel is the only tower in which a late door is higher than the original, seen here with its delicate architrave. (See photos pp. 76, 85.)

Left: Behind the Round Tower is the north transept of the cathedral with a projecting chapel. All the crosses are 19th-century Celtic revival tombstones.

Below: The Rock of Cashel is one of the major set-pieces of Irish antiquity, with its assembly of important ecclesiastical buildings, early medieval, Romanesque and Gothic.

unique among ecclesiastical sites in the richness of the surviving monuments and the sheer drama of its location. Set on the open plain of the Suir valley in the heartland of Tipperary, the area is dominated by a cluster of ancient and partially roofless ruined buildings crammed together on a prominent limestone outcrop, which is visible from a considerable distance. Cashel is the only tower site in an urban situation where the tower has not been absorbed into and subsumed by the architecture of the town, but stands distinct and relatively unencroached upon, although recent building developments around the base of the Rock are undermining this distinction.

Cashel or *Caiseal na Ri*, Cashel of the Kings, or St Patrick's Rock, was a royal enclosure of the Eoghanachta Kings of Munster from the 4th century, which was presented to the church in 1101 by King Muircheartach O'Brien. The site is surrounded by a stone perimeter-wall at its summit, which probably represents the position of the stone enclosure from which the town derives its name. The approach road leads up the south slope of the Rock to the restored 15th-century Vicars Choral, the domestic buildings of the late cathedral. The well-preserved Cormac's Chapel, consecrated in 1134, is the most significant building on the site and represents the finest achievement of Romanesque architecture in Ireland. Cormac's Chapel is dominated by the presence of the 13th-century Gothic cathedral, which interferes with the intended relationship between it and the Round Tower, and make it impossible to see them together except from a distance on the adjoining hills to the east.

The Tower: The Round Tower abuts the north transept of the 13th-century Gothic cathedral, the crossing tower of which rises almost to the full height of the tower, which acted as belfry to the cathedral into which it is incorporated. Cashel is one of the small number of complete towers with an intact roof cone. It appears less impressive than its situation would warrant, because it is overshadowed by the mass of the cathedral. Prior to the cathedral's construction, the outline of the Rock with the Round Tower, with a later steep-roofed church and Cormac's Chapel breaking the skyline, must have been for a hundred years the most extraordinary architectural complex in Ireland. The tower which predates the King's chapel was influential in the manner in which the chapel's two towers were capped. The northern tower has a pyramidal roof and the southern one, now finished by a later parapet, presumably would have been similarly capped, although not necessarily to the same height.

The Rock of Cashel is a metaphor in stone for the overpowering of what Heinrich Böll called 'the spirit of Thebaic asceticism' by the more robust aesthetic of the Continental Gothic world. The view of the Rock from the east, with the cathedral crammed in between the simplicity of the tower and the delicacy of Cormac's Chapel, is an explosion in volume.

The Round Tower faces south-east towards what most probably was the position of the church which predated Cormac's Chapel. The tower is built of well-dressed sandstone ashlars with limestone used erratically throughout, giving it, at close quarters, a rather spotty look. The use of variant types of stone in this manner is seen on many towers, but a lime-plaster rendering would

217

CORMAC'S CHAPEL

Left: Cormac's Chapel is the finest architectural monument created in Ireland before the 13th century, the ambitiousness of its design is without parallel. Now a soberly stony shell, its interior was originally gorgeously decorated with frescoes, some of which survive in the chancel vault. (See photo p. 57.)

Below: The fine ashlar masonry and precisely detailed string-course of the south tower of Cormac's Chapel.

probably have concealed such discrepancies.

The doorway, which faces south-east, is round-arched with seven irregular voussoirs and a broad external architrave-like band on the arch and jambs. The coursing in the area immediately above the door sags off the horizontal, which is recovered slightly higher up the wall. The sagging of the courses at the shoulders of the doorhead suggest that the doorcase stood complete before the upper courses were laid. Putlock holes can be seen to the right of the doorhead. The masonry of the lower left doorjamb, sill and courses immediately below are a 19th-century repair. The tower predates the 1127 commencement date for Cormac's Chapel by perhaps fifty years or less. A second doorway which communicates with the triforium mural passageway of the cathedral was introduced to give access to the tower from within the church.

The windows are lintelled and arranged in a spiralling manner. The four bell-floor windows are triangular-headed and oriented slightly off the cardinal points. Two of these windows have monolithic lintels from which the window-heads have been cut.

Suggested date: 11th century.

Dimensions: height 27.94 metres; diameter at base 5.33 metres; height of door-sill 3.28 metres.

Unique features: none.

Access: no floors or access to the tower; the interior can be seen from the triforium, and the roof cone from the roof of the crossing tower.

(B) Cormac's Chapel, Cashel, Co. Tipperary

The justification for including Cormac's Chapel in an inventory of Round Towers is the light which it casts on both the freestanding and the engaged church towers of the period.

The richness of the chapel's external detailing, with blind arcades and string courses on the body of the church as well as on its two towers, establish it as an important parallel in the study of 12th-century Round Tower architecture. These rectangular towers (**fig. 15e**) are the only contemporary structures with which the towers generally can be compared, outside of the corpus of Round Towers. The use of string courses on the towers of Cormac's Chapel to decorate the exterior of the building, without any relationship to its interior, identifies them as belonging to the same stylistic approach as the decoration of Ardmore Round Tower. While the Cashel string courses are rectangular in profile, with a bevelled upper or lower face, those in Ardmore are formed with a rolled moulding, and are semi-circular in profile. In both cases the choice of detail seems the most appropriate to the differing wall treatments.

If considered independently, the two chapel towers, divorced from the building to which they are attached, are merely rectangular variants of the Round Tower. The chapel's towers differ in appearance and function; the larger, on the north, is capped by a stone pyramid. It is unlit in its upper storeys, while the lower is interconnected with the interior of the nave. Its external wall-surface is divided unequally by seven string courses.

The smaller southern tower is now capped by a flat-topped parapet which is

LIATHMORE

Left: This is a 'new' Round Tower, that is one discovered during archaeological excavations. All that survives are the foundations, which are now protected by a surrounding stone wall. (Photo 1974)

Left: The steep-roofed oratory with antae is probably the church for which the Round Tower was built.

Left: What is now visible is a partial reconstruction of the above-ground level masonry of the tower, constructed of stones found at the site.

probably late medieval. Internally, this is the access tower, and it has a stone spiral staircase like that at Ferns. Externally, it is similarly divided to its northern counterpart, but with eight string courses. While a pair of symmetrically planned chancel towers, projecting transept-like, might be expected to be of uniform height, the southern tower is now taller than the northern one, although this may not represent the original arrangement. The masonry below the parapet appears to be original. The discrepancy in height means that the towers, both similarly capped, would have been of unequal height.

Putlock holes are regularly arranged on the tower walls, as though for decorative effect, and left unplugged, as they are in the abbey-church of Murbach in Alsace, a possible antecedent. A similar treatment can be seen on the Round Tower of Roscam, although here their use was purely structural and they were doubtless plugged and plastered over.

Between the 10th and 12th centuries, all the ecclesiastical towers built in Ireland, freestanding and engaged, with the exception of the Cormac's Chapel pair, are round in whole or in part. Despite their being a product of fresh influences from abroad, the Cormac's Chapel towers are worthy of consideration in the context of Irish 12th-century tower building.

Its stylistic origins probably lie in Anglo-Saxon Britain, although the paired towers seem to derive from Rhineland influences, where prominent arrangements of paired towers are commonplace in 10th-and 11th-century church building. The blind arcading is reminiscent of St Lawrence, Bradford-on-Avon, while the Romanesque parish church in Lullington, Somerset, shares many details with Cormac's Chapel: tangential gable, rosettes, an anthropomorphic tympanum. In plan, the Cashel transeptal towers are reminiscent of Murbach abbey-church.

Numerous architectural details of the chapel correspond to features on Round Towers, placing the reliably dated Chapel in a pivotal position in establishing some tangible datum point in dating other towers in the latter stages of tower building. The string courses, which elide into impost blocks, are similar in detail to the impost blocks of the entrance door at Clonmacnoise I; the single surviving arch of the second range of blind arcading of the south front compares with the decorated doorway of Dromiskin; the idea of a round interior containing a spiral staircase, enclosed in a rectangle, is found at Ferns and Tamlaght.

Date: 12th century (begun 1127 – consecrated 1134).

Dimensions of towers: north tower, base 3.8 x 3.8 metres, height 20 metres; south tower, base 3.1 x 3.1 metres; height approximately 30 metres.

Unique features: unique pair of rectangular early medieval engaged towers.

Access: only to nave and chancel of church; no access to stairs in south tower.

67 Liathmore / Leigh, Co. Tipperary

The site is approached along a private farm road, east from the N8, 6 km south of Urlingford. Liathmore is unusual in being a tower first discovered in the excavations conducted by R. E. Glasscock of Queen's University, Belfast, 1969-70, and one of the small additions to the corpus of towers known since

ROSCREA
Left: The church facade displays an unusual combination of Irish and imported features; the antae are a local manner, while the tangential gables are derived from English Romanesque. The bell cote on the gable end is not original. (See photo p. 63.)

Left: Only the west gable of the 12th-century Romanesque church has been preserved, here seen from behind, with the tower facing it on the far side of the road. A distinctive feature of Roscrea is the quite remarkable size of the second-floor window, almost as large as the entrance door.

the 18th century. It highlights the strong possibility that at other monastic sites where a tower might be expected, but none is evident, further examples will be found through excavation.

Set in a broad expanse of rough farm land, the area is rich in earthworks which date mainly from the 17th century. Two churches stand some distance apart, the smaller an early roofless oratory with antae *c.* 11th century, the larger a mix of rebuildings; of a church with antae converted into a 12th-century nave-and-chancel church with a 15th-century vault and domestic apartments above. The chancel is still vaulted and there is a mural stairs to the upper floor. The monastery was founded by St Mochoemóg in the early 7th century.

The Tower: Liathmore stands equidistant between the two surviving churches, its present appearance dating from a reconstruction carried out by the Office of Public Works subsequent to the excavation in which the foundations of the Round Tower were discovered. A circular stone wall with a small gate has been built around the reconstructed base in order to protect it from cattle. The tower is south-west of the 11th-century church at an extremely acute angle from the west doorway, and due north of the 12th-century church site.

The foundations as excavated went to a depth of 2.6 metres, unusually deep when compared with information available from other towers, where foundations can be as shallow as 60cm (Kilmacduagh). The limestone boulders of which the foundations are constructed are laid doughnut-like, merely as a support wall for the structure above, without any attempt to fill in the entire area with masonry. The foundations give no information as to whether the tower was ever completed or why it might have collapsed – whether by being struck by lightning, by fire, or through later demands for re-usable masonry. Worked ashlars were discovered in the course of the excavation and these have been used in the reconstruction of the above ground section of the tower.

Date: not known.

Dimensions: depth of foundation below ground 2.6 metres; diameter at base; approximately 5.45 metres.

Unique features: a previously unknown tower.

Access: free access to all parts of the site; signposted.

68 Roscrea, Co. Tipperary

The tower is in the centre of Roscrea town, which stands at the crossroads of the N7 and the N62. Roscrea is yet another topless tower, standing at the edge of the Portlaoise road, which separates it from the remainder of the monastic enclosure on the opposite side of the road. This road needs to be relocated before the tower is damaged, or a juggernaut carelessly demolishes the gable of the Romanesque church which stands opposite in an even more precarious position.

The monastery was established by St Cronan in the 7th century. According to the annals, the tower was struck by lightning *c.* 1135. Lightning seems to have been the *bête noire* of Round Towers, and there are numerous annalistic references to towers being damaged by lightning, as well as further late

ARDMORE

Above: Few tower settings can equal that of Ardmore, poised above a bay on the south coast. Below the tower is the cathedral, and to the right can be seen the roof of St Declan's Oratory. (See photo p. 16.)

Left: No tower possesses such a steeply inclined profile as Ardmore, which gives it a character distinctly different from all other Round Towers.

accounts such as the damage to Cloyne in the 18th century and Scattery in the 19th century.

St Cronan's 12th-century church is no more than a façade with its back to the churchyard of the Church of Ireland parish church. The remainder of the body of the church was demolished in 1818. Its façade was obviously preserved for its decorative interest. It has, between antae, a symmetrically arranged series of blind arcades flanking the Romanesque doorway over which, in the tangential gable, is a carved figure of a cleric, presumed to be Cronan the founder, but could also represent Christ in Majesty, with rosettes on either side. This façade may be directly derived from that of the Romanesque church at Lullington, Somerset, which has almost identical decorative elements, but with four rosettes flanking a Christ figure, instead of the pair on St Cronan's.

The Tower: Roscrea stood considerably higher until the 18th century when, in 1798, the upper portion was demolished after an insurgent had used it as a vantage point from which to take pot-shots at the nearby castle. It is constructed of fine coursed sandstone with some exceptionally large stones forming the lower courses below the entrance. The basically horizontal courses occasionally deviate considerably. The sagging is rectified by levelling courses, such as those visible at the base of the second-floor window. There are three offsets at the base, only one of them is now visible. The stonework is well cut to the curve and to the batter.

The entrance door faces south-east across the intervening public road towards the west doorway of the Romanesque church. The tower doorway displays typical round-headed doorcase characteristics of four-stone jambs supporting a tripartite arch. A much-weathered architrival band is carried around the exterior of the doorcase.

The first floor is distinguished by a remarkably large triangle-headed window, illuminating what may be considered as the only usable space in the tower, with the exception of the bell-floor. The positioning of this window indicates that defence was not a consideration since it does not share the same orientation as the door, but faces east. Available light from this window would have made some activity possible on this floor. On the north reveal of the window is a low-relief carving of a single-masted ship, possibly 12th- or 13th-century in style. A similar carving, although more difficult to identify, is higher up. Two small lintelled windows light the remaining third and fourth floors.

Suggested date: 12th century. (Annals reference for 1135.)

Dimensions: height 20 metres; diameter at base 4.7 metres; height of door-sill 2.34 metres.

Unique features: medieval carvings of ships on the window jamb.

Access: free access to the site; there are no internal floors or ladders.

69 Ardmore, Co. Waterford   The tower stands in a churchyard on the hill overlooking the village of Ardmore, reached by the R673, 5 km south-east from the N25. Ardmore may be the last Round Tower to be built and its exceptionally attenuated form is significantly different in spirit from all other towers. It stands in a churchyard which is rich in early medieval buildings, and its location on high ground above Ardmore Bay marks it as a tower and site of above average beauty and interest.

Foundation of the monastic settlement is attributed to the 5th-century St Declan, possibly prior to Patrick's mission. The church buildings of the site are the cathedral and St Declan's Oratory. The 11th – 12th-century cathedral, which appears to have been built in a number of stages, has important architectural and unique sculptural features, both internally and externally. The sculptures that decorate the west gable, thought to have been re-arranged here when the west end was extended, are organised in two ranges under large enclosing arches. Although much weathered, Old and New Testament figures are identifiable: Adam and Eve and the Judgement of Solomon are typical of the subject matter and relate this unique frieze to the bas-relief decorations of the High Crosses. The display of the panels themselves resembles the sculptured reliefs on the exterior of Romanesque churches in France, or more distantly of the Lake Van area of Armenia, more than they do any Irish example. Inside the cathedral the side walls of the nave have unusual Romanesque blind arcading and two ogham stones are displayed, as well as what may be the remainder of the original capstone of the Tower.

St Declan's Oratory, to the east of the cathedral, is a small tomb-shrine of the founder saint, re-roofed during the 18th century.

The Tower: Ardmore is one of the few complete Round Towers which can never be confused with any other – its profile is so distinctive that it must have in its time represented a re-evaluation and development of all previous thought on the subject. While there is no reason to assume that there was any change in Ardmore's function, stylistically it owes more to the detailing of the twin towers of Cormac's Chapel at Cashel (1134) than it does to its predecessors, although it must certainly post-date Cormac's Chapel.

The tower, because of its exceptionally steep batter, diminishes from 5 metres to 3.05 metres under the cornice at the top. There are two offsets at the external base of the wall, which is of fine, well-coursed sandstone ashlars, diagonally comb-finished and well trimmed to the curve and batter.

The door faces north-east towards the chancel of the present cathedral, which was no doubt the position of the original church. The opening is round-headed with a segmental arch of eight voussoirs, the springing of which is based on the horizontal upper courses of the slightly inclined doorjambs. Around the door, an architrave-like rolled moulding with a subsidiary indented roll, is carried up both jambs and over the arch. The sill projects as in the line of the larger moulding and shows signs of wear from the struts of a ladder, but it is not possible to say whether this occurred in antiquity or more recently when the tower was fitted with internal floors, installed during the mid-19th century, but removed some fifty years later.

Two courses above the entrance arch are the first of three string courses which project from the exterior of the tower, dividing its surface into four curiously unequal zones. The positioning of the string courses defies explanation;

ARDMORE
Round-sectioned string courses complement the surface of the tower, features which are unique to Ardmore.

they bear no relationship to the internal floor levels and are purely decorative. As though to adjust the optical illusion created by the height and batter of the tower when seen from close quarters, the external zones graduate from the largest which is at the top, diminishing in the next two stages, yet increasing again for the bottom zone. Perhaps there is a parallel between the introduction of this new detail to the Round Tower, and the long struggle involved in adapting to the idea of the true arch, that it is a motif only partially understood, and the position of the string courses is merely arbitrary.

The batter is not in a straight line from base to cornice, but the wall surface offsets slightly above each string course, similar to the manner in which the Cormac's Chapel towers reduce in width above the string courses.

There are small windows on the second, third and fourth floors, the first two lintelled and with inclined jambs. That on the third floor is round-headed, with its arch cut from a monolithic lintel (like the exterior detail of the Balla basement window), and rests on the string course. The fifth floor is windowless, the bell-floor has four windows facing slightly off the cardinal points. Three are lintelled, that to the south, triangular-headed.

The cap, with steeper sides than any other tower, is surmounted by a cross, placed there in the late 19th century.

Internally, there were six floors over the basement, with offsets to carry three of these. There are numerous non-structural corbels, a number of which have sculpted decorations of human and animal heads and floral decorations. The last mentioned, with paired volutes on the vertical side-faces, looks as though it was intended for hanging satchels on.

Suggested date: mid-to-late 12th century.

Dimensions: height 29.2 metres; diameter at base 5 metres; height of door-sill 3.98 metres.

Unique features: string courses; extreme batter; sculpted corbels.

Access: free access to site, there are no floors or ladders.

70 Ferns, Co. Wexford   Ferns is on the N11, Gorey to Enniscorthy road, 12 km north-east of Enniscorthy. During the 12th century, it was the seat of Dermot MacMurrough, over-king of Leinster, whose rivalry with the O'Rourkes and the O'Connors led to the intervention of the Anglo-Normans in Irish affairs.

At Ferns, the impressive collection of buildings includes the remains of an early 13th-century Norman keep, with a fine circular groined chapel in one of the remaining drum towers. The ecclesiastical site is now the churchyard of the Church of Ireland Cathedral of St Edan, which incorporates portions of the ruins of the 13th-century cathedral. Other remains are that of the Augustinian Priory, founded by MacMurrough, which stands in the middle of an adjoining field, and another church, probably late 16th century. There are a number of fragmentary plain High Crosses, one of which in local folklore is reputed to mark the grave of MacMurrough, who died in 1171. On his death, the kingdom passed, by marriage of MacMurrough's daughter Eva (with Richard de Clare, called Strongbow), to the Anglo-Normans, who ruled the lordship of

FERNS
Left: The tower of Ferns generally escapes inclusion in any inventory of Round Towers, yet in dating, function and structural principles, it belongs with its freestanding and more rotund brethren. A section of the chancel vault of the Romanesque church, to which it is attached, can be seen on the right. (See photo p. 87.)

Left: In the foreground is the base of a High Cross and, in the field beyond it, the Romanesque church with engaged tower. The manner in which the rectangle graduates into a circle is handled similarly at Kinneigh and Kilmacnessan.

Leinster until the 15th century when, briefly, the MacMurroughs regained a portion of their former territory.

The original monastery was founded by St M'Aodhog or Aidan, who died *c.* 626, and whose shrine with corporeal relics, called the Breac Maedhóg, and its leather satchel are now in the National Museum of Ireland, Dublin.

The Tower: In 1152 MacMurrough founded St Mary's Abbey for the Canons Regular. This was burned by the O'Rourkes and O'Connors, but he rebuilt it in 1160, following his return from his appeal to Henry II. This was a nave-and-chancel church with a barrel-vaulted chancel-roof, resembling Cormac's Chapel, to the south of which are the foundations of the cloister. At the west end of the priory is the attached Round Tower, the rectangular base of which projects from the north-west corner. This is the sole example of an attached tower which survives relatively intact. The base rises slightly above the eaves level on which is standing a circular upper portion, apparently without taper. This belongs within the category of attached Round Towers and there is no reason to suppose, considering its date, that it did not have a conical cap. The building post-dates Cormac's Chapel, with which it merits comparison. Internally, there is a stone spiral staircase, as in the south tower of the Chapel.

The tower proper, of a diameter smaller than an orthodox Round Tower, is constructed of well-coursed limestone. Some brick infill of the newel post of the spiral staircase must represent repairs done in the 17th century or later.

Two round-headed doors with vertical jambs and segmental arches, on ground- and first-floor levels, give access to the tower, with a lintelled door with well-defined ashlar jambs and lintel, to the croft level of the nave. There are a number of slit windows in the drum, and four axial lintelled windows on the bell-floor.

Ferns is not generally included in listings of Round Towers, although there is no good reason why it should be excluded; if it is not an early medieval Round Tower, then what is it? Significantly, the manner in which the drum of Ferns is graduated to the rectangular base by the use of corner squinches, is also the case at Kinneigh where the hexagon and circle are combined using the same device.

Suggested date: 12th century (1152-60).

Dimensions: height 18.24 metres; square base 2.9 x 2.9 metres; diameter of base at circular section 2.9 metres.

Unique features: engaged tower; spiral staircase.

Access: free access to site; tower closed by iron-barred gate.

71 Glendalough I, Co. Wicklow   Glendalough is 4 km west of Laragh, 10 km south of Roundwood on the R755. Its Round Tower is probably the most well-known as it forms part of a uniquely important complex of Irish ecclesiastical settlement, known as 'the seven churches of Glendalough', situated in the most beautiful of the Wicklow glens. It remained untouched, if ruinous, until the mid-19th century, and the landscape and environment, while not totally unspoiled, have been tidied up in

GLENDALOUGH I
The setting of Glendalough, despite being a tourist attraction, retains some of its isolated natural grandeur, and the reason for its attraction to an early Christian hermit saint has not been dimmed by the number of modern pilgrims. The cap of the tower is a faithful restoration, using fallen masonry. (See photos pp. 18, 65.)

order to cope with the ever-growing number of visitors. Building development over the last 100 years, other than the ever-expanding modern graveyard, has been fairly restrained. Uniquely, Glendalough possesses three towers, which are freestanding, engaged and attached examples. The beauty of its location, with the two lakes situated below the backdrop of precipitous hills, along with the 12th-century roof-line of the combined towers and churches, must have distinguished Glendalough as one of the primary building complexes of early medieval Ireland.

The foundation of the monastery as a hermitage is ascribed to St Kevin, whose death is recorded in the *Annals of the Four Masters* for the year 617, and it became a significant centre of scholarship and pilgrimage, the latter continuing into the 19th century. The early hermitage was located around the Upper Lake, where there are a number of sites associated with the saint's legend, as well as two significant early buildings, Temple-na-Skellig and Reefert Church. Below the Lower Lake is the main monastic enclosure, one of the most interesting to survive in Ireland, with a superlative Round Tower, a collection of roofless ecclesiastical buildings, and the almost intact St Kevin's Church. The cathedral and Priest's House are individually important; the latter is believed to have been the pilgrimage shrine containing the founder-saint's relics. Among the High Crosses, only one, the Market Cross (*c.* 12th century), bears figurative decoration. It is now preserved in the Interpretative Centre.

The Tower: The tower is the dominant monument of the complex, and the best-preserved. Its cap was rebuilt from the original stones during the late 19th century. This handsome tower has two offsets above the one metre deep foundation pad and a well-executed batter. The fine stonework of the tower, displaying the weathering of seven centuries, as photographed by Dunraven *c.* 1870, before the cap had been rebuilt (1876) and the masonry re-pointed, had a character somewhat more variegated than its appearance today. The masonry is of the local mica-slate with granite dressing, occasional granite courses, and irregular single stones of granite in the wall, which is well worked both to the exceptionally slight batter and to the curve.

Some courses over the upper offset, and slightly to the left of the entrance door above, is a curious and unusual feature, a small channel running horizontally through the wall; its purpose is unknown, but it could function as either an air vent or drain to the basement area of the tower. Similar features are found at Kilmacduagh and Balla, although the latter is certainly a window.

The door faces south-east towards the west doorway of the cathedral. The fine articulated doorcase, with gently inclined jambs, is constructed of granite monoliths, some of which, including both the sill and arch, span the thickness of the wall. The slightly-less-than-round arch of the doorway is composed of a monolithic lintel, cut away on the soffit and on its upper surface to represent a conventional arch.

Internally, there are no floor-offsets or corbels to support the floors, but instead a series of beam-holes in pairs to support each floor, alternating at right angles to each other for successive stages.

GLENDALOUGH I & II
Left: The Round Tower and St Kevin's Church originally stood among the many timber buildings of the monastery which have not survived.
(See photos pp. 54, 85.)

Below: The short tower on the gable of St Kevin's Church is one of the few clues as to the greater variety of early medieval church architecture, most of which has vanished almost without trace.

The windows appear more organised than on other towers, spiralling around the circumference, one to each floor; all are of granite, lintelled and with inclined jambs. The bell-floor windows face the cardinal points, all slightly off to the right of the true points.

Suggested date: 11th century.

Dimensions: height 30.48 metres; diameter at base 4.87 metres; height of door-sill 3.2 metres.

Unique features: basement wall-passage; absence of internal offsets or corbels.

Access: to site, there are no access ladders nor internal floors.

72 Glendalough II, Co. Wicklow

St Kevin's Church, popularly known as 'St Kevin's Kitchen', from the engaged chimney-like tower perched on its west gable, consists of a rectangular church, *c.* 12th century, with a steeply pitched stone roof supported by a corbelled vault, with a true arched section at its centre-point (**fig. 15b**). This supports the floor of a subsidiary corbelled croft in the apex of the pitch. The church has lost its later chancel which adjoined the east gable, but a sacristy of approximately the same dimensions stands attached to the north-east corner of the building. Internally, the vaulted nave was provided with a timber upper floor. An access trapdoor in the vault leads to a roof-croft.

The Tower: The complete miniature Round Tower, which acts as a belfry to the church, is reached from the upper croft chamber of the roof and rises from the west gable. Its masonry is inferior to that of the church, suggesting a slightly later date for its construction. However the skilful manner of its integration into the steep planes of the roof-line is in itself a singular architectural achievement. There are no transitional planes between the surface of the tower and that of the roof-slope. Internally, the narrow tube of the tower is divided in the manner of Round Towers generally into a number of stages. The windows in the drum are small on the first level, large on the second, and face respectively west and east. The bell-floor windows below the cone face the cardinal points.

St Kevin's Church, with its unique Round Tower, is among the most charming and interesting of Irish early medieval church buildings, and like Trinity Church, an example of the developing synthesis of architectural forms which grew out of the refinement and perfection which had been achieved in both tower and church construction by the end of the 11th century.

St Kevin's and Trinity Church at Glendalough, and Kilmacnessan on Ireland's Eye, represent the peak of development in the attempt to combine a rectangular church building with a circular bell-tower before successive waves of international architectural style swept over the island, demonstrating, as in the Romanesque of Cormac's Chapel at Cashel, a more integrated architectonic solution to these aesthetic and technical problems. These three Irish examples capture the Irish church's master builders, poised before the onslaught of new ideas and more classical concepts of symmetry and design, achieving a volumetric mastery which was never to be developed to its full potential. The spirit of these buildings, contemporary with the great Romanesque church

GLENDALOUGH II
The pretty and complete St Kevin's Church is the only example of a building with an engaged tower to stand with its original roof intact.

GLENDALOUGH III
The projecting rectangular cell is a later addition to Trinity Church, and carried a substantial Round Tower on its roof. The vault springing can be seen directly above the arched window in the north wall to the left of the picture.

building of Europe, expresses an unadorned cubic quality which still relates backwards in time. It is more akin to the blankwalled style of Dun Aenghus, than forward looking towards the conceptions of light, space and structural freedom with which Continental masons of the Romanesque and Gothic periods were concerned. During the 12th century, Irish master masons were toying with these problems without the advantage of possessing a coherent theoretical repertoire from which to develop their ideas. This is evident in the experimental manner of all of the developments of the period.

Suggested date: 12th century.

Dimensions: height 14.1 metres; dimensions at base 2 metres.

Unique features: engaged tower.

Access: the church is generally kept locked, with a barred gate, through which the interior may be seen; no access to the tower.

73 Glendalough III, Co. Wicklow

Trinity Church is located 5 km from the Round Tower, directly beside the main road into Glendalough from Laragh, and overlooking the monastic enclosure. It lies on the south side of the road (**fig. 15a**).

The Tower: Although there is now no sign of the round upper portion of the Round Tower which was attached to Trinity Church, the walls of this *c.* 12th-century nave-and-chancel building survive intact, with west and south doorways, respectively lintelled and arched. Here, the chancel is not an addition, as in many cases, but contemporary with the nave. Attached to the west gable, and slightly smaller in plan than the chancel, is a rectangular extension which is entered through what was originally the west door. This vaulted room carried a Round Tower as its superstructure, a reconstruction drawing of which is in Leask (Vol. I, p. 77), based on 18th-century representations. The springing of the supporting vault is still visible on the north and south walls of the tower.

This engaged Round Tower can be clearly seen in an engraving by Paul Sandby (1778) and a drawing by Gabriel Beranger after the Earl of Portarlington's original work (1779). The tower collapsed during a storm in 1818. Its significance, in conjunction with the nearby belfry of St. Kevin's Church, is the light which they cast on the widespread adaptations that were developed in the later period of Round Tower building during the 12th century, with this most satisfactory and aesthetically pleasing form being reinterpreted to fulfil a wider range of needs than those for which it was originally conceived. To the ecclesiastical clients and master masons who planned and constructed these buildings, the distinctive, prestigious and distantly visible form of the Round Tower gained a new life as it became adapted to a wider range of architectural possibilities.

Suggested date: 12th century.

Dimensions: height from springing approximately 15 metres; diameter at base 4 metres.

Unique features: used to have attached tower.

Access: free access to the building.

GLOSSARY

ANTAE: pilaster-like projections which are side walls extended beyond the gable wall surface of a church; their purpose is unclear, but it was probably to support the projecting eaves beams of the gable.

ARCHITRAVE: a plain or moulded frame to a door or window.

ARRIS: the sharp edge formed by the meeting of two planes of masonry.

ARTICULATED: door or window emphasised by the use of finer quality masonry than in the surrounding wall, or by stone of a contrasting colour.

ASHLAR: rectangular, coursed masonry of high quality, with vertical joints.

BATTER: angle of wall which inclines inwards.

BAWN: a fortified enclosure attached to a tower base or plantation manor-house.

BEAD: hemispherical or cylindrical repeating decorative motif.

BIVALLATE, TRIVALLATE: *ráth* or cashel with two or three concentric ramparts.

BULLAUN: boulder with one or more hemispherical, basin-like depressions, usually found in ecclesiastical contexts; their purpose is unclear but they most probably were used as mortars.

CAMPANILE: freestanding Italian church bell-tower.

CASHEL: stone-walled circular or sub-circular enclosure.

CHANCEL: the eastern extension of a church nave where the altar is placed.

CLOCHAN (BEEHIVE HUT): circular or sub-rectangular dry-stone structure with corbelled roof.

CORBEL: stone projecting from the wall surface which may be a wall support over a door-opening, a floor support internally, or may act as a hook for suspending leather satchels or other containers. Some corbels have sculptural decoration.

CORBELLING: a system of dry-stone roofing which depends on courses of stones overhanging those below.

CORNICE: projecting horizontal ledge or capping on masonry, usually at the top of a wall.

CYCLOPEAN: composed of large, irregularly shaped stones.

DOORCASE: stone surround of a door-opening which has been differentiated from the wall masonry by either a change of material or by architectural details.

DRY-STONE: built without mortar.

EMBRASURE: the splayed interior of a door, window opening, or that between the merlons of a parapet.

ENGAGED: feature which would otherwise be freestanding, attached to a larger structure.

ENTASIS: slight convex profile on a column, designed to avoid the optical illusion of a concave outline.

EXTRADOS: the outer curved surface of an arch.

GABLED: with steeply angled sides in the manner of the gable-end of a building.

INTRADOS: the inner or underside curved surface of an arch.

JAMB: the vertical or inclined sides of a door or window.

JOGGLED: coursed masonry in which the horizontal course-lines are not maintained.

LINTEL: horizontal stone spanning a door or window opening.

MANDORLA: almond shaped device enclosing the Christ figure.

MERLON: the upstanding features of a roof parapet with battlements.

MILLIFIORI: glass-mosaic decoration on ornamental metalwork.

MONOLITHIC: composed of a single large stone.

MURAL STAIRS: stairs within the body of a wall.

OFFSET: setback in the surface of a wall.

ORDERS: the receding planes of arches and jambs in Romanesque doors or windows.

PILASTER: column-like wall decoration, rectangular in profile, and attached to a wall.

PLINTH: a distinct and projecting area which forms the base of wall.

PUTLOCK HOLE: hole left in masonry where timber scaffolding had been inserted during construction.

QUOIN: corner stones of a wall or door-opening – alternating long and short on either face; similar treatment of a door-opening.

RENDERING: thin skin of lime mortar on the surface of a wall.

ROMANESQUE: round-arched architecture of the 11th – 12th century, derived from Roman example.

SHEELA-NA-GIG: a crudely carved female figure in a position of genital display, often found on medieval churches and secular buildings.

SILL: the horizontal stone base of a window or door-opening.

SKEUOMORPH: an architectural feature executed in some material other than that in which it was originally made – wood details executed in stone.

SOFFIT: the underside of an arch or lintel.

SPALL: splinters of stone used to pack masonry joints.

SPRINGING: the point from which an arch leaves the vertical plane of a wall.

SQUINCH: angled or curved surface which accommodates a circular form to a square or polygon.

STRING COURSE: decorative projecting horizontal course on masonry.

TANGENTIAL: gable projecting from the curve of an arch.

TAU CROSS: 'T' shaped cross.

TORUS MOULDING: string course, or moulding on a column-base, round in profile.

TRABEATED: window or door-opening covered by a lintel.

TRIFORIUM: space above nave arcade.

TRIPARTITE: composed of three units (as in a three-voussoir arch).

TRIVALLATE: see BIVALLATE

TYMPANUM: area enclosed by an arch, above a doorway.

VOLUTES: decorative motif in the form of a spiral.

VOUSSOIRS: the wedge-shaped stones of an arch.

WESTWORK: the combination of bell-towers, decorated portal and sculpted tympanum found at the west end of Continental Carolingian and Romanesque churches.

BIBLIOGRAPHY

EDITIONS OF THE ANNALS

Hennessey, W. (ed.) (1866) *Chronicum Scotorum*, London: (CS)

Hennessey, W. and B. Mac Carthy, (eds.) (1887) *Annals of Ulster*, Dublin: (AU)

Murphy, D. (ed.) (1896) *The Annals of Clonmacnoise*, Dublin: (AC)

O'Donovan, J. (ed.) (1856) *Annals of the Kingdom of Ireland, by the Four Masters*, Dublin: (AFM)

Ó Hinnse, S. (ed.) (1947) *Miscellaneous Irish Annals*, Dublin: (MIA)

Stokes, W. (ed.) (1895) *The Annals of Tigernach*, Dublin: (AT)

Aalen, F.H.A., M. Stout, K. Whelan, (1997) *Atlas of the Irish Rural Landscape*, Cork

Andrews, J.H., K.M. Davies, A. Simms, (1997) *Irish Historic Towns Atlas*, Dublin

Bannister, Fletcher, Sir, (ed. R.A. Cordingley) (1961) *A History of Architecture on the Comparative Method*, London

Barrow, G.L. (1977) *Irish Round Towers*, Dublin
          (1979) *The Round Towers of Ireland, a study and gazetteer*, Dublin

Barry, T.B. (1987) *The Archaeology of Medieval Ireland*, London

Ben-Dov, M. (1975) 'The Area South of the Temple Mount in the Early Islamic Period', in *Jerusalem Revealed*, Jerusalem

Bitel, L.M. (1993) *Isle of Saints, Monastic Settlement and Christian Community in early Ireland*, Cork

Blades B.S. and N.F. Brannon, (1980) 'Dungiven Bawn Re-edified', in Vol. 43, *Ulster Journal of Archaeology*, Belfast

Böll, H. (1957) *Irish Journal*, London

Butler, L.A.S. and R.K. Morris, (eds.) (1986) *The Anglo-Saxon Church*, CBA Research Report 60, London

Campbell, K. and M. Gowen, (1989-90) 'The excavations at St Michael le Pole, Ship St, Dublin 1981' in *Journal of Irish Archaeology*, Dublin

Casey, C. and A. Rowan, (1993) *The Buildings of Ireland, North Leinster*, London

Champneys, A. C. (1910) *Irish Ecclesiastical Architecture*, London

Clarke, H.B. (ed.) (1990) *Medieval Dublin, The Making of a Metropolis*, Dublin
          (1998) 'Proto-Towns and Towns in Ireland and Britain in the Ninth and Tenth Centuries', in H.B. Clarke, M. Ní Mhaonaigh, R.Ó Floinn (eds.) *Ireland and Scandinavia in the Early Viking Age*, Dublin

Clarke, H.B., and M. Ní Mhaonaigh, R. Ó Floinn, (eds.) (1998) *Ireland and Scandinavia in the Early Viking Age*, Dublin

Conant, K.J. (1959) *Carolingian and Romanesque Architecture, 800-1200*, London

Corlett, C. (1998) 'Interpretation of round towers – public appeal or professional opinion?', No. 44 (Vol. 12, No. 2) *Archaeology Ireland*, Bray

Cox, J.C. and C.B. Ford, (B. Little ed.), 1961 *Parish Churches*, London

Craig, M.J. (1982) *The Architecture of Ireland*, London
          and the Knight of Glin, (1972) *Ireland Observed*, Cork

Crawford, H.S. (1923) 'The Round Tower and Castle of Timahoe', *JRSAI*, Dublin

Creswell, K.A.C. (1970) *Early Muslim Architecture*, Oxford

de Breffny, B. (1976) *The Churches and Abbeys of Ireland*, London de Paor, L. (1967) 'Cormac's Chapel: the beginnings of Irish Romanesque', in E. Rynne (ed.), *North Munster Studies*, Limerick

de Paor, L. (1967), F. Mitchell, P. Harbison, R. Stalley, (1997) *Treasures of Early Irish Art*, New York

de Paor, M & L. (1961) *Early Christian Ireland*, London

Department of the Environment for Northern Ireland (1983, 6th ed.), *Historic Monuments of Northern Ireland*, Belfast

Dikaios, P. (1953) *Khirokitia*, Oxford

Dirsztay, P. (1978) *Church Furnishings, A NAFDAS Guide*, London

Duffy, J. (trans.) (1972) *Patrick in His Own Words*, Dublin

Dunraven, Earl of, (M. Stokes. ed.) (1875-77) *Notes on Irish Architecture*, London

Edwards, N. (1996) *The Archaeology of Early Medieval Ireland*, London

Flanagan, L. (1992) *A Dictionary of Irish Archaeology*, Dublin

Gerald of Wales (J.J. O'Meara trans.) (1982) *The History and Topography of Ireland*, London

Glasscock, R.E. (1970-71) 'Excavations at Liathmore / Mochoemog', *Old Kilkenny Review*, Kilkenny

Hamlin, A. (1976) 'Some further documentary evidence for the Round Tower at Devenish, Co. Fermanagh'. No. 34, *Ulster Journal of Archaeology*, Belfast

Harbison, P. (1988) *Pre-Christian Ireland*, London

(1991) *Pilgrimage in Ireland*, London

(1991) *Beranger's Views of Ireland*, Dublin

(1992) *Guide to National and Historic Monuments of Ireland*, Dublin

(1994) *Irish High Crosses*, Drogheda

Hare, M. and A. Hamlin, (1986) 'The study of early church architecture in Ireland: an Anglo-Saxon viewpoint', in *Anglo-Saxon Archaeology*, Research Report 60, The Council for British Archaeology, London

Harvey, J. (1961) *English Cathedrals*, London

Henry, F. (ed.) (1977) *The Book of Kells*, London

Hillenbrand, R. (1994) *Islamic Architecture*, Edinburgh

Hills, G.M. (1858) 'A review of the architecture and history of the Round Towers of Ireland', *Transactions of the Royal Institute of British Architecture*

Hughes, K. and A. Hamlin, (1997) *The Modern Traveller to the Early Irish Church*, Dublin

Hurl, D.P. (1998) *Adjusting your sites: the ecclesiastical enclosure at Armoy, Co. Antrim*, in Vol. 12 (No. 1, Issue 43) *Archaeology Ireland*, Bray

Huyghe, R. (ed.) (1966) *Larousse Encyclopaedia of Prehistoric and Ancient Art*, London

(1968) *Larousse Encyclopaedia of Byzantine and Medieval Art*, London

Killanin, Lord, and M. V. Duignan, (1967) *The Shell Guide to Ireland*, London

King, H.A. (1998) *Clonmacnoise Studies I*, Dublin

Kjellberg, E. and G. Säflund, (1968) *Greek and Roman Art*, London

Lavell, C. (1998) *Handbook for British and Irish Archaeology; Sources and Resources*, Edinburgh

Lawlor, H.C. (1925) *The Monastery of St Mochaoi of Nendrum*, Belfast

Leask, H.G. (1977) *Glendalough*, Dublin

(1966) *Irish Churches and Monastic Buildings*, Vol. I,

(nd) *St Patrick's Rock, Cashel*, Dublin

and H.A. Wheeler, (nd) *St Patrick's Rock, Cashel*, Dublin

Le Brun, A. (1997) *Khirokitia*, Nicosia

Le Corbusier, (Jeanneret, C.É.) (1927) *Towards a New Architecture,* London

Macdonald, A. (1994) 'Notes on Monastic Archaeology and the Annals of Ulster, 650-1050', in (D. Ó Corráin ed.) *Irish Antiquity,* Dublin

Mallory, J.P. and T.E. McNeill, (1991) *The Archaeology of Ulster,* Belfast

Manning, C. (1985) 'Archaeological excavations at two church sites on Inishmore, Aran Islands', Vol. 115, *JRSAI,* Dublin

        (1994) *Clonmacnoise,* Dublin

        (1995) 'Clonmacnoise Cathedral – The oldest church in Ireland? No. 34 (Vol. 9, No. 4) *Archaeology Ireland,* Bray

        (1997) 'The date of the Round Tower at Clonmacnoise', No. 40 (Vol. 11, No. 2) *Archaeology Ireland,* Bray

        (ed), (1998), *Dublin and Beyond the Pale,* Bray

        (1998) 'Clonmacnoise Cathedral' *in Clonmacnoise Studies I,* (H.A. King ed.) Dublin

        (1998) 'Some notes on the early history and archaeology of Tullaherin', from *In the Shadow of the Steeple* Vol. 6, Kilkenny

McMahon, M. (1991) *Medieval Church Sites of North Dublin,* Dublin

Mellaart, J. (1975) *The Neolithic of the Near East,* London

Mitchell, F. (1976) *The Irish Landscape,* London

Mitchell, F. and M. Ryan, (1997) *Reading the Irish Landscape,* Dublin

Monk, M.A. and J. Sheehan, (ed.) (1998) *Early Medieval Munster, Archaeology, History, Society,* Cork

Moore, F. (1996) *Ireland's Oldest Bridge - at Clonmacnoise,* No. 38 (Vol. 10, No. 4) *Archaeology Ireland,* Bray

Mylonas, G.E. (1967) *Mycenae, a Guide to its Ruins and its History,* Athens

Mytum, H. (1992) *The Origins of Early Christian Ireland,* London

O'Brien, H. (1898) *The Round Towers of Ireland, or the History of the Tuath De -Danaans,* London

Ó Corrain, D. (ed.) (1981) *Irish Antiquity,* Dublin

Ó Croinin, D. (1995) *Early Medieval Ireland,* London

O' Keeffe, T. (1998) 'Architectural Traditions of the Early Medieval Church in Munster', in M.A. Monk and J. Sheehan, *Early Medieval Munster,* Cork

O' Kelly, M. J. (1982) *Newgrange,* London

        (1993) *Early Ireland,* Cambridge

O'Neill, H. (1877) *The Round Towers of Ireland,* Dublin

O'Reilly, S. (1998) 'Birth of a Nation's Symbol: The Revival of Ireland's Round Towers', Vol. 15, *Irish Arts Review Yearbook 1999*

Ó Ríordáin, S.P. (R. de Valera, ed.) (1991) *Antiquities of the Irish Countryside,* London

O'Sullivan, M. (1998) *Seir Kieran,* Offaly

Petrie, G. (1970) *The Round Towers of Ireland,* (a reprint of *The Ecclesiastical Architecture of Ireland Vol. I,* 1845), Shannon

Pochin Mould, D.D.C. (1976) *The Monasteries of Ireland,* London

        (1972) *Ireland from the Air,* Newton Abbot

Richardson, H. and J. Scarry, (1990) *Irish High Crosses,* Cork

Robertson, D. (1969) *Greek and Roman Architecture,* Cambridge

Rodwell, W. (1986) 'Anglo-Saxon church building: aspects of design and construction', in *The Anglo-Saxon Church,* Research Report 60, The Council for British Archaeology, London

Roe, H.M. (1981) *Monasterboice and its Monuments,* Louth

Rowan, A. (1979) *The Buildings of Ireland, North West Ulster,* London

Rudofsky, B. (1965) *Architecture without Architects,* New York

Rynne, C. (1993) *The Archaeology of Cork City and Harbour,* Cork

Rynne, E. (1980) 'The Round Towers of Ireland – a review article', Vol. 22, *North Munster Antiquarian Journal,* Limerick

        (1998) 'The Round Tower, "Evil Eye" and Holy Well at Balla, Co. Mayo', in (C. Manning ed.) *Dublin and Beyond the Pale,* Dublin

Salvadori, R. (1990) *Architects Guide to Rome,* London

Sheehy, J. (1980) *The Rediscovery of Ireland's Past,* London

Spearman, M.R. and J. Higgit, (1993) *The Age of Migrating Ideas,* Edinburgh

Stalley, R.A. (1971) *Architecture and Sculpture in Ireland, 1150-1350,* Dublin

        (1987) *The Cistercian monasteries of Ireland,* New Haven

Stokes, M. (1878) *Early Christian architecture in Ireland,* London

Talbot Rice, D. (1963) *Art of the Byzantine Era,* London

        (1965) *Islamic Art,* London

Toman, R. (ed.) (1997) *Romanesque, Architecture, Sculpture, Painting,* Köln

van der Meer, F. and C. Mohrmann, (1958), *Atlas of the Early Christian World,* London

Vitruvius, (Marcus Vitruvius Pollio), (trans. M.H. Morgan) (1960) *The Ten Books on Architecture,* New York

Wakeman, W.F. (1900) *Cloic Tige or Round Towers of Ancient Ireland,* National Library of Ireland (mss), Dublin

Walker, D. (1995) *The Normans in Britain,* Oxford

Westropp, T.J. (1898-1900) *List of the Round Towers of Ireland, PRIA*

INDEX